Blame Canada

BLAME CANADA!
SOUTH PARK
AND
POPULAR CULTURE

Toni Johnson-Woods

continuum

NEW YORK • LONDON

2007

The Continuum International Publishing Group Inc
80 Maiden Lane, New York, NY 10038

The Continuum International Publishing Group Ltd
The Tower Building, 11 York Road, London SE1 7NX

www.continuumbooks.com

Printed in the United States of America

Library of Congress Cataloging-in-Publication Data

Johnson-Woods, Toni.
  Blame Canada : South park and popular culture / Toni Johnson-Woods.
    p. cm.
  Includes bibliographical references and index.
  ISBN-13: 978-0-8264-1730-5 (hardcover : alk. paper)
  ISBN-10: 0-8264-1730-2 (hardcover : alk. paper)
  ISBN-13: 978-0-8264-1731-2 (pbk. : alk. paper)
  ISBN-10: 0-8264-1731-0 (pbk. : alk. paper)
  I. South Park (Television program) II. Title.

PN1992.77.S665J64 2007
791.45'72--dc22

                                                              2006029497

Contents

Acknowledgments

My humble thanks at the beginning of this book seems little to reward the many people who made the book possible. The University of Queensland provided much-needed funding to support my research, and its Promoting Women Fellowship gave me time to write the book. Many people shared their insights: Ryan Callis, Michael Cust, Jennifer Conary (University of Southern California), John Dempsey, Mike Jeavons, Jessica Knight, Dan Lins, Brian Nomi, and Justin Trevena. Thanks, everyone, for the unending supply of anecdotes, storylines, quotes, and insights. Thanks to Christopher Hassall for checking facts. Extra special thanks to Dr. William Lott for the support, discussions, and TiVo mastery, and to the British Council's Lesley Hayman, who introduced me to some of the complexities and subtleties of Japanese language and culture. Despite all of this help, all I can say is, "Goddamnit, it's my book, Kitty."

Author's Note: Chewbacca Defense

B*lame Canada* is, by and large, limited to the *South Park* television show, *Bigger, Longer and Uncut,* and *Team America*. Only passing reference is made to other creative works by Trey Parker and Matt Stone, such as *That's My Bush, Orgazmo,* and *Cannibal! The Musical*. Each episode was viewed multiple times; excerpts quoted here come from my transcriptions, cross-checked with those at various Web sites, most particularly Willie Westwood's South Park Scriptorium. With respect to Kenny's mumblings, I have only used those that were explicitly clear to me (i.e., "Son of a bitch,"). Any mistakes are mine and mine alone.

As can be imagined, many episodes, incidents, and dialogue support my arguments, but space constraints have restricted me to including only the most relevant. For readers who feel I've missed their favorite episode/incident/quote, I can only say: I haven't referred to many of mine. Any show that develops over ten seasons is bound to contradict itself. I have remained as faithful as I could to the tenor of the series as a whole.

I use episode titles as references rather than numbers (i.e. "Death" rather than 106); the most commonly used abbreviations for titles have been used ("Succubus" rather than "Chef's Mama," and "Big Gay Al" rather than "Big Gay Al's Big Gay Boat Ride"). I have used standardized spellings from the official South Park Web site (for example, Broflovski) and have used names that became clearer in subsequent episodes (Butters Stotch rather than Swanson; Token Black rather than Williams).

South Park is closely aligned with its creators (more than many television shows), but I have tried to avoid marrying the themes and content too closely with the creators' (stated) personal beliefs, especially in regard to politics and religion, mainly because animation shows are team efforts and it is impossible and rather pointless to draw the line been artistic license and personal ideologies.

Blame Canada is divided into three sections. "Oh My God" deals with the *South Park* "facts," its history, media reception, Internet uptake/fandom, and marketing. "You Killed Kenny" covers the show as a televisual artifact, its generic makeup, humor, intertextuality, music, food/drink references, community, and characters. "You Bastards" examines the recurring issues of politics, "difference," religion, and gender/sex. In this way, *Blame Canada* contextualizes *South Park* through its contribution to and reflection of popular culture. A fourth section exists on the Internet—this Web site contains my recaps of all episodes. It is available for viewing at www.continuumbooks .com/download/BlameCanadaEpisodeGuide.pdf.

My apologies to all the students/fans/viewers who read this book and find it ruins what was once a viewing pleasure. Apologies as well to the creators, who will no doubt look on much of my theoretical framework with a healthy skepticism.

Lastly, I am not a fan; or at least I wasn't. The material here has been gathered and disseminated out of scholarly interest; while I have often enjoyed episodes (my personal favorite to date is "Marjorine"), been amused by them, and find myself quoting *South Park*–isms in my media classes, this is not the work of a fan. I came to the series with no preconceived notions or ideas about *South Park*. Therefore, *Blame Canada* comes not from love and admiration but from a healthy respect for the series and for its impact on contemporary culture.

Introduction:
Yesterday's Future Is Today

South Park arrived at a pivotal time in pop-culture history. The golden age of cartoon animation had returned, the Internet was revving up, and Comedy Central needed a signature show. *South Park* slotted in perfectly: it took animation one step backwards aesthetically and five steps forward intellectually, it engaged with its online fans in a maelstrom of Web sites, it stocked shelves with merchandise, and it put Comedy Central on the cable map. It ticked/checked all the popular culture boxes.

South Park is truly a pop-culture phenomenon. When Kim Jong Il makes TV news, chances are a still of his *Team America* persona will be flashed on the screen. It tackles subjects that were long taboo on television and savages celebrities of all kinds. It's a show that leaves viewers gasping, "I can't believe they said that." It's cruelly funny and hysterically satirical—or it's degrading toilet humor, depending upon your point of view. In *South Park*, there is definitely no accounting for taste.

Blame Canada explores South Park's insertion into popular culture. Few who viewed the first program thought they'd be seeing a tenth season celebration. Part of its success is its infusion of popular culture into its episodes. It is another of the hyper-ironic television programs that demand active viewing. Gen X and Gen Y viewers, the creators themselves, have grown up with what is affectionately termed Boomer Humor, and have come to appreciate and even expect highly referential, self-reflective, and cynical entertainment. Add to the mix its ripped-from-the-headlines subject matter, its total irreverence for everything, its audacity, and its off-the-wall humor, then it's not surprising the show continues to be the highest rating show on Comedy Central. The fullest appreciation of *South Park* comes from understanding its subtle nuances and its scathing parodies. *South Park* is the postmodern pastiche par excellence.

At the heart of *South Park*'s philosophy of life is crap. Yes, crap in both meanings of the word. The series pokes fun at the excesses of contemporary life: adoration of celebrities, overenthusiastic support of political correctness, and rabid liberalism. In doing so, it broadcasts toilet-humor images of people crapping and farting, and waves its genitals in the general direction of public discourse. It is difficult not to admire a show that so flies in the face of everything most people hold sacred; even if you disagree with the show's political ideology, even if you find some of the images and subject matter offensive, *South Park* aims at making people think by one of the oldest methods, satire.

Sociologist Peter L. Berger observes that all good satire has four criteria: fantasy (often grotesque), a firm moral standpoint, an object of attack, and an educational purpose.[1] In order to understand *South Park*'s appeal, one must return to the Middle Ages. According to Russian scholar Mikhail Bakhtin:

> For the medieval parodist everything without exception was comic. Laughter was as universal as seriousness; it was directed at the whole world, at history, at all societies, at ideology. It was the world's second truth extended to everything and from which nothing is taken away. It was, as it were, the festive aspect of the whole world in all its elements, the second revelation of the world in play and laughter.[2]

But he would say that—he was a literary theorist.

So what do a television series as potentially offensive as *South Park* and a one-legged Russian have in common? A belief in toilet humor and its anarchical place in society. Russian philosopher and literary critic Bakhtin examined the writings of François Rabelais—the naughty boy of French Renaissance poetry. In the sixteenth century, Rabelais (a monk and a physician) wrote *Gargantua and Pantagruel*, five books documenting the picaresque adventures of two giants, Gargantua and his son Pantagruel, a vinous monk Friar John, and the lecherous scholar Panurge. These books satirize society through scatological humor, gratuitous violence, and crude insults— is this starting to sound familiar? In Rabelais, Gargantua's horse pisses an army away; a woman scares the devil by exposing her vagina; and Pantagruel describes in some detail his experiments in ass wiping. There are pages of incredibly convoluted swear words and crude expressions. Did I mention the chapter on ass wiping? Rabelais is not merely trying to titillate or to shock readers; he takes serious swipes at religious, political, and social pretensions. Precious little escapes the cutting knife of Rabelais' satire. Rabelais had been the *least popular, the least understood and appreciated* of all great writers, claimed Bakhtin. He suffered because of the "deeply rooted demands of literary taste"—in other words, he was just too darned crude.

To truly understand Rabelais, Bakhtin claimed, one had to understand folk culture. Rabelais was best interpreted not through "classical" literature but through popular forms. To understand *South Park*, one should not "read" the show through, say, *Masterpiece Theatre*, but rather through Monty Python. Bakhtin examined folk (or popular) culture and divided it into three distinct forms of humor:

> ritual spectacles: carnival pageants, comic shows of the marketplace
>
> comic verbal compositions: parodies
>
> genres of billingsgate: curses and oaths

"Ritual spectacles" are the carnivals and festivities (feudal, state, or ecclesial) during which inequality was suspended and everyone feasted, ate, drank, and laughed—think Mardi Gras in New Orleans. During festivals, the usual hierarchies were turned on their heads, the fool was crowned king, and vice versa—it was a medieval free-for-all where Jack was allowed to be as "good" as his master. "Comic verbal" compositions have their roots in religious, state, and education discourses. Monkish parodies (as in compiled by monks) such as *The Liturgy of the Gambler* subverted the highly ritualized speeches of the church by rendering religious texts humorous. Parody is of course at the heart of many *South Park* episodes. The "genres of billingsgate" came from the cries and ribaldry of the marketplace. In marketplaces, people joked and conversed in everyday language. Into the linguistic spaces crept abusive, blasphemous, mocking, and obscene words, expressions, and gestures—billingsgate is the language of the streets (or in *South Park*'s case, the language of the playground), not the language of the court, church, or stateroom. These three folk culture forms are imbedded in virtually every *South Park* episode, albeit with contemporary figures and a contemporary sensibility.

All of the above elements form what Bakhtin terms the "carnivalesque," which he described in relation to Rabelais and other writers:

> Carnival brings together, unifies, weds, and combines the sacred with the profane, the lofty with the low, the great with the insignificant, the wise with the stupid. . . . These carnivalistic categories are not abstract thoughts about equality and freedom, the interrelatedness of all things or the unity of opposites. No, these are concretely sensuous ritual-pageant "thoughts" experienced and played out in the form of life itself, "thoughts" that have coalesced and survived for thousands of years among the broadest masses of European mankind. This is why they were able to exercise such an immense formal, genre-shaping influence on literature.[3]

Not to put too fine a point on it, the carnival was a rowdy place—one enjoyed by the "common" folk. At carnivals outrageous behavior and bawdy language ruled and Bakhtin documents some pretty wild events: the mock kings beaten nearly to death by the revelers; the festive flinging of urine, vomit, and excrement at passersby; obscene gestures and words offered as signs of greeting to strangers; public masses in which excrement and urine are used as host and sacramental wine. In *South Park*, similar carnivalesque behaviors occur: Mr. Hankey jumps from toilets to hands to coffee mugs, leaving a shit trail; Stan vomits over Wendy; "shit" not only happens but is repeated over and over again. "Carnivalesque" describes those non-sanctioned spaces on television in which outrageousness provides an antidote to the erudite, the intellectual, and the constrained—think *World Wrestling Federation, Jerry Springer, The Man Show*. To read Rabelais alongside *South Park* is to be amazed at how little things have changed in hundreds of years. Indeed, "*South Park*-esque" is the modern "carnivalesque."

Satire is just one form of carnival laughter, albeit a rather negative form. The other form, festive laughter, is more joyous and inclusive. Festive laughter is of "all the people." As Bakhtin explains, it is universal in scope and "it is directed at all and everyone, including the carnival's participants. The entire world is seen in its droll aspect, in its gay relativity.... This laughter is ambivalent: it is gay, triumphant and at the same time mocking, deriding. It asserts and denies, it buries and revives."[4] However, Bakhtin overstates his case when he claims a universal jocularity, for not everyone laughs. Critics who find *South Park* racist, sexist, childish, insulting, and offensive certainly aren't laughing. It is the contemporary carnival that fairly screams at its audience and it can be strident at times. *South Park*'s scatological reputation isn't entirely deserved. Sure, it has its share of poo-phemisms, Mephisto continues to experiment with four-assed genetics, people still talk shit, and the series continues to have people put fingers and things in butt holes, but, in every case, the role of scat is to show hypocrisy and to question cultural conventions.

Eating, drinking, and roistering went hand in hand during the festivals; fucking, farting, and body excretions were integral to carnival humor. Bakhtin labeled joking about these things as "lower body stratum" humor, because it, well it was about the naughty bits of the body. More importantly, it was the antithesis of the refined, cool, measured wit of the "upper body," the head. Furthermore, Rabelais' focus on the body and its orifices—mouth, loins, and anus—is a rejection of the classical smooth body; instead, the grotesque body and the humor it deploys is important. The grotesque celebrates the:

> ... contradictory and double-faced fullness of life. Negation and destruction (death of the old) are included as an essential phase, inseparable from affirmation, from the birth of something new and better. The very material bodily

lower stratum of the grotesque image (food, wine, the genital force, the organs of the body) bears a deeply positive character. This principle is victorious, for the final result is always abundance, increase.[5]

The grotesque body is constantly active, exceeding its margins: a body in the act of becoming. It is never finished, never completed. It is continually built, created, and builds and creates another body—which is why dismemberment, pregnancy, and elimination of waste (semen, vomit, urine, excrement) reduce loftier philosophy to the base flesh and are inherently part of laughter and humor. The body and the carnival are not innocent places of play, they are inherently political sites—hierarchy and control are subverted. *South Park*'s toilet humor and gratuitous violence are, therefore, part of a rich heritage of subversive crap.

The political nature of the carnival has engrossed critics from a wide range of disciplines. Yes, it was a time for the peasantry to let their hair down, and yes, anarchy ruled (apparently). But was the carnival really a thumbing of noses at the status quo or was it really a sanctioned moment of mayhem—a safety valve allowed by the powers that be to release some of the pent-up energies and frustrations of the common folk? If the latter, then certainly one can read the carnival as containment. These arguments are described by Chris Humphrey in *The Politics of Carnival: Festive Misrule in Medieval England*. If the carnival is sanctioned, then the "anarchy" is only pretense.[6] Scholars have been concerned about the "social" effects and affects of the carnival and how class and gender were acted out during these festivals, but they are not of primary importance for *Blame Canada*. My concern is not how the carnivalesque leads to social change or even how invoking it affects viewers' thinking, but how it is *performed* through the televisual medium. The carnival itself is a performance; it is a theater at which people perform subversive acts. As wildly and sincerely as they are performed, the acting stops when the carnival is over and the world returns to "normal." So it is with *South Park*. The show's exuberance and scatology referencing recreate the carnivalesque for contemporary audiences.

At the end of Rabelais' fifth book, Pantagruel delivers his ultimate condemnation of contemporary society—he eliminates a large shit. So too, *South Park* drops a large one on the world. As Rabelais started his books, so I begin mine:

> *Good friends, my Readers who peruse this Book,*
> *Be not offended whilst on it you look:*
> *Denude yourselves of all depraved affection,*
> *For it contains no badness nor infection:*
> *'Tis true that it brings forth to you no birth*
> *Of any value, but in point of mirth;*

Thinking therefore how sorrow might your mind
Consume, I could no apter subject find;
One inch of joy surmounts of grief a span;
Because to laugh is proper to the man.[7]

Notes

1. *Redeeming Laughter: The Comic Dimension of Human Experience* (Berlin; New York: Walter de Gruyter, 1997).

2. *Rabelais and His World* (1965), trans. Helene Iswolsky (Indiana University Press, 1984), 84.

3. Mikhail Bakhtin, *Problems of Dostoevsky's Poetics*, ed. and trans. Caryl Emerson; introduction by Wayne C. Booth (Minneapolis: University of Minnesota Press, 1984).

4. *Rabelais*, Ibid., 12.

5. *Rabelais*, Ibid., 62.

6. Chris Humphrey, *The Politics of Carnival: Festive Misrule in Medieval England* (Manchester: Manchester University Press, 2001).

7. Francois Rabelais, *Gargantua and Pantagruel*, Book 1, Prologue.

Part One

Oh My God

Chapter 1

Who Cares about a Guy That Makes Beer?: History

In case you've just returned from an alien probing or, even more unimaginable, you haven't heard of *South Park*, this chapter outlines the success story of two young men who go to Hollywood and manage the unthinkable—they sell their idea to a television network and get their own TV series. A series about a talking shit. Seriously. It's the American dream. It's about as likely as a poor hillbilly striking oil in his backyard and moving to Beverly Hills—but that's another show. Despite the general suspicion that *South Park* wouldn't last more than a couple of years, in 2006, its tenth season started. The young men are not so young anymore, but hopefully they're a lot richer. Much of the history of *South Park* is now folklore, but it's worth retelling. The history of *South Park* begins with the histories of Trey Parker and Matt Stone.

Believe it or not, *South Park* is a real geographical place: "It's in a perfectly circular valley in the middle of the Rocky Mountains, and because of that there's, like, the most UFO sightings, and cattle mutilations, and Bigfoot sightings,"[1] according to Trey Parker. And he should know—he grew up in a small mountain town in Colorado. He claims the isolation encouraged him to make movies because there wasn't a movie theater in town. Parker is the youngest son of a government geologist (Randy) and an insurance broker (Sharon); he has an older sister (Shelley). Hmm, so he's really Stan Marsh. He is a talented musician and attended Berklee College of Music in Boston, Massachusetts, but transferred to the University of Colorado in Boulder (UCB). At UCB he met Matt Stone.

Matt Stone was born in Houston, Texas, but moved to Littleton, Colorado, when he was young. Stone's dad, Gerald, is a semi-retired economics professor, and mom Sheila is a homemaker. His sister, Rachel, is a social worker.

Rachel? There isn't a Rachel in *South Park*. So Matt is basically Kyle Broflovski. "My parents think I'm completely warped . . . but my dad is probably our biggest fan."[2] At the time Stone and Parker met (1989), Parker was making *The Giant Beaver of Southern Sri Lanka* (sound familiar? "Mexican Staring Frog") for a class assignment and the two began to collaborate on various projects.

Beginnings

Even in elementary school, Parker was given to shocking people. His first effort was a sketch, "The Dentist Parker," in which he "drilled holes in his classmate's head" and much fake blood ensued—he later had to explain to the traumatized first and second graders that the dentist was their friend.[3] In high school, he doodled pictures of people with butts for heads during class (also familiar? "How to Eat with Your Butt"). So naturally, at UCB he was going to push filmic barriers. His first animated[4] piece (with Chris Graves), *American History,* was done for an animation class at UCB (1991) and won a silver medal for animation in the Student Academy Awards in 1993. The next year, he did a three-minute fake trailer of *Cannibal! The Musical* for a film production class.

He pretended *Cannibal!* was the short for a real project, so when people kept asking him about it, he decided to go ahead and make it. He, Stone, and others formed a production company, Avenging Conscience, raised the money, and made the film. When their trailer was rejected by Sundance Film Festival organizers (January 1993), a fact satirized in "Chef's Salty Balls," the pair sidestepped Sundance and gave a private showing attended by Brian Graden of Foxlab. The pressure of filming was too great for Parker, who dropped out in his senior year. With *Cannibal!* finished, Stone graduated (with a degree in mathematics) and the two moved to Los Angeles in March 1994.

For nearly two years, they had an agent, a lawyer, and a film, but no success. They relied on the kindness of others. Camping on friends' couches and sharing a 1985 Buick, they worked as landscapers and production assistants and continued to write scripts.[5] While working with a BBC crew shooting a documentary on the porn industry, they made contacts that led to three porno-esque films (*Orgazmo, Profiles for the Young and Horny,* and *Sex for Life*). Parker directed a short, *Your Studio and You.*

In 1995, Parker and Stone did the rounds pitching *The Mr. Hankey Show* to various channels, but the response was basically: "Okay, that does it, screw you guys I'm going home. Talking poo is where I draw the line" ("Mr. Hankey, the Christmas Poo"). Brian Graden suggested the show focus on the four boys and not on Mr. Hankey, and the show was renamed *South Park*. Graden commissioned them to create a Christmas videocard for him.

Back home for Christmas, Parker and Stone made Graden's card while their family members prepared for Christmas. Parker recalls his mother was "mashing yams or something" (she was making fudge), while downstairs the two boys were "screaming as loud as we could 'You [bleep]ing son of a [bleep]!'"[6]—the experience is immortalized in "A Very Crappy Christmas." Graden sent *The Spirit of Christmas: Jesus vs. Santa* to friends; soon bootleg copies were circulating and George Clooney received a copy, which he distributed widely. The clip became a cult hit; excerpts were spotted at rock concerts.

By 1996, the duo had turned down development deals by New Line, Warner Brothers, DreamWorks. As it happens, a newcomer at Comedy Central,[7] Deborah Liebling was looking for a new property and had heard the buzz about *The Spirit of Christmas*. They pitched to her and, in March 1996, she commissioned a pilot. The pilot did not go smoothly and though Nancy Cartwright (voice of Bart Simpson) walked out in disgust. The pilot was finished in October 1996. However, the show wasn't immediately picked up because the pilot did not fare well with focus groups. But Parker and Stone were encouraged to keep working on scripts. They wrote "Weight Gain 4000" and then Comedy Central decided to give the show a try. During the filming of *Orgazmo*[8] (February 1997), Trey and Matt learned that the pilot was accepted. Still skeptical about its chances of success, they agreed to star in another movie, *BASEketball*. They recalled:

> TREY: Last July, David Zucker called and wanted me to direct *BASEketball*. And I said I can't, we're doing this TV show . . . And he went, "Well, when that falls apart?"
>
> MATT: Yeah, they said, "We'll get you out of doing that show so you can come work for us." We were like, "Why would we want to get out of this? It's the coolest thing!"
>
> TREY: Then he called back and said, "How about if you guys act in it?" I said, "I don't know if we have time to do that, either." He said, "We're not shooting until February." We were like, Fuck, *South Park* will be done by then. No way it's gonna still be on the air in February.[9]

The first episode aired on August 13, 1997, and sixty-five thousand households tuned in—for the first time in six and a half years, Comedy Central had a top-rated television show. After four episodes, *South Park* was picked up for another thirteen episodes. In the summer of 1999, a feature film, *South Park: Bigger, Longer and Uncut* was released, and "Blame Canada" (Trey Parker and Marc Shaiman) was nominated for Best Song at the Academy Awards. The show continued to break ratings records at Comedy Central and, in 2005, Parker and Stone renegotiated their contracts through 2008—the twelfth season.

FAQs

Compared to network budgets, cable budgets are modest. A half-hour sitcom episode usually costs anywhere from $800,000 to $1.5 million,[10] depending on the stars' salaries. Of course, animation is slightly different. Even so, *South Park* is cheap. *The Simpsons* costs about $1.2 million per episode;[11] the first thirteen episodes of *South Park,* including production costs and the creators' salaries, cost $3.25 million,[12] around $400,000 per episode.

Who pays these costs? Mainly advertisers. And how do you get advertisers to shell out big bucks? You have a show with high ratings; the higher the ratings, the more expensive the advertising slot. At the end of 1997, four months after the first *South Park* episode, Comedy Central recorded its first profit (less than $10 million) in its six and a half year history.[13]

On August 13, the show premiered with a 1.3[14] Nielsen Media Research rating. By its sixth episode, the rating had climbed to 1.7, the highest of any original series shown on Comedy Central. Previously, Comedy Central shows averaged 0.6 rating in prime time.[15] This is not unusual; cable channels do not attract the same high ratings as free-to-air channels; "CNN has to have a worldwide disaster to come up with a 1.4."[16] The ratings continued to rise and the Halloween episode ("Starvin' Marvin") earned an "astonishing 4.8."[17] From October, *South Park* averaged about 2.3 million viewers per episode in a cable universe of about 46 million homes.[18] In December, a poll asked kids to name their favorite show, and *South Park* scored in the top three.[19]

By the next year, *South Park* claimed the "highest ratings for any series in basic-cable history."[20] Reruns of the first nine episodes helped to make the show a "cult hit," drawing "five or six times" Comedy Central's usual audience.[21] When "Damien" aired in February 1998, another record toppled and the ratings reached 6.4, an increase of 19 percent from the last new episode ("Mr Hankey the Christmas Poo," December 17, 1997).[22] In the final two weeks of February, 5.2 million viewers watched. The show even managed to outperform ABC's *PrimeTime Live.*[23] The best ratings were for "Cartman's Mom Is Still a Dirty Slut." The episode aired on the April 22 and achieved an 8.2 rating, or 6.2 million viewers, breaking the previous cable record, USA Network's 8.1, for the first installment of *Moby Dick,*[24] and was the highest-rated non-sports show on cable television.[25] Less than forty-eight hours after the episode, Parker and Stone signed another agreement that anchored them to Comedy Central until 2000.[26] They also negotiated a deal to write and produce a full-length feature film, *South Park: Bigger, Longer and Uncut*. The film was released the following year, 1999.

Much to Comedy Central's delight, they had an "appointment show"; groups of fans were congregating to watch it.[27] *South Park*'s phenomenal success was the talk of the industry and the media; few cable network shows attracted so many viewers or such media attention. Before the second season started, the show was featured on the covers of *Rolling Stone, Spin, Newsweek,* and *TV Guide*; it even rated an article in the UK's *Guardian.*[28]

By the third season, the show's success seemed to be wavering. The ratings had fallen. The third-season premiere (April 7, 1999) drew 3.4 million viewers, a "dramatic" drop from the 5.5 million for the previous year's opener, "Not Without My Anus," and the 6.2 million for the second episode, "Cartman's Mother Is Still a Dirty Slut."[29] In total, the first three episodes of the third season had lost "64% of its teen viewers and 39% of its 18-to-34 viewers."[30] Perhaps the poor quality of the second season did not help; the stress of making *Bigger, Longer and Uncut* had sapped Stone and Parker of their creative vitality (see season two DVD commentaries). Still, *South Park* was number twelve in Lycos's top search items for 1999.[31] The creators believed the incredible media hype had inflated the show's ratings, and that the third-season ratings reflected its "true" fan base. By 2000, original episodes averaged "just north of 1.5" million homes.[32] In July 2001, the ratings climbed to 2.3 million, largely attributed to late-night fraternity viewership.[33] By the sixth season (2002), around 2.8 million tuned in. The ratings continue to hover around the 2.7 figure, 3 million viewers; the one hundredth episode (April 9, 2003) grabbed a 2.7, as did the eighth (2.7[34]) and ninth (2.6[35]) seasons. Comedy Central has been surprised by *South Park*'s "ability to hang on"—it was the channel's most-watched original series in its sixth season.[36] Moreover, *South Park* draws more dedicated viewers to the channel; they stay and watch other shows. In April 1999, an overall increase of 16 percent in the channel's prime-time audience was recorded;[37] and in May 2004, the prime-time ratings were 26 percent higher than those of May 1998.[38]

Once upon a time, syndication was no big TV deal. Now syndication reels in hefty revenue dollars. Reports have claimed that *South Park* syndication realized around $100 million "over five years."[39] When syndication started in September 2005, the ratings were not spectacular: "In its first week, *South Park* pulled in a 1.4 household rating and averaged 1.87 million viewers. It dipped somewhat to a 1.3/4 in week-three overnight ratings. . . . Nationally, however, *South Park* is down 19% from its lead-ins.[40] Because of its content, the show airs at later time slots—between 11 p.m. and 1:30 a.m.—no doubt this contributes to the low ratings. The show now airs on "135 stations, reaching 86% of the country," and more new viewers potentially translates into an increased audience for original episodes.

As a consequence of healthy ratings, Comedy Central advertising revenues have steadily increased from $76 million in 1997 to $129 million in 1998, $163 million in 1999, $240 million in 2001, and $283 million in 2002. Comedy Central is now among the top fifteen grossing basic-cable networks.[41] But ratings is only part of the economic health of a channel. Because of *South Park*'s success, more cable companies opted to carry Comedy Central, and it became one of the fastest-growing cable channels, jumping from 9.1 million households in 1997 to 50 million in June 1998, 64.6 million in May 2000, 70.1 million in 2001,[42] and 82 million in 2003.[43] Cable operators pay monthly license fees to Comedy Central; the fees jumped from $51 million in 1998 to $56 million 1999.[44] Overall, the series has done for Comedy Central what *The Simpsons* did for Fox. It *made* Comedy Central.

"Tian-ah! Kenny bei guadiao!"

When *South Park*'s success became global knowledge, television stations around the world were keen to buy it. In the United Kingdom, Sky bought *South Park* in September 1997, a few weeks after its US debut. It started airing on Sky One in March 1998 and on free-to-air Channel 4 in July 1998. Paramount Comedy picked up the UK rights from Sky in March 2005, and the new episodes premiered in April 2005.[45] In both the UK (Channel 4) and Australia (SBS), *South Park* airs on channels noted for risk taking, for example SBS offers *The Iron Chef*, *Queer as Folk*, and *Mythbusters*.

In Australia, *South Park* airs on SBS, a free-to-air network. The first season was rated PG (Parental Guidance, content should not harm or disturb children under 15[46]) and aired at 8:00 p.m., but for the second season, it was moved to 9:30 p.m. and given an M rating (Mature, not recommended for those under 15). One option was to edit the series to maintain the old classification, but SBS feared the reaction of the strong fan base. As a spokesman pointed out, "[W]e wouldn't get out of the building alive."[47] Around a million viewers watched the show and, in Sydney, reruns average 226,400 viewers.[48] When the commercial free-to-air stations saw *South Park*'s success, they tried to outbid SBS for the second season, but Comedy Central remained loyal to the station that took a risk—SBS had paid almost $1 million (Australian).[49] *South Park* has boosted SBS's advertising revenue: "Since *South Park* was first broadcast, advertising revenues have soared from $16.4 million in 1996–97 to $21.2 million in 1997–98, and $19.2 million in 1998–99, according to various SBS Annual

Reports."[50] In 2001, Australian cable channel Comedy Central launched *South Park*. It shows reruns; SBS still has the rights to air original episodes.

South Park aired on Canada's free-to-air network Global Television in September 1997. Originally, it aired at 9:30 p.m. but, following complaints, it was bumped to midnight and still managed to rate in the top ten.[51] Nearly a year later it made its cable debut on Canada's Comedy Network. In August 1998, the first season's episodes were shown back-to-back over thirteen nights. The show airs ninety minutes earlier on cable, at 10:30 p.m.

In France, the show premiered one year after its US debut (July 7, 1998). It airs on cable channel Canal Plus (+) at the relatively early 6:25 p.m. The following year, the show started in Germany (RTL) and South Africa (M-Net).

Hong Kong-based StarTV picked up the show, which became a surprise hit "among Taiwan's latte-sipping, cynicism-dripping youth."[52] As can be imagined, the script has resisted "straight translation." Local writers have translated it into Mandarin Chinese and interpolated Taiwanese pop culture references, current events, and Chinese puns. For example, in "Big Gay Al's Boat Ride," Stan's gay dog is told to attend "a Leslie Cheung concert." Cheung is a "well-known gay actor-singer" from Hong Kong. The show's title has been altered to *Nanfang Sijianke* or *South Park's Four Slackers*, which in Mandarin also sounds like *The Four Musketeers*.

The *South Park* world includes New Zealand, Brazil, Scandinavia, Italy, Germany, Switzerland, Belgium, the Netherlands, Latin America, Mexico, and Israel.

Programming

To ensure success, a show has to air on the right channel and at the right time. Programming is not a science but an art, and many a show has languished in the wrong time slot until it attracts enough viewers. In *South Park*'s case, the TV-MA rating it received at Comedy Central means that it is not supposed to air before 10 p.m.[53] Thanks to *South Park*'s success, the channel now enjoys a reputation for cutting-edge comedy and, in 2005, it hosted some of the edgiest shows on television: *Drawn Together, The Dave Chapelle Show*, and *The Daily Show with Jon Stewart*.

Programmers must also consider what shows surround it for maximum impact. In the US, episodes are usually paired with *The Daily Show with Jon Stewart*, which satirizes recent news items and contemporary culture—this coupling highlights *South Park*'s satiric political elements. In 2005, it was preceded by *Drawn Together*, foregrounding the shows' animation and adult content. In pairing the two, programmers were using an old programming trick to create an audience for the new *Drawn Together*. When it went to syndication, it aired in much later time slots with limited success; Allison Romano thought WKBD Detroit's strategy of placing it after *The Simpsons* a "winning" one.[54]

Despite having similar names, comedy cable networks around the world demonstrate remarkably dissimilar line-ups. In the UK, the Paramount Comedy favors rather old-fashioned US sitcoms such as *Soap, Mork & Mindy, The Wonder Years, Happy Days, Roseanne*.[55] As many of these shows are mentioned in *South Park*, this lineup creates a nostalgic anchor. In Australia, the Comedy Channel airs US comedies such as *Arrested Development, Curb Your Enthusiasm, The Man Show*, thus linking *South Park* with more experimental comedy. Because of its adult content, *South Park* is aired late at night in Canada and the UK, thus effectively foregrounding the show's taboo content. Not so in Australia where it can be seen at all hours.

Thanks to remote controls, viewers can create their own viewing experiences by watching several shows simultaneously. In Australia, the lover of sitcoms could "watch" *South Park, The Flintstones, Who's the Boss*, and *That '70s Show* simultaneously—providing a potentially fascinating viewing of representations of the American family. The adventurous viewer could opt for *Dr. Quinn Medicine Woman, Law and Order, The Price Is Right*, and *M.A.S.H.*—goodness knows what kind of cultural message that viewer would decode. The relatively commercial-free cable channels further complicate scheduling. The US rigidly adheres to an hour/half-hour schedule (usually using advertisements as a stop-gap device), but in the UK, Canada, and Australia, *South Park* starts at differing times creating a headache for the channel surfer.

Programming is a consummate skill—a program must work on both axes of the programming grid. It must complement the station's viewing line-up and compete successfully with the competition. A clever programmer arranges the viewing day most appropriate for the channel's regular viewers and works to attract new ones. In these days of the remote control, viewers have learned the art of judging a show in a matter of seconds—the action, look, and sounds have to tempt viewers to stop.

Rewards of Creation

Comedy Central owns *South Park*; Trey Parker and Matt Stone do not. The two do not even own the images. They are employees who are paid to write, direct, and produce the weekly animation. Parker explains, "They could fire us tomorrow and continue doing the show, and we wouldn't be able to do a thing about it."[56] Yet Parker and Stone are firmly anchored to the show; 41 percent of the *South Park* articles in Factiva.com included "Trey Parker" (5,382 of 13,026), and 37 percent refer to "Matt Stone" (4,936).[57] Why do Stone and Parker receive so much attention?

The *South Park* creators' story smacks of Horatio Alger: two talented young men leave their small Midwestern towns and come to Hollywood, where they find fame and fortune. Well, fame at least. In September 1997, Parker admitted that they were earning comfortable incomes but were "not insanely rich, but rich by our standards."[58] In March 1998, a *Newsweek* interview provided glimpses of their discontent as Parker complained, "I have a friend who writes for *Just Shoot Me* who makes more a week than I do. . . . Thirty million in t-shirt sales, and I got a check for $7,000."[59] When it came time to renew their contract in April 1998, Parker and Stone were more money savvy, upped the ante for another forty episodes, and increased their share of merchandise revenues (approximately $130 million). No exact salary figures were given, but *Daily Variety* reckoned "the producing duos various deals which also include a couple of other unrelated films are worth a minimum of $15 million."[60] However, Parker and Stone soon squashed the $15 million figure on *The Tonight Show*:

T: . . . it came out someplace that we made 15 million dollars, which is—

M: Everyone pictures like a check

T: Yeah . . .

J: You didn't?

M AND T: No, no . . .

T: I mean we're getting like way better money than we did when we started and it's totally cool and Comedy Central's been great to us.

J: What kinda dough we talking? What kinda money?

T: It literally would break down to probably like still 50 grand a year.[61]

Comedy Central enigmatically said, "they're being handsomely paid."[62] A couple of years later, it was reported that Parker and Stone receive $500,000 for each new episode.[63] Money, however, is of secondary concern to fans, who are more worried about the show remaining on the air.

Fans speculated that the two would not sign again with Comedy Central and with good reason—the duo had said so on a number of occasions. In March 2000, they claimed they would not sign another long-term deal.[64] A year later, in a KROQ (Los Angeles) interview (April 4, 2001), they said they would quit at 120 episodes, but they continue to commit themselves and in 2005 they signed on until 2008. They re-signed after *Team America*; apparently, the filming was such an unpleasant experience that they vowed not to work with organizations other than Comedy Central. Parker explained: "After doing this movie [*Team America*], we realized what a great gig we have with *South Park*. As long as they let us, we'll keep making it. We started and thought we'd get up to six episodes maximum and now we have 120."[65] Yet, only a few weeks earlier, Trey Parker admitted that he "hates" making the show. "It's super stressful. I'm always miserable. I want to kill myself every week."[66]

Parker and Stone are the public faces of *South Park* for a good reason. Not only is their material innovative, controversial, and new; they are two young(ish), attractive males who are upbeat and amusing. They perform the *enfant terrible* role well. Because of their multiple talents as directors, writers, and composers for movies and television, they have a large body of work. They do the talk-show circuit several times a year, whether to promote *South Park*, or their latest movie, or to respond to the latest criticisms. For instance, their appearance schedule for the month of October 2005 (just before the launch of the second half of the ninth season) reads like this:

> *The Tonight Show with Jay Leno* – October 5
>
> MTV, *Making the Movie* – October 8
>
> *Access Hollywood* – October 12
>
> *60 Minutes* – October 13
>
> *Late Night with Conan O'Brien* – October 13
>
> CNN, *Anderson Cooper 360* – October 14
>
> *Ebert & Roeper* – October 17
>
> *Last Call with Carson Daly* – October 22

Their irreverent attitude strikes the right note and reflects their Gen X sophisticated understanding of the processes of fame and television. They resist merchandising by creating lame characters such as Towelie. Their repeated celebrity bashing reminds viewers that celebrities are only human too and sometimes not very nice humans. Perhaps their most memorable rejection of the film industry was their appearance at the 72nd Academy Awards. Both Parker and Stone wore dresses, but not any dresses—they donned designer clothes linked to specific stars.[67] The outfits demonstrated a healthy skepticism for the bloated Academy Awards system and the spectacle of the red carpet. They flouted gender conventions; their choice of designer garments refused acceptance of product placement on stars' bodies. But even they admit the prank was not easy to pull off:

> Q: How drunk were you guys the day you wore dresses to the Oscars?
>
> STONE: We weren't drunk at all, we were on acid.

PARKER: We were on acid that day. And not that we take, because we don't take a lot . . . [*sic*]

STONE: That's the last time I ever took it.

PARKER: That was the last time I've taken acid. And we hadn't done it for a few years before that, but that seemed like the right time to do it.[68]

Despite the fact that the two creators have produced an enviable body of work in a short period of time, they continue to be typecast as "slackers" and drug users,[69] a mantle they relish and encourage. They make it sound easy by repeating that they write episodes at the last minute; that they start on Thursday for the following week's show. But part of the perception problem stems from the populist perception of comedy. Writing for television sounds like fun, doesn't it? But only a fool would think the creators are lazy. Deborah Liebling emphasized their work ethic in her introduction at the 1998 US Comedy Festival: "They work around the clock, paying attention to every detail on the show, both on-air and off-air. They're prolific writers."[70] She then listed the projects they'd undertaken in the first eight months of *South Park*, and the list is impressive:

> written, directed, produced, and starred in *Orgazmo*
>
> started writing the prequel to *Dumb and Dumber*
>
> starred in *BASEketball*
>
> in talks about a feature film, which was to become *Bigger, Longer and Uncut*
>
> producing a *South Park* soundtrack album
>
> performing in their band DVDA
>
> dozens of media appearances and interviews

Their hero, David Zucker, witnessed their heavy workload while filming *BASEketball*. He said the two stars were "up all hours. They work all day on this movie, then they go and write *South Park*. They have people on the set constantly coming up to them with plotlines and other things that demand their direction."[71] The two-part *South Park* schedule[72] allows the creators a midyear "break" to pursue other projects, such as *My Bush*, *Orgazmo*, *BASEketball*, *Bigger, Longer and Uncut*, and *Team America: World Police*. They've also signed with Paramount Pictures for three years,[73] so it seems unlikely they will be able to relax for some time to come.

So, How Is *South Park* Made?

CHARLIE BROWN: Good Grief! We need a Christmas tree for our play.

CARTMAN: Oh, Jesus, not this thing again.

STAN: How come everyone in cartoons has such big heads?

CHARLIE: Alright, everyone, we've got to get on with our play!

KYLE: Jesus, this sucks! All they keep doin' is dancing around!

CARTMAN: Yeah, this thing really falls apart in the second act.

STAN: And why is it that on Charlie Brown cartoons, everyone talks like this.

CARTMAN: My mom could make a better Christmas special than this!

KYLE: Hey, that's it. Oh, my God, that's totally it! It's so simple!

STAN: What, dude?

KYLE: We can get everyone back into the Christmas spirit by making our very own animated Christmas special, and showing it to everybody in town!

STAN: We don't know anything about animation.

KYLE: How hard can it be? Look at it.

CARTMAN: Hey yeah! We can make a little animated Santa Claus and Jesus, and it can star us instead of these little round-headed guys!

KENNY:

STAN: Yeah! And we can call it . . . "The Spirit of Christmas."

"A Very Crappy Christmas" recreates the painstaking story of *The Spirit of Christmas* videocard. In the *South Park* version, Butters makes cardboard cutouts of the characters, and the boys take the cutouts to a photographic shop where they begin the laborious process of arranging the figures and then photographing them. The boys have to manipulate the cutouts scene by scene and the mouths syllable by syllable. Their excitement soon turns to boredom as the reality of creating an animation by hand sets in. It is tedious to say the least; it's even tedious to watch. But things have changed dramatically since Parker and Stone did *The Spirit of Christmas*.

Unlike other animated shows, *South Park* is created quickly and in the US.[74] It's a frenetic pace. As Trey Parker explains:

We take a lot of time before just to come up with broad ideas, but until the Thursday before that Wednesday, that's when we really sit down and go 'OK, how can we tell this story?'. . . . A lot of times on a Thursday, we'll sit down and go, "hey, have you seen this Terri Schiavo thing? This is huge, we should do a story about that. . . . Matt and I really do most everything. We still write, direct and edit every episode ourselves. We can sit there on a Tuesday night and (rewrite the third act), run into the booth next door, record all the voices, get the storyboards together, edit it and see it in a couple of hours.[75]

However, obviously there are some big gaps in Parker's account. There are around sixty people at South Park Studios, so what are they doing? Basically, Trey Parker writes the first draft of the script. During the first recording, the editor (Tom Vogt[76]) sits in on the session:

> to see if there are any notes that are made to the script while they're recording the voices. That also gives me a feel for what Trey's intention for the show is going to be, which is kind of my job. I'm supposed to interpret that and get as close to his idea for the show at the beginning . . . After that, I get the audio that was recorded, . . . the storyboards, and then I build a skeleton of the show up to that point.[77]

The animatic[78] is made and passed to the director of animation (Eric Stough). Stough notes difficulties in staging or continuity and "finesses" the animatic. The postproduction supervisor (Karin Perrotta) marks the scenes while the animators and technical directors view the tape. During the course of production, the animatic is updated with completed animation so that everyone can see how the whole thing is developing. After production is finished with the storyboards, they are returned to the editor, who divides the story and assigns various parts to people in the storyboard department. Artists either choose or are allocated what they'll do. Adrien Beard, storyboard and production artist supervisor, explains: "Tony [Postma, storyboard artist], since he's studied trans (transportation design) at Art Center, I might give him a scene that has a lot of vehicles, or anything that's kind of technical. Keo is really good at action, so he can do a lot of the action sequences. Greg [Postma, storyboard artist] is really good at character scenes where there is a lot of talking."[79] Computer technology does most of the menial work. Originally, the construction paper cutouts were scanned into a computer and replicas were built in Alias Wavefront's PowerAnimator. Now, Silicon Graphics workstations run Maya software to create a virtual plane—in 3D space—on which the "flat" computer-generated characters are animated. "Trey drew all the original characters in Corel Draw," says Stough. "We actually take those illustrator curves directly into Alias PowerAnimator 8.5 and build what we call smart puppets." With the characters constructed, Stough and company then tap into the Expressions function of Alias to manipulate specific body movements. "We animate all the visibility—the front heads, the side heads, the mouths—they're all on these little sliders you push back and forth which make different mouths visible." To keep up with the fast turnaround needed, the production department relies on a variety of SGJ boxes.[80]

Technical directors construct the layout, backgrounds, and props, and lip-synchers animate the mouths. Even the texture of construction paper is applied via computer. While the process is to keep the animation from looking too sophisticated, astute viewers can spot the differences between earlier and later episodes—virtually gone is the "no-platen" or "shadow" look.

After the animation gets Trey's approval, it is sent with the audio to be edited and mixed using Avid Media Composer. Sounds easy? Well, Tom Vogt expounds on particularly "challenging" episodes:

> "Spooky Fish" was one, "Chef Aid" was another. "Spooky Fish," because we weren't sure if the story should be told all at once because there was an A, B, and C story. First, there was the story establishing the fish as being evil, and then you're crossing over to the parallel universe. To me it was one of the more complicated stories because of the way the act links broke, and the way that certain parts of the stories were revealed, and how those parts were resolved. I think they all came together quite nicely in the end. "Chef Aid" was difficult because you were dealing with a lot of new characters, namely musical artists who did the voices. We had a pretty big pre-production period as far as new setups and character designs were concerned, and then we had to wait on the audio for the songs. I feel like I always get the trickier shows (oh, wah!), but I like that challenge.[81]

Fifteen to thirty people work on each episode. It can (and has been) done in a week; but according to the South Park Studios Web site FAQs, it takes two to three weeks. An almost finished episode can be revised within days if necessary; for example, "Quintuplets."[82]

At the end of 2005, the South Park Studios Web site added blogs which provide insight into the production madness. Anne Garefino, executive producer, wrote:

> All's quiet in the studio tonight. People are feeling the effects of three weeks of crazy hours. Even Toni isn't running her usual marathon from one animation station to the other. They'll perk up when the fast food shows up in a couple of hours.

> Keep lit scented candles in the edit bay to combat the smell of all the stinky bodies in there. By this time on Tuesday nights, the edit bay is the place to be. Everyone is in there trying to get a clue about what shape the show's in.

> The Storyboard dept. brought some designs into the writer's room for a potential show. (Writer's meeting just wrapped at 11:30 p.m.) As soon as he saw them, Trey was sold on the story for next week. They're hilarious. The designs are of Cartman and that's all I'll say about that.

> The shot update. This week at midnight we're 52 shots out. That's good news except that we have a few shots that will take a while to set up and animate.

(They have lots of people in them and a fancy camera move too.) Those shots will cost us a couple of hours easy.

Trey has written a song for this week's show. One of my favorite things about South Park is the music and I love watching Trey record. He obviously records "in character" and it's a great thing to see. "FOLLOW THAT EGG" Posted: Tue Nov 01, 2005 9:00 pm.[83]

We just finished group. There were THREE females in the booth tonight. We hardly ever have women available for ADR. In general, women are in the minority here at South Park. . . . Matt directed and Lydia cut it all in to the show as we recorded—flawless as usual.

It's midnight and Frank just came in . . . We're 39 shots out. We've got a few hours to go but overall, things look good *unless Trey continues to write.* So good in fact Ryan even has time to animate a shot. He's been so busy lately trying to manage the floor, (sitting in on the retake sessions, making shot assignments and answering a million questions), that he hardly has time to do what he likes most, animate!

The writer's meeting broke up at about 10:30 again tonight. I am crazy about the ideas for the next episode. All I can say is . . . , it's too hot to even tease. . . .

Stopped into the Storyboard dept. to see what they were doing. While we were in the writer's meeting, I saw the entire department leave the building and then return a while later with Tower Records bags. They had a break and went on a field trip to buy some music. Greg loves Ninja Academy. Tony is sick—which means that by next Tuesday the entire building will have what he's got. Before I got in the room he was napping under his desk. Now he's up and they are all working on new characters for next week's show. ("Ginger Kids," November 9, 2005)[84]

The firsthand account of smelly bodies, fast food, and late nights sleeping under desks certainly does not conform to the glamorous world many associate with television. Rarely does the public glimpse such details about the intimate workings of a television production.

After the show is finished, it is uploaded by satellite to the East Coast, usually on Wednesday afternoon, the day it airs. Because of the tight schedules, there is no time to catch, let alone correct, mistakes. Fans are of course quick to note errors, which are remedied for the second airing,[85] typically on Saturday; for example, Willie Westwood notes the following changes at his *South Park* Web site:

"Memememee!"—When Cartman says this on Wednesday his voice is deep. On Saturday, it's normal. The number of insane boy terrorists was corrected to four. The length of time since the word "veal" was officially changed to "little tortured baby cow" drops from six days to 24 hours. It should've dropped to 36 hours or so . . .[86]

Presumably, other countries receive the corrected versions.

Occasionally, episodes are aired out of numerical order. This happens for a variety of reasons. The particular episode might require a new look and thus additional production work. Charles Song at South Park Studios summarized the main differences:

> *An entirely unique look.* Sometimes they're extremely complicated and require extra time, like #405 "Pip" which aired after #414. Everything in "Pip" had to be built from scratch, including the new mouths with rotted out teeth that were used for most of the characters. Since Trey and Matt were looking for an entirely new look for Pip's England (in the same way that Terrance and Phillip's Canada had its own, unique look), everything had to go through a laborious approval process. In addition, *Live-action sequences.* "Pip" had live action sequences with the actor Malcolm McDowell, which involved casting, scheduling, additional planning, and post-production. These things take time, something we didn't have that summer. South Park had a run of consecutive episodes ending with #411 "Probably," and a hiatus for cast and crew. When a new run of episodes, "The Fourth Grade," began in September, there was time to finish the remainder of work on "Pip" in between the new episodes.

> *Special effects* are another reason why certain episodes are delayed, like #310 "Chinpokomon" (which aired after #312) and #311 "Starvin' Marvin in Space" (which aired after #313).

> *Holidays.* Other times holiday scheduling is a factor, as when #110 "Mr. Hankey, The Christmas Poo" delayed #108 "Damien" from airing for several months. #312 "Korn's Groovy Pirate Ghost Mystery" is a unique example where work on the episode began near the beginning of the season, but wasn't given an episode number because of its late air date (Halloween).

> *Guest Stars.* And lastly, certain episodes include the participation of special guest stars, as with #501 and Radiohead, whose busy schedules require careful planning.[87]

Victims of their own timeliness, everyone wants to know how the show remains so topical.

Conclusion

In January 1999, the t-shirts were still everywhere, but the media claimed "the buzz was over" and people weren't looking forward to Wednesday nights anymore.[88] In Internet parlance, *South Park* had jumped the shark. The show continues to attract media attention and money. Indeed, if media appearances and articles are any indication, the ninth and tenth seasons have seen *South Park* reclaim some lost ground. Comedy Central's profits continue to rise, and Parker and Stone can be seen chatting with Jay Leno, Charlie Rose, and Larry King. People remotely related to the show are coupled with it: Johnnie Cochrane's obit mentions his *South Park* "appearance"; Liane Adamo (Parker's ex-fiancée) has her own entry at the Internet Movie Database. The cult of celebrity runs deep in *South Park* culture. The continued popularity of the show is demonstrated in its name as signifier.

After completing nearly an entire decade, the show has become a staple. *Daily Variety* still runs stories describing the corporate headquarters of South Park Studios.[89] The show now appears in nostalgic reminiscences about teen years![90] Though the show's demise has often been predicted, it has been signed until at least 2008. It ranked sixth in Lycos's most popular television search term for 2005. As fan Coop warned all the naysayers: "And to all you people who say the show is going to end, please be nice and shut up. I'd rather watch the worst episode of *South Park* than nearly anything else on TV."[91]

"*South Park* is a show you should be proud to admit watching, I love it!" —Drew Carey

"To date, *South Park* still holds the Guinness World Record for 'Most swearing in animated series.'"

"Now, remember: there are no losers at the Cable Ace Awards, only people who are less likely to have another season." —Kyle

---

Notes

1. Gail Pennington, "A Cartoon about Kids," *St. Louis Post-Dispatch*, August 13, 1997, E6. Stone quoted in Paula Span, "On the Cussing Edge: 'South Park' Pushes the Taste Envelope," *Washington Post*, September 14, 1997, G8.

2. Elizabeth Snead, "The Masters of the Chaotic 'South Park' Universe," *USA Today*, August 27, 1997, D3.

3. Michael Mehle, "Eight Year Old with an Attitude," *Rocky Mountain News*, February 1, 1998, 12.

4. Because he couldn't draw, he resorted to construction paper cutouts.

5. Paula Span, "On the Cussing Edge."

6. Ibid.

7. Comedy Central came from the merger of HBO's Comedy Channel and MTV's Ha! in 1991.

8. A parody about a Mormon porn star, *Orgazmo* (1997) was a hit at the 1997 Toronto International Film Festival and at Slamdance in January 1998.

9. E! Online interview, http://www.southparkcows.com/interviews/eonline.html, accessed October 22, 2006.

10. Phil Kloer, "Networks Turned on by Tuning in to Toons," *Atlanta Journal and Constitution*, March 26, 1999, F6.

11. Ibid.

12. Span, "On the Cussing Edge."

13. Ray Richmond, "Comedy Central Finally Parks Itself in the Black," *Variety*, October 6, 1997, 38.

14. A rating point is the percentage of the 48 million homes capable of getting the channel. A rating point for Comedy Central represents 460,000 homes. Bill Carter, "Comedy Central Makes the Most of an Irreverent, and Profitable, New Cartoon Hit," *New York Times*, November 10, 1997, D11.

15. Ibid.

16. Span, "On the Cussing Edge."

17. Stuart Miller, "Comedy Central's 'South Park' Shocks Cable," *Multichannel News*, December 15, 1997, 54.

18. Sylvia Rubin, "TV's Foul-Mouthed Funnies," *San Francisco Chronicle*, January 26, 1998, D1.

19. "Kids Rate Their Favorite New Shows," *Milwaukee Journal Sentinel*, December 1, 1997, 4.

20. Annette Cardwell, "'South Park' Flush with Success," *Boston Herald*, May 20, 1998, 52.

21. Tom Feran, "'South Park' a Runaway Cult Hit," *Cleveland Plain Dealer*, February 3, 1998, E5.

22. Tim Cuprisin, "'South Park' Isn't for Everyone," *Milwaukee Journal Sentinel*, February 9, 1998, 8.

23. Rick Marin, "The Rude Tube," *Newsweek*, March 23, 1998, 56.

24. Richard Huff, "South Park Shows Plenty of Pop in the Nielsens," *New York Daily News*, April 24, 1998, 130.

25. Robert McNatt and Joan Oleck, "South Park's Canny Bait-and-Switch," *Business Week*, April 27, 1998.

26. *Hollywood Reporter*, April 28, 1998.

27. Ibid.; Lauri Githens, "With 'South Park,' a Cult Following Is Born," *Buffalo News*, December 28, 1997, F1; "'South Park'—It's a Gas," *Boston Globe*, January 28, 1998, D1; Kevin M. Williams, "'South Park' Soirees," *Chicago Sun-Times*, February 11, 1998, 49.

28. Stuart Jeffries, "Move over, Homer," *The Guardian*, July 16, 1997.

29. "*South Park*'s Ratings Drop Dramatically," *St. Petersburg Times* (Florida), April 20, 1999, 7D.

30. Jenny Hontz, "Genre-Action Gap Hits Sitcoms," *Variety*, April 26, 1999, 1.

31. "Lycos 15 Most Popular Search Terms of 1999," *USA Today*, February 10, 2000, D11.

32. "More South Park, We Swear," *New York Daily News*, May 2, 2000, 78.

33. John Dempsey, "Latenight Yuks for Youth," *Variety*, July 23, 2001, 15.

34. "Animated Comedy Rocks Ratings," *Multichannel News*, November 5, 2004.

35. "Ratings," *Cablefax*, March 11, 2005.

36. Donna Petrozzello, "Park and Ride," *New York Daily News*, June 14, 2002, 150.

37. John Dempsey, "Comedy Web Smiling over Sub Increases," *Variety*, April 12, 1999, 27.

38. Alan James Frutkin, "Comedy Central 2.0 Laugh Net Launching Originals in Search for Next 'South Park,'" *Mediaweek*, June 12, 2000.

39. Linda Moss, "Belles of the Syndie Ball," *Multichannel News*, January 17, 2005, 43.

40. Allison Romano, "Naughty Is Nice: *Sex and the City*, *South Park* Work for Stations," *Broadcasting & Cable*, October 17, 2005, 11.

41. Dempsey, "Latenight Yuks for Youth," 15.

42. Dateline Viacom 2001, http://www.viacom.com/pdf/dl01q1.pdf;jsessionid=POYOO J2QY0CTWCQBAHIQ4CY, accessed October 22, 2006.

43. Dateline Viacom 2001, http://66.102.7.104/search?q=cache:7rghKtJrxwAJ:www.viacom .com/pdf/dl03q2.pdf+%22south+park%22+nielsen+ratings+2003&hl=en, accessed October 22, 2006.

44. Dempsey, "Comedy Web Smiling."

45. Neil Wilkes, http://www.digitalspy.co.uk/article/ds19757.html, accessed October 22, 2006.

46. *Bigger, Longer and Uncut* also received a milder rating in Australia, an MA (Mature) rating as opposed to R (Restricted) in the USA. Comedy Channel also aired *Cannibal! The Musical* in July 2001.

47. Mike McDaniel, "Pushing the Limit," *Houston Chronicle*, April 5, 2000, 10.

48. Simon Yeaman, "Park Life," *Daily Telegraph*, August 27, 1998, 35.

49. Stuart Clarke, "Bigger than Jesus," *Rolling Stone Yearbook 1998* (Australia), 55.

50. John Field, "Public Broadcasting and the Profit Motive: The Effects of Advertising on SBS," *Policy* (Autumn 2001), 13–18, http://www.cis.org.au/Policy/aut2001/polaut01-3.htm, accessed October 22, 2006.

51. Claire Bickley, "Hot Series *South Park* bumped to midnight," *Jam Showbiz*, October 9, 1997, http://jam.canoe.ca/Television/TV_Shows/S/South_Park/1997/10/09/735414.html, accessed October 22, 2006. Keith Marder, "Welcome to South Park," *The Globe and Mail*, February 21, 1998, C1; Paul McCann, "Talking Poo on a Screen Near You," *London Independent*, January 26, 1998.

52. Henry Chu, "Taiwan Goes South," *Los Angeles Times*, December 27, 2000.

53. Of course, the late time slot is based on Eastern Time; in Central Time, *South Park* runs at 9 p.m.

54. Romano, "Naughty Is Nice."

55. Based on the TV guide for London at Yahoo.com.co.uk.

56. Matthew Sweet, "Who Ruined Kenny?" *London Independent*, April 22, 1999, 12.

57. Most of the articles without their names are reviews of upcoming episodes.

58. Span, "On the Cussing Edge."

59. Marin, "The Rude Tube."

60. Quoted in Richard Huff, "Parker Gets Multi-Season Deal," *New York Daily News*, April 28, 1998, 74.

61. Interview, May 1998, from "South Park Cows" Web site, http://www.southparkcows .com/interviews/tonightshow.html, accessed October 22, 2006.

62. Huff, "Parker Gets Multi-Season Deal."

63. Linda Moss, "*South Park* Creators Renew at Comedy Central," *Multichannel News*, May 8, 2000, 18.

64. Richard Huff, "'South Park' Won't Be Fenced In," *New York Daily News*, March 31, 2000, 122,

65. James Ellis, "Sixty Second Interview," Metro Café, www.metro.co.uk/metro/interviews/ interview.html?in_page_id=8&in_interview_id=1000, accessed October 22, 2006.

66. Kate Aurthur, "Those Boys Are Back, as Timely as Ever," *New York Times*, October 19, 2005, Arts 1.

67. A copy of the Ralph Lauren dress worn by previous year's Best Actress Gwyneth Paltrow and a copy of the controversial green Versace dress worn by Jennifer Lopez to the 2000 Grammy Awards.

68. Jeff Otto, "Interview with Trey Parker and Matt Stone," IGN Filmforce, http://filmforce .ign.com/articles/612/612094p1.html, accessed October 22, 2006.

69. Vicki Mabrey, *Sixty Minutes* interview, aired October 13, 2004.

70. Deborah Liebling at the US Comedy Festival, February 1998.

71. Jeffrey Ressner, "Gross and Grosser," *Time*, March 23, 1998, 74.

72. The first half of the season airs March/April to June/July, and the second half recommences around October/November to December.

73. "Paramount Signs South Park Duo," *Guardian Online*, http://film.guardian.co.uk/news/story/0,12589,1645725,00.html, accessed October 22, 2006.

74. For a full explanation of the production process and the staff, visit the official Web site, www.southparkstudios.com.

75. Associated Press, "Q & A with Matt Stone and Trey Parker," October 18, 2005.

76. South Park Studios, http://www.southparkstudios.com/behind/interviews.php?tab =20#4, accessed October 22, 2006.

77. Ibid.

78. An "animatic" is the filmed version of the storyboard. It can be still images pasted together in sequence and can have dialogue. The animatic determines timing, scene lengths, and so on for the animators and technical directors.

79. http://www.southparkstudios.com/behind/interviews.php?tab=20#4, accessed October 22, 2006.

80. Wendy Jackson, "Dig This," *Animation World Magazine*, September 1, 1998, http://mag.awn.com/index.php?ltype=search&sval=south+park&article_no=411, accessed October 22, 2006.

81. South Park Studios, http://www.southparkstudios.com/behind/interviews.php?tab =20&sid=sid=b0133fcc5769675a8de8d415a6fa6a2d, accessed October 22, 2006.

82. South Park Scriptorium, http://www.spscriptorium.com/SPinfo/SPStudiosFAQIndex .htm, accessed October 22, 2006.

83. South Park Studios, http://www.southparkstudios.com/fans/bbs/viewtopic.php?t=14 877&sid=188d8a4dea07e8730658c5bcc9ade0f1, accessed October 22, 2006.

84. Daily blog at http://www.southparkstudios.com/show/blog.php?tab=10, accessed October 22, 2006.

85. Matt Cheplic, "The Method Behind the Madness of *South Park*," *Millimeter Magazine*, May 1, 1998.

86. South Park Scriptorium, www.scriptorium.com, in the "Secrets" section of the relevant episodes.

87. March 4, 2002, http://www.spscriptorium.com/SPinfo/TableOfColumns.htm#Some FAQs, accessed November 12, 2005.

88. Virginia Rohan, "Looking Ahead to 1999 Television: What's Next," *The Record* (Hackensack NJ), January 3, 1999, 3.

89. "Corporate Punks," *Daily Variety*, January 9, 2006.

90. "Toons of Our Teen Years," *Philippine Daily Inquirer*, January 25, 2006, C2.

91. Coop, South Park Alliance, March 31, 2005, http://spalliance.net/content.php?sub action=showcomments&id=1110382179&archive=&start_from=&ucat=4&go=episodeguide 9, accessed October 22, 2006. http://www.njmg.com/contact/advertising.php, accessed October 22, 2006.

South Park Award Nominations			
Year	Award Association	Episode/Film	Award *Winner
2005	FactNet	912, "Trapped in the Closet"	Person/s of the Year for debunking Scientology
2005	Primetime Emmy Creative Arts	904, "Best Friends Forever"	Outstanding Animated Program*
2004	American Film Institute	South Park	Television Program of the Year*
2004	Primetime Emmy Creative Arts	715, "Christmas in Canada"	Outstanding Animated Program
2003	Santa Monica Film Festival	Maverick Filmmakers	Persistence of Vision*
2002	Primetime Emmy Creative Arts	509, "Osama Bin Laden Has Farty Pants"	Outstanding Animated Program
2000	Primetime Emmy Creative Arts	310, "Chinpokomon"	Outstanding Animated Program
2000	MTV Movie Awards	South Park: Bigger, Longer and Uncut	Best Musical Performance*
2000	Chicago Film Critics Association	South Park: Bigger, Longer and Uncut	Best Original Score*
2000	Academy Awards	South Park: Bigger, Longer and Uncut	Best Original Song: "Blame Canada"
1999	Los Angeles Film Critics Association	South Park: Bigger, Longer and Uncut	Best Music*
1999	Annie	South Park: Bigger, Longer and Uncut	Outstanding Individual Achievement for Writing in an Animated Feature Production
1998	PGA Golden Laurel	South Park	NOVA Award* (honors promising producers and new talent)
1998	Primetime Emmy Creative Arts	104, "Big Gay Al's Big Gay Boat Ride"	Outstanding Animated Program
1997	CableACE	South Park	Animated Program*
1997	Florida Film Festival	Spirit of Christmas	Best Short*
1997	Los Angeles Film Critics Association	Spirit of Christmas	Best Animation*

Chapter 2

Towelie Ban: *South Park* in the Media

Ｉf a TV show is considered a popular culture phenomenon, how is it measured? By ratings? Number of t-shirts sold? People quoting lines *ad nau-
seum*? Yes, and more. In this world of hypermedia and almost
instantaneous global transmission, the press, television, radio, and the Internet are not merely barometers of the popular, but seminal to popular culture.
If it appears on the covers of *Time, MAD Magazine, Newsweek,* and *Rolling
Stone,* then it's hot—even if *you* haven't heard of it. Cult hits become mainstream with a wave of the media wand.

One thing's for sure, *South Park* made a media splash. Before August
1997, "South Park" was a county in Colorado, a town in Pennsylvania, and a
public school in Utah. A few hundred press notices, mainly in local papers,
celebrated local events, football teams, and graduations. All that changed.
Between January and June in 1997, a Factiva database search for "South
Park" yielded 1,223 articles, and from July to December that number had
nearly doubled (2,042). The following year, triple the number of entries
appeared (7,369).[1]

Even before the first episode aired, the industry was buzzing. In January,
the *Hollywood Reporter* noted:

> "We have produced a pilot with Trey Parker and Matt Stone called 'South Park,'
> which is our twisted 'Peanuts,'" explains Comedy Central's senior vp of pro-
> gramming Eileen Katz. "In the next few weeks we'll decide whether to go
> series." It utilizes construction paper cutouts and involves the comic adventures
> of a space alien and an alien abductee in a quiet Colorado mountain town.[2]

Then there was silence for several months until Comedy Central distributed
copies of the first episodes with a press release. As a result, the show snagged a
mention in *TV Guide* (June 6, 1997) and articles in numerous newspapers

around the US: *Tulsa World, Portland Oregonian, Florida Times-Union, Pittsburgh Post-Gazette, Buffalo News, Sarasota Herald-Tribune, Dallas Morning News, New Orleans Times-Picayune, Milwaukee Journal Sentinel.* News crossed the Atlantic, and the UK *Guardian* mentioned *South Park* nearly one month before its US premier.[3]

Reaction to the first episodes was surprisingly uniform. Stuart Miller observed that "everywhere from *TV Guide* to *Newsweek* to *USA Today,*" the show enjoyed "positive reviews."[4] Critics called it "devilishly original,"[5] and "most daring, most unpredictable."[6] They delighted in the show's "twisted exploits," which were "deliciously demented"[7] and part of its "spurious, perverted charm."[8] Most were amused and found "hearty laughs and many wry chuckles."[9] Others found it "hilarious"[10] and "laugh-out-loud funny."[11] Eric Mink of the *New York Daily News* felt *South Park* displayed a "joyous lack of self-restraint . . . stridently, relentlessly gloriously and hilariously outrageous."[12] Many proclaimed the show a "classic in the making"[13] and predicted it was going to be the newest "cult hit."[14] Others paid tribute to the creators' "comic genius" and their "vehement creativity."[15] They saw past the swearing and the crude humor and appreciated the show's "bitter social satire."[16] Matthew Gilbert points out:

> No matter how nasty and scatological it gets, it's never just dumb and dumber. Besides all the bathroom humor, the show is built on clever, equal-opportunity satire as it stomps over every politically correct sensitivity of the past decade. . . . "South Park" doesn't tiptoe around, and that's a sometimes refreshing switch from most TV fare. Environmentalism, the fragility of childhood, death—they are all detonated in the subversive fantasia that is "South Park." It's as if the cartoon's creators, Trey Parker and Matt Stone, have taken the dark paranoia of tabloid-obsessed culture—from UFOs to weight-gain products—and dropped it on a bucolic Colorado landscape and into the silly mouths of babes. The result is jarring, illuminating, and sometimes hysterical.[17]

Most observed its duality: "South Park is immature, gross, violent and crass."[18] But "it's hilarious, too."[19] They predicted viewers would enjoy it as a "guilty pleasure"[20] or would "run screaming for shelter."[21] Chris Vognar's response is typical, "Time will tell how well the *South Park* kids maintain the ability to shock and entertain. In the meantime, sidle up to the TV for some big-boned laughs—or get ready to write your cable company in protest."[22]

Though Tom Shales of the *Washington Post* was not amused by the first episodes, he warmed to later ones:

> "Park" gets off to a ghastly start . . . Most of the alleged humor on the premiere is self-conscious and self-congratulatory in its vulgarity: flatulence

jokes, repeated use of the word "dildo" (in the literal as well as pejorative sense) and a general air of malicious unpleasantness. . . . But the third episode in the series, airing two weeks from tonight, is rather funny and even verges on the satirical.[23]

Of course, not everyone reviewed the early episodes positively. *Entertainment Weekly*'s Ken Tucker yawned: "'South Park' is the essence of a novelty act. If you've seen one episode, you've seen 'em all";[24] one year later he had changed his mind: "I admit it took the brilliant *South Park* feature film for me to appreciate how good the TV series is. This year's parody of the *Passion of the Christ* only confirmed its ongoing excellence. . . ."[25] Seattle's Hal Boedeker thought the series "unfunny . . . abrasive, tasteless" and felt it didn't have "staying power."[26] The *Buffalo News* agreed that it was "unfunny . . . and lame."[27] But they were in the minority.

Early articles about *South Park* are so uniform, they're formulaic: they tell the history of the show's creators, its uptake by Comedy Central, outline the characters, and mention Kenny's deaths, Cartman's big-boned ass, and Isaac Hayes as Chef. They express concerns about swearing and content but heap praise for the riotous humor. In various wordings, they revise Comedy Central's press release. This South African excerpt is typical:

> The scatological, computer-generated, cardboard-cutout characters are the creation of two Denver filmmakers, Trey Parker, 28, and Matt Stone, 26. Both studied film at the University of Colorado, although Parker was expelled for cutting classes. He was busy making his own films. (He grew up in the real South Park County in Colorado, which has the highest per capita UFO sightings of the US.)[28]

Press releases are of course critical for the television critic, because they bring to their media cousins the latest products, neatly packaged.

Overseas Responses

The British press largely ignored the company line and engaged more critically with the show's content. They used *South Park* to compare and contrast differences in British versus American humor. Toilet-humor? Ha, we're British, we invented it, Toby Young crowed in the *Sunday Times*: "[*South Park*] specialises in the kind of scatological offensive humour that British audiences are used to but has rarely been seen on US television screens before."[29] And what about that other great British literary tradition, the satire? According to Meg Carter of the *London Independent*, James Baker (head of programming at Sky One) claimed surprise at *South Park*'s social satire; apparently, he hadn't seen it in an American TV show before.[30] Aside from the nationalistic posturing, British critics noted the show's underlying tenderness (something few American articles noted) and subtlety; apparently, subtlety is "virtually unheard of in a British adult television animation series."[31]

South Park also provided the press the opportunity to consider the differences between British comedy productions and American ones. Articles were suffused with a subtle rhetoric of nationalism:

> Unlike American sitcoms, which have too many cooks in the kitchen, the British writer usually has more control over his six to eight episodes. . . . The British writer has time to polish, rewrite and get it right while maintaining a single vision. . . . In America, you have to squeeze a lot of situations out of a series, which drains it of freshness and spontaneity, but the Brits tend to stop—or take several years off—when they run out of ideas.[32]

In other words, the British produce fewer but better sitcoms. Furthermore, British animations are of a better quality, "The British have different expectations of animation. We tend to concentrate on the quality of the visuals. The Americans go more for minimalist animation but very, very strong writing,"[33] Colin Rose, head of the BBC's animation unit, explained. Basically, the Brits were alarmed because *South Park* outstripped anything the Brits were doing animation-wise, "[T]he series's impact underlines the fact that despite our reputation for world-class animation . . . British TV has yet to finance a long-running adult animation show."[34] Seven years later (August 2005), *Bromwell High*,[35] "an animated comedy following the adventures of three exceptionally naughty school girls, one maverick headmaster and a bunch of desperate teachers," aired on Channel 4.

The Australian press had another boat to row. It was not concerned about the show's content nor did it posture about the superiority of local television productions, comedy writing, or animation. American television imperialism is a given. Rather, the local press focused on the station that bought the show, SBS; reportage favored stories about *South Park*'s place in the SBS lineup and its ratings' impact on revenue. SBS is partially funded by taxpayers, newspapers reminded readers, and so when SBS paid $1 million (Australian) for the second series, media reaction was mixed.[36]

Everything *South Park* attracts press attention whether it's the release of movies *Bigger, Longer and Uncut* (1999) and *Team America: World Police* (2004), the creators' new comedy *That's My Bush* (2001), syndication (2003), re-signings by the creators, books (2005 Brian C. Anderson's book *South Park Conservatives*), and of course controversial episodes. By 2006, the show had evolved media-wise. The press had invoked the grand television narratives, from the fairytale beginnings to business reports, TV ratings, and product merchandising. After all, it had been a movie, made a bundle in merchandising, and been nominated for an Academy Award and multiple Emmys. *South Park* was no longer the innovative and shocking cartoon, but part of cartoon establishment.

Controversies

The first season offered content to offend everyone, from insulting celebrities (Barbra Streisand and Sally Struthers being the most notable attacks), to gay dogs ("Big Gay Al's Big Gay Boat Ride"), to an elephant fucking a pig ("Elephant Fucks a Pig"), and blasphemy ("Damien"). Viewers saw Stan vomiting, Cartman being anally probed ("Cartman Gets an Anal Probe"), and a Christmas crap singing ("Mr. Hankey, the Christmas Poo"). But media reports of complaints were few and far between. No wonder newspapers puzzled at the show's ability to avoid controversy[37]:

> Since "South Park's" debut in August . . . the show hasn't generated complaints, despite its raunchy content. "It's totally out of place for what your eyes are showing you," said Greg Collins, a Seattle "South Park" fan and men's college basketball editor at ESPN's SportsZone. "It's this really simplistic cartoon. Then, when you hear what's coming out of these kids' mouths . . . it just doesn't fit at all. I just kind of shake my head and go, 'How'd that get past the censors?' Then I think, 'What kind of mind is thinking up these things and getting them into this format?'"[38]

To media observers, and even to the creators themselves, *South Park* seemed Teflon coated—whatever they said or did failed to register on the moral panic scale. Of course, the show hasn't been trouble free—episodes have had fingers wagged (or waved?) at them about swearing ("It Hits the Fan"), representations of religion ("Red Hot Catholic Love" and "Bloody Mary"), and celebrities ("Trapped in the Closet")—it's a typical *South Park* mix.

With more than 160 repetitions of the word "shit," "It Hits the Fan" caught the press's eye. It was fun to see the reporters scrambling to find euphemisms for shit. The *New York Times* wrote the "dung-related" word,[39] U.S. Newswire tried "a common four-letter word for fecal matter,"[40] but most were happy to call it "un-bleeped utterances of the word s—." So many letters when a simple four will do. They couldn't even agree on the number of times it was said. Missing the moral of the episode, *Cleveland Plain Dealer*'s Phillip Morris was incensed and called the show "pathetic" and "teetering on the verge of a delinquent meltdown."[41] But he was about the only one. Rather than offend, the episode prompted thoughtful engagement—which is, of course, the role of effective satire.[42]

It hit the fan again two seasons later when one episode took on the Catholic Church's sexual abuse scandals. "Red Hot Catholic Love" offended the Catholic League for Religious and Civil Rights, whose president issued a statement after seeing episode promotions:

> The scandal in the church is not about priests having sex with prepubescent boys. It is about priests having sex with post-pubescent young men. The former is called pedophilia and the latter is called homosexuality. If Stone and Parker really had guts, they would do a show on gay priests. But, of course, like so many other intellectually dishonest elites in our society, they will go to any length to protect homosexuals.[43]

Unfortunately, the league's rather bizarre response only confirmed that the church is out of touch and misjudged public feeling at the time of the sex abuse scandals. Not ones to miss an opportunity, executives at Comedy Central used the league's response in press releases and pre-show promotions encouraging viewers to watch what "the Catholic Church doesn't want you to see." Worse was yet to come. In the 2006 "Bloody Mary," the final episode of the ninth season, a statue of the Virgin Mary bleeds from her ass and the Catholic League released two outraged responses.[44] In one, it requested that Comedy Central not air the episode again;[45] in the second, it crowed when the episode did not appear in the traditional end-of-the-year marathon.[46]

But when it comes to media attention, a bleeding Virgin Mary cannot hold a candle to super-celeb Tom Cruise. When *South Park* begged Tom Cruise to come out of the closet nearly fifty times ("Trapped in the Closet"), the press around the world sat up and paid attention. A shade over four hundred articles on the Factiva database mention the episode. Irish, Indian, Australian, and British press reported that the show was banned from re-airing. Litigious Cruise had apparently contacted Paramount (owner of *South Park* and his latest production) and complained; however, in a year of media strangeness from Cruise, things didn't go as planned. As "Trapped in the Closet" aired in Australia and in the UK,[47] it can only be assumed that the "rumor" that Paramount "agreed not to show the episode again, after Cruise complained" was just that, a rumor.[48] The attack on Scientology also stirred the media pot when voice-over regular Isaac Hayes, a Scientologist, resigned.[49]

Aftermath

Not all of the print media focuses on *South Park* as television show. Its success has become ribosomatic. The creators' public appearances are assiduously recorded.[50] Their other projects and private lives earn column space. Isaac Hayes, singer, songwriter, actor, musician, and disc jockey, has found his career revived though *South Park* and will probably be remembered by a generation for his role as Chef:

> At Clive Davis' iconic Grammy bash, musician, actor and radio jock Isaac Hayes riffed about another hat he wears. The white one. "Doing the voice of the chef on 'South Park,' that's adding to my longevity," said the Moses of soul. "Now my fan base has expanded from 6 to 96." Hayes said his biggest kicks come from meeting families familiar with both ends of his 35-year career spectrum. "The kids come up to me and say, 'Wow, you da chef.' And their parents go, 'Wow, you da Shaft.' They're all mesmerized."[51]

Those celebrities, A or Z grade, who "appear" on the show are inexorably linked with *South Park*. Brian Boitano talks of "the future for skating" but cannot escape the inevitable *South Park* question.[52] It becomes their coda and sometimes their touchstone, with younger viewers, anyway.

It's hard not to be amused at the inventive ways the media invokes *South Park*. Cartman is both a cartoon character and a poster child for misguided prejudice.[53] Democratic presidential hopeful Carol Moseley Braun said, "Even if your mother is Cartman's mom, you ought to be able to go and get a quality education."[54] In 2003, the *Sydney Morning Herald* contained an article about the role of potatoes in history, including the "fact" that Kenny's heart was replaced by one in *Bigger, Longer and Uncut*.[55] Saddam Hussein as Satan's lover is recast as wishful thinking.[56] Few topics avoid a *South Park* observation or quote.

There are even articles about the articles; specifically, the controversy surrounding the *Spin* cover that did not have official sanction and prompted Trey Parker to challenge *Spin* editor Michael Hirschorn to "an eight-round boxing match any time in the next three months."[57] In March 1988, *Newsweek* and *Time* faced a similar rivalry; both had features in their March 28 issues, but *Newsweek* appeared one day earlier and with the *South Park* characters on the cover: "Planning a *South Park* cover? Better act fast. That's the lesson *Time* learned last week after being scooped by *Newsweek*. Both books had geared up for *South Park* packages and both wanted to get their stories on the stands before the show's April 1 special episode. But *Newsweek* beat *Time* to the punch by one day."[58]

Dozens of articles note the growing cultural currency of *South Park*, largely by its coverage on magazine covers.[59] In the cultural cycle, a cult hit attracts media attention, which then ratifies its popularity.

South Park reportage makes for strange bedfellows. *South Park* was never relegated solely to youth-inspired magazines such as *Rolling Stone* and *MAD Magazine*; it ran the gamut, from industry staples *TV Guide* and *Broadcasting*

& Cable to the populist, gossipy *Entertainment Weekly* (in October 1997 and January 2000) and establishment magazines such as *Time*, *Newsweek*, and *Fortune*. *Mean Magazine* (May 2000), *PC Gamer*, and *Casino Player* also found the series newsworthy. The show's merchandising hype meant dozens of marketing magazines—*Discount Store News*, *Brandweek*, *Licensing Letter*, *Sports Style*, *Consumer Media Report*, and *Brand Strategy*, among others—applauded the show's success, tried to learn from it, and considered it an exemplar of merchandising. Even academic articles embraced the series, covering topics like marketing and underpants gnomes, racism and Chef, sexuality/gender and Garrison, religion and ridicule, humor and Rabelais. Newspapers, populist publications, specialist magazines, and academic journals all contributed to the *South Park* phenomenon. It is not often one gets to bracket *Audio Week*, *Women's Wear Daily*, and *Gambling News* together.

Other Media

Print is, of course, only one form of media. As a child of the World Wide Web, it is only natural that *South Park* has a huge and varied online presence: newsy articles appear in online versions of print newspaper articles and at entertainment news sites such as E! Online, Ain't It Cool News, and IMDB. Specialist e-zines such as *Webuser*[60] and *Animation World*[61] contain material appealing to their readers. Other sites contain fans' contemplative essays,[62] reviews of the latest DVD and CD releases, information and gossip about Matt and Trey, and behind-the-scenes production information.[63]

The rather lone voice raised in protest came from the Internet. In 1997, L. Brent Bozell, founder and president of the Media Research Center and Parents Television Council (and the Conservative Communications Center), found the show "sordid" and called it "filth."[64] He ended his column with the warning that "as we cross the bridge to the 21st century, there will be no cultural barriers left" (which is rather confusing, since breaking down cultural barriers sounds like a good thing). His argument is a version of the end-of-civilization-as-we-know-it type heard during the black days of sensational TV talk shows and the early days of reality TV shows.[65] Bozell revisited the show several months later in an effort to see if he'd misjudged it; the verdict was no, he hadn't, and he stood by his previous criticism.[66] While the American Family Association boasts that it persuaded Geico, Best Buy, Foot Locker, and Finish Line to stop advertising on *South Park*, it also concedes that its campaigns have had little to no effect on TV programming.[67] Bozell continues to crusade against *South Park*.[68]

Case Study: *Variety*

Variety is considered the industry standard print media for gossip, stories, and the latest in television and movie worlds. It is, therefore, the most appropriate place to trace *South Park*'s media evolution. According to Factiva, *South Park* has had 256 mentions in *Variety* between April 21, 1997, and September 2005.[69] References to the show occur across a broad spectrum, from obituaries[70] to stage plays and marketing.[71]

The show first appeared as a blip in the summer schedule forecasts.[72] Four months later, it was previewed. Like so many other articles, the review briefly outlined the cartoon's history, gave a brief biography of the creators ("geniuses"), compared it to other cartoons (*Beavis and Butt-head*), and described the characters. The article speculated that "a lot of people just ain't gonna get it" and predicted a backlash against the show because of its content.[73] All in all, a fairly typical *South Park* review.

Within months of its first appearance, *South Park* was inserted into articles whenever crude humor or low comedy (i.e., performances of Aristophanes' *The Birds*[74]) was mentioned: "If all this seems a tad sophomoric, well, it is. Strip away the graphic excess (which, truth be told, is not so graphic or excessive that most won't have seen it all before—the simulated anal sex in 'Angels in America,' the puking on Comedy Central's 'South Park')."[75]

Soon, *South Park* entered the animation canon; *Variety* described *Bob and Margaret* as "not as outrageous as 'South Park.'"[76] And of course, there was *Family Guy*: "MacFarlane, a graduate of the Rhode Island School of Design, is being hailed as nothing less than the second coming of 'South Park' creators Matt Stone and Trey Parker (but younger)."[77] Each year when cartoons rolled out for the new season, the hope was for the next *South Park*:[78] "'Tripping the Rift' was a 'South Park'-like animated half-hour for the Sci Fi Channel that lampoons socially responsible space operas."[79] Eventually, *Variety* elevated *South Park* to the rarified status of the *über* cartoon, *The Simpsons*: "Yet . . . this [*Family Guy*] and 'American Dad' (whose latest installment is mildly improved vs. the unimpressive pilot introduced following the Super Bowl) will never be 'The Simpsons' or even 'South Park.'"[80] The crappy show was now the benchmark for other animations:

> Though not in the elite technical class of Japanese animation—background characters bobble about a la "South Park"—"Nitaboh" scores top marks in storytelling.[81]

> When earthbound characters, afterlife denizens and J.T. in limbo all join to stand erect with fists clenched, solemnly singing their plea to God for the hero's young life in "Not This Day," the turgid "Les Miz" ripoff involuntarily

delivers one of the most hilarious skewerings of overwrought musical emotion since the "South Park" movie.[82]

South Park has become contemporary cultural shorthand for success, for scatological content, and for animation style. It's no longer the new kid on the block but the yardstick.

Conclusion

After almost a decade, *South Park* has become a television "classic." The show appears in lists such as "100 Moments That Rocked TV,"[83] "TV Land's 100 Most Unexpected Moments on TV,"[84] "50 Best Cartoon Characters,"[85] and the whole cast makes it into the "Top Ten Gay Cartoon Characters."[86] It regularly has an entry in the various "top TV moments" of the past year. Whenever a new animation is released, *South Park* is trotted out, especially if the new show is at all controversial. For example:

> MTV's new series, *Clone High USA* . . . is tamer than *Beavis and Butt-head*, more family-friendly than *South Park*.[87]

> It drives him "nuts" when people say producer Greg Lawrence is ripping off *South Park* for his Comedy Network hit *Kevin Spencer*.[88]

Comedy Central has managed to keep the publicity treadmill moving, and the creators power walk with their steady stream of controversial episodes and other creative projects. *South Park* could not have been better packaged for contemporary media consumption. The show's content continues to be controversial, and the attractive and biddable creators manage to remain the darlings of the talk show circuit.

"We got a letter from a kid in Mississippi who said he was in a school play about Rosa Parks and played the bus driver as Cartman," Parker says. "Which shows how kids get it."

"It appears to be that [South Australian Premier Mike] Rann's thinking on alien contact has been profoundly influenced by *South Park*—and the episode "Cartman Gets an Anal Probe." –crikey.com.au

---

Notes

1. Factiva results continue to vary as the database adds new titles; the research for this chapter was conducted in three periods, January–March 2005, September–November 2005, and January–February 2006.

2. Alan Waldman, "Tube Groove Cable Cartoon Programs," *Hollywood Reporter*, January 14, 1997, 8.

3. Stuart Jeffries, "Move Over, Homer," *The Guardian*, July 16, 1997, 19.

4. Stuart Miller, "Comedy Central's 'South Park' Shocks Cable," *Multichannel News*, December 15, 1997.

5. Monica Collins, "'South Park' Unconventional, even for a Cartoon," *Pittsburgh Post-Gazette*, August 12, 1997, C10.

6. Shane Danielsen, "That's Not All, Folks," *The Australian*, December 29, 1997.

7. Mark Lorando, "Cartoon Craziness: You'll Need a Baby Sitter for an Outing to 'South Park,'" *New Orleans Times-Picayune*, October 29, 1997, E1.

8. Monica Collins, "Toons in the Hood," *Boston Herald*, October 28, 1997, 32.

9. Lorando, "Cartoon Craziness."

10. Jim Minge, "Comedy Central's 'South Park' Pushes Lots of Parental Buttons," *Omaha World Herald*, August 7, 1997, Living Today 42.

11. Joanne Ostrow, "Weird, Funny Adult Cartoon Series Has Colorado Roots," *Denver Post*, July 15, 1997, E1.

12. Eric Mink, "'South Park' Comes Up a Hallo-Winner," *New York Daily News*, October 29, 1997, 89.

13. Ibid.

14. Gail Pennington, "A Cartoon about Kids That Isn't for Them," *St. Louis Post-Dispatch*, August 13, 1997, 6E.

15. "Ernest Tucker," *Chicago Sun-Times*, August 11, 1997, 37.

16. Jeff Simon, "Who's Really the Butt of All Cable Jokes?" *Buffalo News*, August 3, 1997, TV 2; Collins, "Toons in the Hood."

17. Matthew Gilbert, "Cute but Crude, Sly Kids Can Kick 'Butt-head,'" *Boston Globe*, January 28, 1998, D1.

18. Ibid.

19. Lorando, "Cartoon Craziness."

20. Tom Shales, "'South Park' Falls Flatulent," *Washington Post*, August 13, 1997, C1.

21. Pennington, "A Cartoon about Kids."

22. Chris Vognar, "'South Park': Having Some Fun in the Gutter," *Dallas Morning News*, August 11, 1997, C1.

23. Shales, "'South Park' Falls Flatulent."

24. January 16, 1998, quoted in Don Aucoin, "'South' Creators Do It for Laughs," *Boston Globe*, January 20, 1998.

25. Ken Tucker, "Second Opinion," *Entertainment Weekly*, August 20, 2004, 114.

26. Hal Boedeker, "Comedy Central's 'South Park' Series Takes Adult-Aimed Humor a Bit Too Far," *Seattle Times*, August 13, 1997, F6.

27. "'South Park' Cartoon Characters Aren't for Children," *Buffalo News*, August 12, 1997, C5.

28. Cas St. Leger, "Out of the (Foul) Mouths of Babes," *Sunday Times*, April 4, 1999.

29. Toby Young. "Charm Offensive—Television," *Sunday Times*, February 8, 1998.

30. Meg Carter, "Comedy Bites in South Park," *London Independent*, March 17, 1998.

31. Steve Clarke, "It's as if Roald Dahl Had Dropped an Ecstasy Tab and Set a Story in Dysfunctional America," *The Guardian*, March 16, 1998, 108.

32. Alan Waldman, "Hidden Treasure," *Hollywood Reporter*, March 3, 1998, S1 (British article).

33. Carter, "Comedy Bites in South Park."

34. Clarke, "It's as if Roald Dahl Had Dropped an Ecstasy Tab."

35. A "British" show produced in Canada.

36. "Bidding War for Cartoon," *Herald-Sun*, September 2, 1998, 4; Jacqueline Lee Lewes, "Minnow Calls the 'Toon," *Daily Telegraph*, October 15, 1998; "Oh My God! Risky Business," *Daily Telegraph*, November 26, 1998.

37. Tom Feran, "'South Park' A Runaway Cult Hit," *Cleveland Plain Dealer*, February 3, 1998, E5; Lauri Githens, "With *South Park*, a Cult Following Is Born," *Buffalo News*, December 28, 1997, F1.

38. Melanie McFarland, "Those Darn Kids!" *Seattle Times*, November 11, 1997, E1.

39. James Bone, "TV Taboo Broken 162 Times," *New York Times*, June 30, 2001, 18.

40. U.S. Newswire, "*South Park*'s Use of Bathroom Language Is Another Reason for Congress to Extend Broadcast Decency Law to Basic Cable," June 22, 2001.

41. Phillip Morris, "We're Bludgeoned by Profanity," *Cleveland Plain Dealer*, June 26, 2001, B9.

42. Robert Philpot, "TV Dares to Defy the Taboos We Swear By," various newspapers, including the *San Diego Union-Tribune* and the *Fort Worth Star-Telegram*, November 3, 2001, E5.

43. Anthony Violanti, "Talking Trash," *Buffalo News*, July 8, 2001, E1; "South Park Angers Catholic League," *Montreal Gazette*, July 14, 2002, A12.

44. Don Kaplan, "*South Park* Defends Bloody Cut," *New York Post*, January 10, 2006, 83.

45. "Vile South Park Episode Pulled," http://www.catholicleague.org/05press_releases/quarter%204/051230_Southpark_pulled.htm, accessed October 24, 2006.

46. Catholic League, "Virgin Mary Defiled on South Park," http://www.catholicleague.org/05press_releases/quarter%204/051208_south_park.htm.

47. Guy Adams, "Falkender Sees Red over Wheen's 'Lavender List,'" *The Independent*, May 17, 2006, http://news.independent.co.uk/people/pandora/article485463.ece.

48. "Cruise *South Park* Show Censored," *Irish Examiner*, January 20, 2006; "Cruise gets 'South Park' Episode Censored," *Hindustan Times*, January 21, 2006; "The Lens," *Courier Mail Guide*, January 26, 2006, 2.

49. "Hayes Out of South Park," JamBase, http://www.jambase.com/headsup.asp?storyID=8147, March 31, 2006.

50. "Aspen Comedy Festival" mentions Matt and Trey's appearance at the Aspen Comedy Festival in 1998. *Denver Post*, February 23, 2003.

51. "Pre-Awards Soirees Sound Good to Guests," *New York Newsday*, February 23, 2003.

52. "Boitano Talks of Future for Skating," *Daily Herald* (Arlington Heights, IL), February 10, 2003.

53. Rick Marin, "The Rude Tube," *Newsweek*, March 23, 1998, 56.

54. "Campaign Trail Mix," *Atlanta Journal-Constitution*, December 15, 2003.

55. "No. 1 Mash Hits," *Sydney Morning Herald*, January 11, 2003.

56. "Saddam to Siberia? Residents Reveal Their Wishes for Iraq Leader," *Bluefield Daily Telegraph* (Bluefield, WV), January 27, 2003.

57. "'South Park' Creator Is Fighting Mad," *Pittsburgh Post-Gazette*, February 20, 1998, 35.

58. "Dude, That Sucks—Newsweek Beats Out Time on South Park," *Mediaweek*, March 23, 1998.

59. ". . . they got pissed off because we wanted the cover of *Rolling Stone*. And so they decided to release a cover at the same time to piss us off." http://www.southparkcows.com/interviews/uscomedy.html.

60. Top 20 *South Park* Web sites, October 23, 2001.

61. Dominic Schreiber, "Cult Heroes and Their Secrets," April 1, 1998, http://mag.awn.com/index.php?ltype=search&sval=south+park&article_no=547&page=1.

62. Juliet Brownell, "South Park and Socrates: South Park Symposium," http://core-relations.uchicago.edu/VolumeIIpages/southpark.html, dead.

63. Matt Cheplic "The Method Behind the Madness of South Park," *Millimeter Magazine*, May 1, 1998.

64. "TV's New Nightmare," August 20, 1997. http://www.mrc.org/BozellColumns/enter tainmentcolumn/1997/col19970820.asp, accessed October 25, 2006.

65. Toni Johnson-Woods, *Big Bother: Why Did That Reality TV Show Become a Phenomenon?* (St. Lucia, Australia: University of Queensland Press, 2002).

66. Parents Television Council, "'South Park' Reconsidered, Sort Of," February 11, 1998, http://www.parentstv.org/PTC/publications/lbbcolumns/1998/col19980211.asp, accessed November 21, 2005.

67. Jack Neff, "Christian Group Spooks Advertisers," *Advertising Age*, October 25, 2004, 1.

68. Parents Television Council, "Sleazy Sequels on 'South Park,'" August 22, 2001, http://www.parentstv.org/PTC/publications/lbbcolumns/2001/col20010807.asp, accessed November 22, 2005; Town Hall Winners and Losers, January 3, 2004, http://www.townhall.com/opinion/columns/brentbozell/2005/01/03/14123.html.

69. Trey Parker is mentioned in seventeen; Matt Stone in seven; and Comedy Central in five.

70. Steve Irwin, *Variety*, September 11, 2006, 67; Stanley Desantis, license holder of South Park t-shirts, *Variety*, August 29, 2005, 85; lawyer Johnnie Cochran, *Variety*, April 4, 2005, 80.

71. Ray Richmond, "One-Hit Nets Find Cable Carriage Won't Speed Up," *Variety*, February 16, 1998, 38; Paul Sweeting, "'Titanic' Floats Vid Biz Hopes," *Variety*, August 10, 1998, 10; Marc Graser, "'Wars' Sparks Summer Toy Stories," *Variety*, October 5, 1998, 7–9; Marc Graser, "New Playground for Studios," *Variety*, May 17, 1999, 9.

72. Ray Richmond, "Cablers Position Skeds for Moment in the Sun," *Variety*, April 21, 1997, 27–28.

73. Ray Richmond, "South Park," *Variety*, August 11, 1997, 28.

74. Charles Isherwood, "The Birds," *Variety*, February 2, 1998, 47.

75. Greg Evans, "Shopping and Fucking," *Variety*, February 9, 1998, 80.

76. Brendan Kelly, "Production Closeup: 'Bob and Margaret,'" *Variety*, January 25, 1999, 66.

77. Ray Richmond, "Family Guy," *Variety*, February 1, 1999, 29.

78. Denise Martin, "Cable Toons Get Kapowed by Auds," *Daily Variety*, December 15, 2003, 30.

79. John Dempsey, "Cablers Turn Tables: Edgy Fare Helps Niche Nets Beat Out Broadcast Rivals," *Daily Variety*, December 15, 2003, 1–2.

80. Brian Lowry, "Family Guy," *Daily Variety*, May 2, 2005, 71.

81. *Variety*, August 22, 2005, 1.

82. David Rooney, "Sugar-Coated 'Life' Delivers Giant Lemon," *Variety*, October 24–30, 2005, 32–33.

83. VH1 and *TV Guide*'s "100 Moments That Rocked TV," PR Newswire, January 9, 2003.

84. http://en.wikipedia.org/wiki/The_100_Most_Unexpected_TV_Moments , accessed October 25, 2006.

85. *TV Guide*, July 29, 2002.

86. January 30, 2004, http://www.thisislondon.co.uk/entertainment/articles/8842878?source=Metro, accessed October 25, 2006.

87. "Double Whammy," *Miami Herald*, January 20, 2003.

88. John McKay, "Perverse Humour of Animated Kevin Spencer," *Canadian Press*, January 31, 2003.

Chapter 3

Trapper Keeper: Internet and Fandom

He's fat, he's obsessive, he speaks fluent Klingon, his favorite Web site is alt.nerd.obsessive, and he owns a comic book store. Yes, Jeff Albertson is the contemporary image of the "fan":

CBG: Last night's Itchy & Scratchy was, without a doubt, the worst episode ever. Rest assured I was on the Internet within minutes registering my disgust throughout the world.

BART: Hey, I know it wasn't great, but what right do you have to complain?

CBG: As a loyal viewer, I feel they owe me.

BART: What? They're giving you thousands of hours of entertainment for free. What could they possibly owe you? I mean, if anything, you owe them.

CBG: Worst episode ever.[1]

His uptake of the Internet to voice his "disgust" and catchphrase "Worst. Episode. Ever." encapsulate not only the obsessive but also the critical nature of the fan. Unflattering as the portrait is, *The Simpson's* Comic Book Guy was common enough to have become a recognizable stereotype, as early as 1991—the earliest days of the Internet.

South Park is the Internet's first love child. Comedy Central saw the cult status *The Spirit of Christmas* had achieved simply by being digitized. It realized the Internet's potential to make show success and co-opted (or exploited) fans from the first episode.

At the core of the Web activity is the fan. People log in to recap episodes,[2] discuss their favorite episodes, visit Web sites, and blog about their favorite shows. Many download and watch the latest episodes. More dedicated fans are proactive and develop dedicated fansites which aren't merely shrines for TV shows, but are personal showcases of the fan's programming and creative talents. And while the quality might be questionable (see Excessive Fansites at http://www.ggower.com/fans/), the sheer quantity indicates a show's popularity. Conversely, when a show wanes, the sites shut down and steal away like a circus. *South Park* had hundreds of Web sites within months; today only a handful remain active. Thousands of fanfic and fan art pieces crush into Web sites such as http://www.fanfiction.net and http://www.fanart-central.net. Fans actively participate in the creation of the mythos that becomes part of the show; a viewer watches a show, but a fan celebrates it.

The early Internet was a chaotic Babel of voices transformed. It was a virtual carnival. People celebrated the new, virtually ungoverned space. It was fairly democratic—as long as one had the technology and skills to access it. Soon its very popularity drew criticism, content started to be censored, copyright issues became problematic, money exchanged hands, and the temple roar was subdued. During the turbulent days of the Web, *The Spirit of Christmas* was digitized and distributed among thousands of people. No one sought permission, no one thought of copyright or ownership. A cult was born.

How better to understand the Internet than to examine its social agency as mediated through cybercommunities? That's exactly what Brian Ott did when he "traveled" through the *South Park* cybercommunity.[3] In his quest to explore the relationship between the show and the Internet, Ott examined 31 of the hundreds of fansites in 1998 and again in 2001. Focusing on seven key principles, "connectivity, interactivity, originality, master, iconicity, marketability, and adaptability,"[4] Ott describes what he found at these Web sites to explain the show's relationship to its fans and more generally how the Internet works for fans. His safari started at the largest Web site, www.beef -cake.com, and he surfed from there. Alas, Taison Tan's www.beef-cake.com doesn't exist anymore; of Ott's core 31 Web sites, only 3 remain active (and one of those is the official Comedy Channel site). The "webring" sites display the same attrition. In 1998, Ott found 247 sites; these had slumped to 67 in 2001, and to 31 listed under "The Original South Park Webring" in January 2006. Of the 31, none were currently updated.[5] Ott proposed three causes for the dwindling numbers: the decline in popularity of the show, the increased age of the Web owners (whose tastes may have changed), or because the sites were too "time-consuming" and "could not compete (technically) with more elaborate and advanced Web sites, which were more communally prestigious."[6] His last point is one I wish to investigate more thoroughly. I agree that many websters had grown up, moved on, and become bored, but I would like to consider another factor. Based upon my observations in 2004–2005 and Web-archived material, the *South Park* Web site graveyard continues to fill because the webmasters couldn't and didn't compete with the official Web sites at Comedy Central and South Park Studios.

South Park Fansites

Nearly twelve months before the show aired, the first *South Park* Web site, a digitized *The Spirit of Christmas*, was on the Internet (December 1996).[7] Six months after the first episode, *Newsweek* claimed "more than 250 unofficial Web sites . . . sprung up."[8] It's an impressive number. Even more impressive is the Internet's role as a conduit in creating fans: "Without the Internet I doubt I would have ever even heard about it [*South Park*]," Oskar Horyd e-mailed Rick Marin.[9] Why not?

Though *South Park* was airing weekly, Comedy Central was on few cable networks. The Internet allowed people who could not view the show to access *South Park* material; sound bytes, video files, graphics, text scripts, and the latest gossip were a few clicks away. In the halcyon days before Napster and copyright fears, netsters freely admitted to downloading and sharing *South Park* material: "Weingold and a few of his co-workers sometimes watch a CD-ROM containing all the episodes of 'South Park,' which they downloaded from one of the handful of Web sites that make them available."[10] Comedy Central didn't seem to object, not at the start, anyway.

At first, Comedy Central allowed images and sounds to remain on Web sites and even distributed official transcripts; however, in October 1997 (two months after the show's premier) Comedy Central urged Web sites to stop webcasting.[11] Six months later, February 1998, the network considered "going after fansites that sell ads."[12] Exactly why is unclear. But for the websters, advertising offset the expense of producing and maintaining a Web site. Later the same year, Comedy Central moved to copyright images with Parable's ThingMaker, a new software program which would prevent the "unauthorized use of images, animations and sounds."[13] Then Comedy Central sent out letters demanding fans remove full-length episodes and sounds (end 1999). Justin Trevena (whose distinctive 3D *South Park* style was celebrated and reproduced on many Web sites[14]) received a cease-and-desist letter when he advertised that he would do "3D caricatures of people in *South Park* style." He asked for more clarification but "never" heard back from CC.[15]

In swift succession, more Web sites (Mr. Hat's Hell Hole, South Park Central, and No. 1 South Park Street) received cease-and-desist orders. The

Justin Trevena 3D Graphic

Internet retaliated with a one-day blackout by seventy-five sites[16], which ultimately proved ineffective because, like the boys' band strike in "Christian Hard Rock," no one really cared. Comedy Central had been added to many cable networks and no longer needed the Internet to disseminate *South Park* material. Comedy Central was taking control back from its unwieldy netizens. Graphics that had been distributed free were now jealously guarded. Its authoritative stance was to prove disruptive to the *South Park* cybercommunity.

The cybercommunity, which as Ott points out is not a homogenous one, became a distinctly divided one. Three webmasters argued over content and the *South Park* community split between Mr. Hat's Hell Hole (www.thehell hole.com) and Beef-cake (www.beef-cake.com).[17] One of the key figures is Taison Tan, "a 21-year-old senior at the California Institute of Technology."[18] Tan was the first famous cyber-fan, largely as a result of his ten thousand-visitors-a-day South Park Information Center. Tracking his movements demonstrates the increasing control exerted by Comedy Central.

Comedy Central Steps In

Taison Tan's first *South Park* Web site was up in April 1997; two months later, one week before the show's premier, he launched "A South Park Information Center."[19] His Web site was filled with little-known information, such as changes made to the pilot and mentions of George Clooney and Kathy Lee Gifford. Tan's ability to garner news snippets earned him the sobriquet "king of the news." Parker and Stone were "amazed" at his inside info.[20] Tan even received an admiring letter from Parker which he posted on his site.

In January 1998, Tan's "Information Center" and two other *South Park* fansites, Jonathan "Elvis" Davis' "Beefcake Sound Archive" and Shannon "Blackbart" Greene's "Blackbart's South Park Page" combined resources at "A SP Information Center, Blackbart's South Park Page, and the SP Sound Archive" which eventually became beef-cake.com.[21] The *South Park* cyber-community flocked to beef-cake.com because of its insider gossip, and its selection of sounds and images. It also offered contests and discussion boards. It had incredible cultural capital. But all was not well in the *South Park* networld.

In February 1999, beef-cake.com stopped distributing sounds to its mirror sites. Other fansites, particularly Mr. Hat's Hell Hole (Vin Casale and Matt Godfroy), protested; *South Park* sounds were hot property. Hellhole remonstrated that beef-cake would not be able to handle the requests for sounds; mirror sites took the strain off the bandwidth.[22] The three met online but the discussion was unproductive;[23] it was a real "my bandwidth's bigger than yours" argument. Beef-cake hinted things were afoot, "changes visible and invisible," not the least being a new server. Hellhole rejected the argument and, over the next few months, the two sites staged a virtual mud-slinging match. Beef-cake.com went down in August and came back online in September with "a new layout and several missing areas." One of the missing areas presumably was the "sounds" area, for reasons which will become apparent.

In April 2001, Tan, as part of Kung Fu Design, started work at South Park Studios, designing its Web site.[24] Beef-cake closed down while he was away. Willie Westwood summarized the movements:

April 18, 2001 – Taison Tan and Jonathan "Elvis" Davis get positions at the South Park Studios, via Kung Fu Design, so they close Beef-cake down to work on SPStudios. Elvis reported on Beef-cake earlier that these were volunteer positions, so maybe neither he nor Taison were to be paid. *They bring the sounds with them* and give their images to Sweeet.com. *They discard the scripts*, as the Studios have the originals and export them to PDF for fans to download. Also, KeriAnn Martin, from DTISFU,[25] gets a position at the

Studios, and she's going to be paid. This means that maybe the Beef-Cake guys will be paid, too—we'll have to wait and see. There's no more needling the guys at the Hellhole, as Taison and Elvis have gone on to the official SP site. That South Park Studios exists, and that Taison and Jon work there, are testament to Trey and Matt's regard for Beef-Cake. Trey and Matt used to go to Beef-Cake to see what was going on in the SP world—Taison usually had the news before anyone else—and they liked his site a lot. But it wasn't the official site, and so they determined to put up a site that would have the latest South Park news direct from themselves and the studios they work at.[26]

Clearly, a deal had been struck; the major players of the largest South Park Web site were seconded as designers for an official Web site. In return for their new jobs, they transferred all their valuable South Park material to the official Web site. But things didn't work out and Tan returned to the fan community, only it was too late. The Internet had moved on.[27]

Taison Tan serves as an e-moral. He was a conduit for Comedy Central to its Internet fan base; he closed down his own Web site to help develop the official one. By co-opting Tan to develop the official Web site, Comedy Central drew upon his technical skills and removed one of their chief competitor sites. Valuable contraband material was returned to official governance, effectively limiting material available for downloading and ensuring that only sanctioned material would be available. South Park Studios and Comedy Central regained control of *South Park* on the Internet and eliminated their main competition.

Ironically, Comedy Central got more than it bargained for. Their *South Park* Web pages attracted too much traffic. It tried to curtail traffic by dropping digests and discussion boards, and eventually decided the show warranted its own Web site. South Park Studios became the official South Park Web site in April 2001. As the South Park Studios site grew, so did fan disenchantment. The site is slow. According to the statistics at Alexa.com, 81 percent of sites are faster (Comedy Central's is even slower—90 percent of sites are faster). Longtime fans prefer the more community-focused fansites and find the discussion boards at South Park Studios too large and unwieldy; however, it remains the popular site for up-to-the minute information and offers online chats with creators and behind-the-scenes information such as interviews with staff and staff blogs.[28]

South Park arrived on the cusp of the World Wide Web boom, and its Internet history is a prototype for the increasing interest in the Net not as a site for personal fun but one for corporate interest. No wonder, the Internet is big business. In 1998, Melonee McKinney pointed out, "over 1.8 mil *South Park* searches are made every 30 days" at Yahoo.com;[29] the Comedy Central

Web site attracted "one million hits a day, about 40 percent for "South Park."[30] All of these hits are potential customers. Rather than the democratic space of play and dissident voices, the Internet has become increasingly controlled and controlling; Lincoln Dahlberg observed in 2000 that "online commerce has rapidly colonized cyberspace since the privatization and commercialization of the Internet in the early nineteen nineties."[31] By the end of the 1990s, Napster™ had alerted commercial interests to the potential of lost profits. It is no wonder that Comedy Central needed and wanted to control its most profitable product.[32]

South Park Sites One Decade Later

Google "South Park" and the first ten Web sites listed demonstrate that the official Web sites rule. Two link to South Park Studios, two to Comedy Central, and two to Internet Movie Data Base. Of the remaining four, two link to Wikipedia, one links to a German site (www.planearium.de), only one links to an English Web site, Mr. Twig's net. In other words, official Web sites dominate the Google search engine. In 2005, I investigated the non-official sites. Using South Park X[33] as a jumping-off point, I examined the following fansites:

1. South Park X: http://www.southparkx.net lists six affiliates: South Park Complete, Cartmanland, SPG Archives, TKKS, Cartman's World, and SP Alliance
2. South Park Complete: http://www.spcomplete.com
3. Cartmanland: http://www.awesomo.net
4. South Park Games Archives: http://www.spgarchives.com
5. South Park HTML: http://www.sphtml.com
6. You Bastards: http://you-bastards.net, in limbo since April 2006
7. South Park Scriptorium: http://www.spscriptorium.com
8. TKKS (The Krazy Kenny Show): http://www.thekrazykennyshow.net, in limbo December 2005 then died October 2006
9. Cartman's World: http://www.cartmansworld.net, in limbo since January 2006
10. South Park Alliance: http://spalliance.net

During the months I monitored these Web sites (September 2005–October 2006), the sites were often down; some went into limbo (online but not updated) and some died.[34] When a new series is airing, the active sites are busy—outside these times, most of them remain dormant. The mutable state of fansites is worthy of a PhD in itself.

South Park X weathered the great 1999 fan site plague. The mainstay of the site is its downloadable material, material that comes with a rather vague disclaimer: "All of these files are Copyright of their respective owners,"[35] but official approval for downloading is claimed in the FAQs section:

> Q. Is downloading these Episodes legal?
> Matt and Trey do not mind when fans download their episodes off the Internet; they feel that it's good when people watch the show no matter how they do it. *Note: This is official.* Posted on the South Park Studios FAQ August 2003.[36]

This official sanction is posted at other Web sites.[37] Web sites can roughly be divided into two groups: those that offer episode downloads and those that don't. Because of contentious copyright issues, it can often be difficult to locate sites that offer episode downloads. Because of their popularity, sites often exceed bandwidth and are shut down by hosts.

Surviving in the *South Park* cybercommunity is not just a matter of programming talent; Web sites require constant updating. When new episodes are airing, a Web site needs to supply the latest gossip, media articles, and episode information, not to mention scripts and episode files.

Generally, fansites offer pretty much the same content: a history of the show, information about staff (Matt and Trey usually), outlines of episodes, descriptions of main characters, news items, and downloads (sounds, images, videos). Some offer different tidbits. The South Park Games Archive offers *South Park*-themed games to download, nearly three hundred of them. South Park Alliance (SPA) offers the latest netology, including weekly podcasts and Frappr (Rising Concepts "friend mapper," people register and are placed on a map). In January 2006, it ran weekly contests with $500 worth of *South Park* products as prizes; *South Park* is of course the sponsor of the contests.[38]

Aesthetics and Web Sites

Aesthetically, *South Park* fansites have changed considerably over time. Many of the early pages are simple one-page homages, filled with animated gifs, graphics of uneven size, and demonstrating a preference for black backgrounds and electric-colored text. They are often poorly organized and difficult to read—South Park Kenny Conspiracy is typical.[39] They are, to the seasoned Net user, archaic. Today's Web sites demonstrate a higher level of sophistication in both execution and design. They tend to adopt simple design features (a banner heading flanked by menu columns to the left and right) and iconic graphics (most often the *South Park* sign and a montage of various characters), and use colors associated with the characters. The reading has thus gone from left to right (i.e., across the page) to bytes layered top to bottom—replicating the "scrolling down the page" of online reading.

South Park X proudly proclaims "that [it] has been on the internet since February 1999."[40] Since then South Park X has undergone several updates and has a slick professional look. It knows what fans seek and gets them there in an intuitive way. It is a template for how a good Web site should work and look. Most of the Web sites are user friendly because they have evolved through several versions. Ryan Callis at Cartman's World revamped his site four times,[41] and TKKS had four versions archived.[42] Cartmanland documents its evolution: "The site has gone through a few owners and now it's owned by Kyle who has had the site since about late April 2003. It has gone through 2 name changes, and about 7 designs, some of which didn't last long; some were rips of other sites, and the rest sucked, except version 2 and 3, but 3 was a rip."[43] Even the official Web sites have gone through several versions as well.

The Net world is not a static one; not only do Web people have to revamp to accommodate new areas of fan interest (i.e., fan fiction, games, and so on), but also new technologies. When new technologies are added, for example, BitTorrents and podcasts, the Web sites provide instructions and links to sites for downloading appropriate software. In general, the *South Park* fan sites display a sympathy for and an understanding of end users.

A much-ignored aspect of Internet fandom is the economics of hosting a fan site. Owners need the Web skills, Web space, and basic computer equipment (thereby, in some instances, limiting fandom to the technologically capable and the cashed up). How owners pay for their sites is uncertain; especially, if they have episodes to download. Noah reports that it costs him around $30 per month to host TKKS. Once upon a time, money could be made from on-site advertising. Justin "Juz" Trevena remembers the days of sponsored advertising: "I brought Sweeet across to their [Stomped] network. They had an advertising deal with IGN at the time which was paying about $3 per 1000 adviews. . . . At its peak Sweeet was getting 3 million hits a month. To put this into advertising dollars, the site was earning roughly US$9,000! I didn't see this money, as I was earning a salary from Stomped."[44] Fan sites, therefore, need sponsors. Amazon and Google ads, and/or PayPal donations are the usual options. Justin explained why he moved from advertisements to PayPal:

> Most of you have probably heard or seen the results of the drop in the advertising economy online—well the amount of revenue that ads generate these days isn't particularly high, so I've decided to try out a paypal donation system. . . . If you think Sweeet deserves a payment of some kind, using paypal

Comedy Central's South Park Mini-Site

> you can make a small (or large!) payment to show your appreciation. Dona-
> tions can be as little as US$1 and as far as I know are completely refundable
> (within 30 days) if you decide to change your mind. Any money that is col-
> lected will go towards features and upgrades for the site. Depending on the
> response I might even make a "Friends of Sweeet" page/section listing the
> people who have made donations (if they allow it). Saturday, July 7, 2001.[45]

Justin's apologetic tone reflects his distaste for recompense; the Web site was
"purely a love job." While the site earned $9,000 a month, he failed to receive
any money. After shutting down www.sweeet.com, Toyzz contacted him and
he sold his site to them for $900. *South Park* fans shy away from economic
gain even though their devotion may occupy many hours and demand considerable skill—it is, in Henry Jenkin's terminology, a "week-end only
world."[46] However, sometimes the rewards are more tangible.

Popular site owners have found their skills segue into employment. As
mentioned earlier, Taison Tan and Jonathan Elvis Davis of beef-cake.com
were co-opted by Comedy Central. Justin Trevena reports that not only did
Davis not get the webmaster position—he was never paid. Paul Wein became
moderator of Official South Park Booster Club Digest (for which he received
a modest fee), and Breayle Riess became the webmistress at South Park Studios between 2000 and 2004. So though employed, none of the above people
seem to have made a career from being a fan. Comedy Central had conferred

perhaps the greatest accolade any fan can receive, recognition by the producers/creators of the product they endorse. However flattering this might be, it does not make a good basis for a business relationship.

What Is a Fan?

Fans tend to get a bad rap. While the merchandisers woo them with a plethora of merchandising opportunities, the media portrayals of them are far from flattering; generally they are deranged, obsessive people, usually synonymous with stalkers. No wonder few people label themselves "fans." The definition of a fan is somewhat open—but, I consider fans the people who watch *South Park* regularly (rather than religiously) and who have been involved in more than one meta-watching activity (participating in discussion boards, building fansites, reading or writing fanfic, purchasing themed merchandise, buying videos, CDs, or DVDs), and people who label themselves "fan."

Fans do not dress the same, look the same, or profess a singular political/social ideology, except for a devotion to the show, which, if threatened, can cause them to become political (*Cagney and Lacey* fans saved the show from being axed). Fans belong to a virtual community of people who watch the same television show. They may meet in real time or on the Internet. Fans are the lifeblood of the television industry and don't always get the respect they deserve. Many of them devote hours to their passion, with few rewards; some simply watch the show.

Some fans become well known outside the cybercommunity. Taison Tan's South Park Information Center "made him something of a 'South Park' figure."[47] Veteran South Parker Willie Westwood, operator of the South Park Scriptorium,[48] is a long-term fan who maintains a comprehensive Web site, posts at a number of *South Park* forums, and moderates on quite a few too, not the least being the official bulletin boards at South Park Studios. He was the acknowledged "alt.tv.southpark guru" and remains a stalwart of fandom. But he is the exception rather than the rule, Noah of TKKS Web site is a typical *South Park* fan. He is young (18) and started a Web site to feed his fan appetite; the site enabled him to refine and flex his Web skills.

Brian Nomi and Dan Lins are typical South Park fans. They have watched the show since the start, have joined fan discussions lists, and have been involved in meta-*South Park* activities such as the South Park Convention.[49] Dan Lins tells how the show has actually given him not only a virtual family but a real-life one:

> My wife Kandice and I met through the South Park Fan Club. . . . We met in-person for the very first time at the first South Park Convention. Soon after,

she moved from Texas to Chicago, IL, and into my apartment. By the second convention, we had a 1 month old baby named Coltrane who came along with us to the convention. I'm sure he's probably the youngest person ever to attend such a convention. He's also (as far as I know) still the ONLY child born to two people who met through South Park. . . . Because we now have a family, I have little time for posting and chatting, but I occasionally make an appearance, or send a post. . . . Paul Wein, the last moderator of the Comedy Central Digest, was called the "Mod-Father". That's also because of Coltrane, my son. You see, we asked Paul to be Cole's godfather. And since Paul was already known as "The Mod" (short for "Moderator", obviously), "The Mod" and the new "God-father" just fit together nicely, giving the fans "The Mod-Father".[50]

Both men are proud of their fan roles and their fan knowledge. Brian can name names and has specific details, such as Paul Wein's salary. Dan instigated the idea of a conference and of his status as one of the handful of people who have attended all conferences. Both Dan and Brian reject Comedy Central's official status; they are disgruntled by the network's indifference and lack of support. But what is of real importance to fans is that Trey and Matt support them; Comedy Central is merely the cable company and fans are faithful to the show, not to the institution. Brian demonstrates the fan's discerning taste: he knows which discussion groups are good and which "suck balls." He counters the "mad fan" stereotype and is not the cultural dupe people like to associate with fandom.

Fan Participation on the Internet

Of course, the Internet is not simply a collection of Web sites, nor is it used that way by fans. Henry Jenkins, Kristen Pullen, Nancy Baym, and Matthew Hills delved into fan cultures such as *Star Trek*, *Xena*, and soap operas, and have examined the contributions of fans to the Internet as a collective intelligence and as a communicative sphere.[51] *South Park* fans are prototypical fans. Their uses of the Internet for fandom are as varied as the fans themselves; they search for information, engage in discussions groups, create blogs, maintain Web sites, download/upload material, critique episodes, transcribe scripts, and create/read fan fiction/art. Some engage in one activity, some in all. And over time, of course, their engagement has been shaped by new technologies.

Why do fans spend more time discussing rather than watching their favorite shows? Baym posits that fans are "motivated by epistemophilia," which she defines as "pleasure in exchanging knowledge," but its more negative dictionary definition is an "abnormal preoccupation with knowledge." Because multilayered shows such as *Seinfield*, *The Simpsons*, and

South Park drip with cultural referents, pleasure comes from identifying these intertextual and metatextual moments. Fans who spot the cultural cues not only derive pleasure decoding these moments, but also gain power that comes from sharing their knowledge. Like gossip, being the first to be "in the know" is a powerful position.[52] Most of this exchange of information happens in three ways: real-time chat, news discussion groups, and posted commentary.

One of the first uses of real-time chatting was the World of South Park at The Palace. At the time of the *South Park* premier, The Palace was *the* meeting place for netsters. The Palace was a virtual world that hosted hundreds of thematic "sites" where people of like interests gathered.[53] Each "palace" reflected the owner's concept of a virtual world: in most cases, they resembled a typical meeting place, a bar or a house. People chose avatars (small icons representing themselves) and entered their chosen palace; once inside the palace, they visited various rooms or areas and chatted to people in real time. The South Park Palace began with thirty sets and "grew over the next three years to include over two hundred graphical locations from America's favorite Colorado mountain town."[54] Avatars closely resembled *South Park* characters because the "goal of the site was to bring people inside the world of *South Park*, as close as possible to the one on their TV screens."

It was Comedy Central-driven, and As If Productions "produced more than two hundred original programs for the site's regular weekly schedule. These experiments in 'simulated television' ranged from the laudable to the laughable, and were 'broadcast' by the fictional television station SPPA (South Park Public Access)."[55] People who logged in automatically appeared and acted out their roles as either "Stan the ring leader," "Kyle the Jew," "Kenny the doomed," or "Cartman the chunky bigot" who could obliterate nearby avatars with flaming farts. They could also kick the baby, kill Kenny, and make Stan puke. The Palace was so popular, that Trey Parker visited a number of times but was ignored—fans could not believe that Trey Parker would actually visit.[56] The site also had guest moderators who worked on the show. The South Park Palace was still active in August 2000[57] and closed in December 2005. For those interested, The Palace of November 2005 has over three thousand palaces. Just over two thousand users were online when I visited, mostly in the main palace. It remains popular with adults seeking a quiet place to chat—many of the Web sites are "Adults Only." The South Park Palace site is one of those cultural artifacts that defined a moment in Internet time—like Tribal Voice's Pow Wow.[58] Unfortunately, the chats don't seem to be archived, though there are moves afoot to reclaim The Palace for posterity.

One *South Park* Palace "Set"

The South Park Palace allowed for chat in real time,[59] but less immediate forms of communication, "discussion groups,"[60] remain one of the most popular ways to share knowledge. Comedy Central's digest was the first official "digest"; it started in 1998—at the time when *South Park* was at its hottest. Brian Nomi recalls:

> ... this Digest was sent to thousands of people all over the world. The mailing list was huge, as anyone who came to CC's website could simply input their email address, and become a subscriber to the Digest. Nobody knows how many people did subscribe ... reading the posts from this digest was magical. I formed many friendships with *South Park* fans all over the world through this Digest, and I know others did the same.[61]

While the digest drew fans to its Web site, Comedy Central tired of maintaining it and eventually cancelled it. Nomi continues:

> CC decided to cancel the official digest probably because they didn't like spending the money to maintain this project. They did pay a south park fan $500 a month to handle this. The last mod was a guy named Paul Wein, who is fondly known as the "Mod Father." After the official CC digest ended, a couple of unofficial digests sprang up. They united about 3 years ago, and

they are now the South Park Daily Marklar. The MSN Group and my Yahoo group have been in existence since January 2001, and they are another unofficial place for fans to gather. We can use naughty words at these groups, and nobody gives a fuck. There is no governance at all from CC over us. We have tried to get some recognition, but CC could care less and has never responded to any of our petitions.

The regular posters were clearly angered at Comedy Central; again, Comedy Central had courted fans until they realized there was no benefit in hosting a discussion board. Brian hints at Comedy Central censorship, and the South Park Daily Marklar (SPDM) Web site has a more complete version in the "About Us" section:

> But after a short time, members of the [CC] digest noticed certain amounts of "editing" being done. . . . There were strict rules in place to keep the subject matter and the language in line with Comedy Central's "Standards."[62]

The discussion group has become more than a place of collective intelligence; it offers opportunities for technological advancement and is, in effect, a socio-emotional warehouse.[63] One of the sociological outcomes has been the coming together in real time of some *South Park* fan communities. The SPDM digest is more than simply fans swapping *South Park* information; it is a friendly newsletter that includes cultural references, *South Park* trivia, fan verse/songs, and personal information. There is only one rule: "be nice." Brian emphasizes the unity of the group and its special status:

> The key point about the groups I've referenced is that they are the only group of Fans who ever get together to meet. We're a great, big-hearted group of fans and friends. So far there have been 4 conventions in Denver, Colorado (not too far from South Park), and many, many mini-conventions. . . . The fan club on Southparkstudios tends to suck balls. It's mostly kids and weirdos posting one-line put-downs and bizarre stuff. You never know who you're really dealing with. There are probably over a hundred other *South Park* Fan groups out there, the large majority of which are totally dead.[64]

As Brian states, the official Web sites are crowded and boisterous. Official bulletin boards are readily accessible, which is both part of their allure and part of their problem. Of the half-dozen South Park discussion boards active in October 2006,[65] South Park Studios has the largest group of participants, over 423,000 registered users (the bulletin board has recorded 1,200 users online at any one time)[66] and countless "guests" who can log on and post without any identification and usually outnumber registered users. The discussion board has over 60,000 postings to the more than 850 topics.[67] So many postings make it almost impossible to keep current, and endless postings asking for "your favorite *South Park* moment" tire the experienced fan.

Fan Fiction

Henry Jenkins coined the phrase "textual poaching" to describe fans' appropriation of material that they refashion into their own narratives. The most commonly known form is filking.[68] For the uninitiated, textual poaching presents a complex world of new words[69] and specialized knowledges. *South Park* poaching comes in three broad forms: fan fiction (written songs, plays, episodes, stories, musicals), visual fan art (graphics, computer wallpaper, and even *South Park*-esque animations), and fan games (PC games using *South Park* events, characters, and themes).

In the olden days of the 1970s, fan fiction remained buried in the pages of printed fanzines circulated among a handful of dedicated fans. The earliest fan fiction celebrated texts and characters such as The *Lord of the Rings*, Sherlock Holmes, and later cult TV shows like *Star Trek* and *Doctor Who*. Along came the Internet, and these creative outpourings had a worldwide forum. Since then, the genre fan fiction has developed its own subgenres and characters. There is crossover fiction, which blends two differing, separate stories or shows; slash fiction, which romantically links characters of the same gender; femslash or Saffic[70]; oneshots, Mary Sues (new characters added to the story, derided for its obviousness as a plot device), and even songfic (Love and Other Four Letter Words).

Instead of lingering on the fansites, fans have their own—Fanfiction.net[71] houses hundreds if not thousands of fandicraft. It has eight categories, including TV shows, films, animes, and cartoons. In the cartoon category, over 150 TV shows are represented; *South Park* is one of the most popular, with nearly 700 contributions (*Teen Titans* leads at around 150,000 entries). Here, *South Park* fans post their fan material, including novel-length fiction and oneshots, with a brief synopsis and other vital statistics. It's a highly codified place; a typical entry reads:

> Reunions by robert3A-SN *reviews*
>   In this fic set in the future, Butters is crushed when Wendy is killed in a horrible accident, and when [*sic*] Stan takes his own life soon after. But then the ghost of Wendy appears to ask Butters for help in reuniting her with Stan in the afterlife. Fiction Rated: T – English – Drama/Supernatural – Chapters: 18 – Words: 70008 – Reviews: 46 – Updated: 8-3-04 – Published: 7-14-04[72]

"Reunions" is "T" rated (meaning it is not suitable for children under 13[73]), written in English, and combines two genres (drama and supernatural). It is long at 70,000 words—fan fiction varies from a few hundred words to book length. Chapters? Well, though written in novel style, Robert has divided

"Reunions" into acts and scenes rather than chapters. This reflects the filmic heritage of the concept. Forty-six people have read "Reunions" and reviewed it. Given the Web's predilection for flaming, the reviewers at Fanfiction.net are overwhelmingly positive (no matter how casual the fiction's spelling, punctuation, and grammar):

> Once again, another fantastic cluster.[74] . . . I think that, as far as entertainment is concerned, this cluster was probably the best of the lot. . . . isn't it fitting that the final review you'll ever get from me (here, at least) is a review of, in my opinion, the greatest *South Park* fan fiction ever written? . . . As far as the "Best Fan Fiction" award is concerned, you've got it in the bag with "Reunions". I can't wait to read the final cluster; if it is as good as the rest, which I do not doubt, then it's going to be excellent! That's all from me . . . UNTERMENSCHEN 2004-08-09 ch 18[75]

"Untermenschen" is unversed in traditional literary-speak but is clearly well aware of the review genre. What is striking is the laudatory nature of the review. Other fanfic reviews are equally supportive and encouraging:

> total misanthrope: ah! stan!! that was so damn cool! you're amazing! I'M AFRAID OF YOUR POWER and ability to freak me out. . . . i cant wait for your next story![76]

> Indiana Beach Bum: Okay, your stories are AMAZING, beginning to end. I am always anxious to read about the drama you have instilled, and this is just another pefect [sic] example. Kind of leaves you breathless at the end. . . . Seriously, GOOD JOB[76]

The contrast between comments posted at general fansites and those at fanfic Web sites are marked. Clearly, fanfic is a supportive community and highlights the differential nature of the Internet and of fandom.

Fan Art

Those fans without literary leanings can pay homage to *South Park* with graphics. Perhaps the best-known fan art is that done by Justin Trevena. His 3D images were state of the art and still adorn many pages, even though his own Web site has long since closed down. Not everyone has Trevena's computer skills. At Fan Art Central,[77] most of the art is not computer created; the art ranges from what appear to be children's hand-drawn imitative characters and scenes to the more sophisticated anime interpretations. A surprising number contain kissing scenes (boys/girls and boy/boys), a few are sexually explicit, and some capture the toilet humor.

The more technologically gifted, Ted Bracewell and Ayaz Asif, made the fan-vid *Park Wars: The Little Menace*, an eleven-minute animation that marries *Star Wars* with *South Park*. Their plans for a one-hour animation were abandoned when someone at Lucasfilm warned them that a production of an hour turns parody into rip-off. The question of copyright and fandom is still a tricky one. Generally, owners of copyrights and trademarks turn a blind eye; but when the Internet became economically viable, cease-and-desist letters started. Paramount did it to *Star Trek* Web sites in 1996, Fox did it to a *Simpsons* fan, and, as previously mentioned, Comedy Central did it to www.beef-cake.com. While it's tempting to demonize the lawyers, fans can distribute and take payment for someone else's creative work. There are even Web articles informing fans about the legal minefield (http://www.salon .com/tech/feature/2000/12/13/fandom/index.html and http://www.whoosh.org/ issue25/lee1.html). Fandom is a battlefield.

Conclusion

The Internet of today is not the Internet of a decade ago. Increasingly, the homemade fansites or homepages have been replaced—the technology has increased so that a little html knowledge doesn't get you much these days. Buffeted by a decade of Comedy Central's attempts at control, fans have seen their favorite Web sites and downloads restricted. They feel used and their demands for authenticity have increased. In retaliation, fans have skirted the official Web site and instead patronize those done by one of "them" or create their own.

South Park came at a pivotal time in Internet history. *Yahoo! Internet Life* magazine claimed that *South Park* was the "the highest Web site-to-episode ratio in television history." At one point, over three thousand *South Park* Web sites existed.[78] Taison Tan claimed tens of thousands of visitors a day. Once upon a time, the World Wide Web was a democratic space. Today, the Net is much more institutionalized and governed. Fears of copyright infringement and similar threats have tamed the free economy of the Web. Today's Web is still an uneasy blend of rebellion (especially in blogs) and acquiescence. Debates continue to rage about Internet governance.[79] Only those with the cultural currency, the technological skills, and the financial resources can survive. Those who remember the halcyon days of idiosyncratic pages and Pow Wow sigh. Unfortunately, almost completely erased from popular memory are the Fourassmonkey Web site, the Aliens Stuck Things Up Your Butt! fan site, and Stan's Insult Generator.

Ari @ 21 Apr 2004 05:52 pm

shit, my computer is broken. stuck on my dads slow ass pc.
Fuck! i guess i have to watch [South Park] on TV . . .

Notes

1. *The Simpsons*, "The Itchy & Scratchy & Poochie Show," 4F12. First aired May 9, 1991.

2. One of the burgeoning areas of television on the Internet has been the growth of episode information. This information comes in two forms: actual transcripts of episode (scripts) or plot summaries (synopses). Both provide different types of information. The transcript is the "official" version, which is painstakingly transcribed and posted. The synopses/recaps can be colored by the writers' editorializing, found on sites like www.televisionwithout pity.com (TWoP). The most comprehensive TV Web sites, such as www.tv.com, contain factual information about the show (staff, number of episodes), summaries and recaps (the difference between the two is quite blurred), popular culture references, continuity goofs, trivia, and quotes from each episode. To date, most of the episode recaps, like book reviews at Amazon and film reviews at IMDB, have been a healthy part of networking. Fans such as those on TWoP have become paid recappers and have thus created another layer of fandom, the professional fan. But with an increasing awareness of user-generated media, will it be long before sites such as Amazon copyright reviewers' comments? It's already been touted as a possibility.

3. Brian L. Ott, "Oh My God, They Digitized Kenny!: Travels in the South Park Cybercommunity V4.0," *Prime Time Animation: Television Animation and American Culture*, ed. Carol A. Stabile and Mark Harrison (London: Routledge, 2003), 220–42.

4. Ibid., 235.

5. The WebRing page lists five South Park webrings (http://dir.webring.com/rw?d=Enter tainment___Arts/Television/Genres/Comedies/Titles/South_Park, accessed October 22, 2006); none of the Web sites at any of the five webrings had been updated since 2003; the majority have been in limbo since the second season.

6. Ott, "Oh my God," 235.

7. SOXMAS, http://www.killfile.org/soxmas, accessed November 20, 2005.

8. Rick Marin, "The Rude Tube," *Newsweek*, March 23, 1998, 56. Brian Ott misquotes Rick Marin when he claims 250 Web sites are before the show aired, in fact, Marin guesstimates numbers *after* the show's premier.

9. Ibid.

10. Nathan Cobb, "'South Park'—It's a Gas," *Boston Globe*, January 28, 1998, D1.

11. http://www.spscriptorium.com/SPinfo/SPTimelineIndex.htm, accessed October 22, 2006.

12. Ibid.

13. Dianne See, "Stamping Out 'South Park' Imposters," *The Industry Standard*, November 9, 1998, http://www.idg.net/go.cgi?id=147433, accessed November 20, 2005.

14. http://e-mats.org/sweeet/notenough1024x768.jpg, accessed October 22, 2006; http://www.geocities.com/Heartland/Flats/6661/southpark.html, accessed October 22, 2006.

15. E-mail, January 31, 2006.

16. February 21, 2000.

17. For more about the split between Mr. Hat's Hell Hole and Beef-cake, see January and February 1999 entries at http://www.spscriptorium.com/SPinfo/SPTimelineIndex.htm, accessed October 22, 2006.

18. Cobb, "'South Park'—It's a Gas."

19. http://www.ugcs.caltech.edu/~ttant/SouthPark. Now defunct.

20. Comedy Arts Festival, March 1998, http://www.spscriptorium.com/SPinfo/SPTimelineIndex.htm.

21. http://web.archive.org/web/19990428144811/www.beef-cake.com/taison/, accessed October 22, 2006.

22. http://web.archive.org/web/20000229044246/www.beef-cake.com/faq.html, accessed October 22, 2006.

23. For a full transcript, see http://web.archive.org/web/20010428075154/www.beef-cake.com/beef-cake_vs_thh.htm.

24. Originally, the South Park Studios Web site was to open in October 2000; it opened April 17, 2001.

25. "Dude This Is So Fucked Up," another early and popular Web site.

26. http://www.spscriptorium.com/SPinfo/SPTimelineIndex.htm.

27. Davis reopened beef-cake.com in June 2001, but the site struggled and never fully recovered its former glory. The site closed in November 2001. A year later it returned with both Davis and Tan, but continued to struggle. The death knell sounded in 2003. In October 2005, www.beef-cake.com was a dead site; Mr. Hat's Hell Hole is a commercial site selling toys (http://fortknox.portline.com).

28. South Park Studios, "Production Blog," http://www.southparkstudios.com/show/blog.php?tab=10, accessed November 14, 2005.

29. Melonee McKinney, "Licensees Do Cartwheels to Get a Piece of Cartman and 'South Park' Gang," *Daily News Record*, June 1, 1998, 18.

30. H. B. Koplowitz, "Lost in Cyberspace: Cyber 'South Park,'" archived at http://web.archive.org/web/20000821100429/http://onyx.he.net/~hotmoves/LIC/southpark.html, October 24, 2006.

31. Lincoln Dahlberg, "Democratic Participation through the Internet: A Brief Survey," *Media/Culture Reviews*, http://reviews.media-culture.org.au/features/politics/participation.html, accessed November 12, 2005.

32. For those who are interested, many of the defunct Web sites are available at The Web Archive: Sweeet, http://web.archive.org/web/*/http://www.sweeet.com (1998–2004); Beef-cake, http://web.archive.org/web/*/http://www.beef-cake.com (1998–2004); Mr. Hat's Hell Hole, http://web.archive.org/web/*/www.mrhatshellhole.com (1999–2004).

33. Which was the only active site in the top ten googled in September 2005.

34. When I started writing this chapter in 2004, I chose a dozen Web sites. Only two remained active (South Park Scriptorium and South Park X). Because of the constant changes, I decided it was more productive to write this section as close to publication as possible in the hope that some would remain active.

35. http://www.southparkx.net/multimedia/programs, accessed October 22, 2006.

36. http://www.southparkx.net/faq/is-downloading-legal, accessed October 22, 2006.

37. South Park Complete, http://www.spcomplete.com/index.php?pg=faq, accessed November 13, 2005.

38. http://spalliance.net/content.php?go=apperances, accessed October 22, 2006.

39. http://members.tripod.com/~AlienBeliever/index.html, accessed October 24, 2006.

40. http://www.southparkx.net/others/about-south-park-x, http://spalliance.net/content.php?go=apperances, http://members.tripod.com/~AlienBeliever/index.html

41. E-mail, November 12, 2005.

42. http://www.thekrazykennyshow.net/index.php?page=previousdesigns, dead.

43. http://www.awesomo.net/index.php?act=faq, accessed October 24, 2006.

44. E-mail, January 31, 2006.

45. http://web.archive.org/web/20010709101330/http://sweeet.com, accessed October 24, 2006.

46. Henry Jenkins, *Textual Poachers: Television Fans and Participatory Culture* (New York: Routledge, 1992), 20.

47. Cobb, "'South Park'—It's a Gas."

48. http://www.spscriptorium.com.

49. E-mail, June 1, 2005.

50. E-mail, October 1, 2005.

51. Henry Jenkins, "Interactive Audiences, the 'Collective Intelligence' of Media Fans," http://web.mit.edu/cms/People/henry3/collective%20intelligence.html; and *Textual Poachers: Television Fans and Participatory Culture* (New York: Routledge, 1992); Kristen Pullen, "I-Love-Xena.Com: Creating Online Fan Communities," in David Gauntlett, ed., *Web.Studies: Rewiring Media Studies for the Digital Age* (London: Arnold, 2000); Nancy K. Baym, *Tune In, Log On: Soaps, Fandom, and Online Community* (Thousand Oaks, CA: Sage, 2000); Matt Hills, *Fan Cultures* (London: Routledge, 2002).

52. Max Gluckman, "Gossip and Scandal," *Current Anthropology,* 4 no.3 (1963): 307-316.

53. For more Palace history, see http://www.jbum.com/history/index.html, accessed October 24, 2006.

54. http://www.asifproductions.com/southpark.html, accessed October 24, 2006.

55. http://www.asifproductions.com/southpark/avatars.html#palette, http://www.jbum.com/history/index.html.

56. South Park Scriptorium, http://www.spscriptorium.com/SPinfo/SPTimeline1990s.htm, accessed October 24, 2006.

57. "August 30, 2000 – A few weeks ago The South Park Digest had announced a special moderator for today's Palace chat, but the moderator, a SP producer, cancelled due to new episode production."

58. Pow-Wow was a popular Windows-based chat program, see http://en.wikipedia.org/wiki/PowWow_(chat_program).

59. Like IRC (Internet relay chat), ICQ (I seek you), chat rooms, instant messaging, and so on.

60. I'm using "discussion group" as an umbrella term for various forms of Internet discussions, including newsgroups, bulletin boards, Web forums, message boards, etc.

61. E-mail, January 6, 2005.

62. http://sp4u.netfirms.com/about.html, accessed October 24, 2006.

63. To appropriate Nina Baym, *Tune In, Log On.*

64. E-mail, January 6, 2005.

65. Tv.com (http://www.tv.com/south-park/show/344/forums.html), City Wok (http://awesomo.net/forum), Chef's Kitchen (http://chef.spcomplete.com), Tick's South Park Madness (http://groups.msn.com/TicksSouthParkMadness), and Go Timmy Go (http://www.gotimmygo.com/forum).

66. At 8–11 p.m. (US) on Sunday, November 27, 2005, there were 8 registered users and 124 guests on the official bulletin board.

67. Over 850 topics include episodes, bloopers, fanfics, fansites, fan art, polls, voting, production blogs, related media, merchandise information, games, collectibles, feedback.

68. Originally a typo, filking means to create folk-type song parodies, particularly in relation to science fiction.

69. The Fan Fiction Glossary, http://www.subreality.com/glossary/terms.htm#M, accessed October 25, 2001.

70. The sexualized nature of fanfic is quite extraordinary.

71. http://www.fanfiction.net, accessed November 28, 2005, dead.

72. http://www.fanfiction.net/l/5/13/11/1/1/60/0/0/0/0/1, accessed October 25, 2005.

73. http://www.fictionratings.com/guide.php, accessed October 24, 2006.

74. Because the fiction is usually an ongoing project, fans post as they complete chapters or "clusters."

75. http://www.fanfiction.net/r/1962599/0/1, accessed November 28, 2005, dead.

76. http://www.fanfiction.net/r/2519489/0/1, accessed November 28, 2005, dead.

77. http://www.fanart-central.net, accessed October 25, 2006.

78. http://whatsonthe.net/southparkmks.htm, accessed October 25, 2006.

79. Kenneth Neil Cukier, "Who Will Control the Internet?" *Foreign Affairs*, November/December 2005, http://www.foreignaffairs.org/20051101facomment84602/kenneth-neil-cukier/who-will-control-the-internet.html, accessed October 25, 2006.

Chapter 4

Collect Underpants: Marketing

One thing's for sure, *South Park* sells. Forget a sexy woman or a virile man—put Cartman on the cover of something to attract sales. Before the series premiered, Comedy Central had appointed Hamilton Projects as sole licensor of the *South Park* products. Hamilton Projects unveiled a two-year marketing plan and launched the first products "simultaneously with the launch of the series."[1] As soon as the show aired, the company started receiving calls from prospective licensees.[2] Eleven licenses were signed (with another twenty pending) in April 1998.[3] In the following year, more than sixty-five new licenses were signed between January and June 1999.[4] By 2003, over five thousand individual products had been prepared by nearly two hundred licensees. Spurred by *South Park*'s success, Comedy Central hired a twenty-strong sales force to spearhead merchandising and advertising sales.[5] By the end of 1997, sales had been phenomenal and Comedy Central recorded its first-ever profit.

Marketing's hottest demographic are tweenagers and teenagers. Studies show that much of the $111 billion of teens' "discretionary income" goes towards "entertainment products."[6] This brand-mad generation expects movies and television shows to be accompanied by a raft of merchandise, and Comedy Central postulates, "it actually hurts a show if there's not merchandise to buy. Kids approach with that expectation."[7] Of course, each piece of merchandise, whether it be a t-shirt, DVD, or coffee mug, is another advertisement for the program.

The onslaught of products during the first season did not go unnoticed by media. Four weeks after the first episode, Paula Span notes the "forthcoming raft of licensed 'South Park' merchandise, from T-shirts and caps and books to a snow globe."[8] A little over a month later, Comedy Central claimed that the merchandise "was selling briskly."[9] But what exactly was selling?

Marketing the Primary Product

The most obvious sales product is the show. Five episodes into the first season, Comedy Central advised that episodes would be released on video (September 14, 1997), but fans would have to wait until May of the following year before they could actually buy them. Within a few weeks of the first VHS release, more than 700,000 copies had been sold in the US.[10] In the UK, 400,000 boxed VHS sets were sold in ten weeks, sales topped £1.2 million by the end of 1998.[11] Warner Brothers released the first season's boxed DVD set in November 2002 (re-released by Paramount in 2004). *South Park* couldn't have been better timed. Sales of television DVDs have steadily climbed since 1997 and are the "fastest growing trend in the home video business."[12] This trend has created a new level of cult popularity for shows such as *Firefly* (which didn't finish its first season) and *Family Guy* (which was reinstated after its DVD sales surprised Fox executives).[13] Sales of TV DVDs account for 10% of all DVD purchases and currently earn about $2 billion per year.

Despite the sophistication of the marketing plans, the video and DVD releases were clumsily handled. Originally, Rhino Entertainment handled the video releases but when Warner Brothers took over, they decided to release thematic VHS tapes (*Christmas in South Park, Insult to Injuries,* and *The Chef Experience* in November 2000), much to the annoyance of the fans. Fans responded with a petition:

> [I]f you want your eps in order when they come out on VHS and DVD, go and <u>sign this petition</u>. When Rhino was handling the releases it released the eps in order, by season. Then Warner Brothers took it over and switched to themed releases, which really fucks things up for people who want to collect the eps as they came out, in order. Many other shows release their eps in order; *South Park* should be able to do so as well.[14]

Warner Brothers further angered fans when they dropped the commentaries on the DVDs. One reviewer explained:

> Parker and Stone recorded 13 separate tracks for the discs release, each addressing the specifics of individual episodes. Why they were dropped is God's own private mystery. There is nothing outrageous or remotely scandalous about them. . . . Hoping to recoup a little positive publicity, Comedy Central offered a chance to pick up the alternative audio tracks on a five CD

set that costs $3.95 to order directly, or one gets them free if they order the DVD set through the cable channel's online store.[15]

But Comedy Central ran out of the separate DVDs. Some people who ordered them didn't receive them. The South Park Studios' solution? Pick up a secondhand one at eBay. Fans had come to expect additional features and they felt gypped. Fans wanted the commentaries because they provided valuable behind-the-scenes information and insights into the show. Furthermore, Amazon.com's season three and four DVDs (February 2002) wouldn't play on US DVD players. Apparently, they were intended for overseas buyers only, and US fans were not happy to realize that other countries had earlier access. Was this really just incompetence on Warner Brothers' part or part of a masterful manipulation of fans? Effectively, Warner Brothers had created repeat customers—people could potentially buy four versions of the same product: a VHS tape, a DVD without commentary, and one with it, and one which wouldn't play at all.

Still, after these initial teething problems, fans eagerly await each new season's release. Willie Westwood keeps visitors updated with the latest release dates, cover art, and best prices, and urges fans to make the purchase:

> October 12, 2005 – An eventful week starting today. :) Get your season six DVD sets if you didn't get them yesterday. Here's the schedule of events: October 11 – Season 6 DVD boxed set is out.
> November 7, 2002 – Amazon has the SP Season 1 DVDs on sale for $30, CD Now has them for $28. Compare to $40 at Comedy Central's store.[16]

In doing so, he acts as a *de facto* salesperson for Comedy Central. As a *South Park* guru addressing other fans, his inadvertent salesmanship is more compelling.

Despite the Net-wide availability of episodes to download,[17] *South Park* videos and DVDs continue to realize healthy sales. Advertisements for the sets appear on the very fan sites that have downloaded episodes available (for example, http://www.southparkx.net). Which begs the question—why buy the expensive Comedy Central boxed sets when free downloadable episodes are free and more readily available? Clearly, there is more at stake than simply having the episodes to watch. First, the quality of the downloads is still fairly poor—small screens and uneven quality. There are several possibilities. Not everyone has the technical resources or skills to download RealAudio (ra) or AVI files off the Internet. Besides, downloading doesn't offer fans the chance to support their favorite TV show. Finally, there is the consumerist pleasure of owning an attractive cultural artifact. The DVDs are aesthetically well presented and (now) offer added extras (such as Parker and Stone's mini-commentaries). Also, the boxed sets make ideal gifts for a fan or from a fan wishing to spread some *South Park* cheer. For whatever reasons, seasons one through six have sold more than 3.5 million units on DVD.[18] Season five was among the top ten best-selling TV titles in 2005.[19]

Music provides another item for Comedy Central to easily rip from the show and translate into merchandise. Albums include *Chef Aid: The South Park Album* (1998),[20] *South Park: Better, Longer and Uncut* soundtrack (1999), and *Mr. Hankey's Christmas Classics* (1999). Singles "Timmy & the Lords of the Underworld" and "Timmy Livin' a Lie" were available online for $2.49 each in ASF format (July 19, 2000). In 1999 Chef's "Chocolate Salty Balls" toppled the Spice Girls from the lucrative Christmas top spot in the UK, and the movie soundtrack outsold *Titanic* and Oasis.

Distribution is critical to achieve maximum sales. Primary materials such as VHS tapes, CDs, and DVDs were available from the usual outlets; secondary items were another matter. As a strategy to reach brand-conscious teens and tweens, the items had to be available in the right places. Mass distribution is the death of branded products; the movement from specialty stores to retail chains is a sign that "a hot trend is about to cool down."[21] So discount stores are a no-no. *South Park* items are suited to specialty stores such as Hot Topics, Foot Locker, and Gadzooks. Hot Topic found that *South Park* was their number one licensed property in the fourth quarter of 1997.[22] By Thanksgiving of the following year, the material was relegated to the "second tier,"[23] and Hamilton Projects/Comedy Central allowed mass retailer Target to sell a limited amount of *South Park*-licensed merchandise.[24] The rules are fairly restrictive: products get no advertising in retail circulars or on television and will not be discounted; nor will Targets sell items that have been exclusive to specialty shops such as Spencer and Musicland, or to department stores Mervyns and J.C. Penny. Never fear, J.C. Penney did not want *South Park* merchandise after receiving "negative feedback from customers"[25] and complaints on Web sites such as the Christian Family Network.[26]

Secondary Products

South Park started with licenses for t-shirts and baseball caps.[27] Newbury Comics, a Boston-based eighteen-outlet pop-culture chain, reported selling six thousand t-shirts in December 1997. "That's like five times larger than a Pearl Jam or a Metallica," effused co-owner Mike Dreese.[28] T-shirts accounted for more than $26 million in sales by February 1998.[29] The popularity of t-shirts meant that the show's status shifted from cult to mainstream. As one reporter reasoned, "If there are enough of you out there to buy $25 million worth of T-shirts, are you still a cult?"[30] *South Park* fan Taison 'Ian's t-shirt went from a "what's that?" t-shirt to "where can I get one?"

South Park soon graduated to more sophisticated, and male, wearing apparel. Novelty neckwear leader Ralph Marlin signed with Hamilton Projects to produce ties, boxers, and suspenders. The neckwear hit the market in time for the second season (April 1998) and sales were phenomenal; some retailers received the product on Friday and had to reorder on Monday. Dennis Abramczyk, executive vice president for Ralph Marlin, said *South Park* was bigger than the other extremely successful *Star Wars* and *Dilbert*.[31] In the UK, cufflinks were added to the *South Park* suite of merchandise.

While videos, DVDs, and t-shirts are standard grist for the merchandising mill, Comedy Central also offered fans a cornucopia of spending opportunities: calendars, coffee mugs, magnets, boxer shorts, and bumper stickers. All of which, according to Boston's Newbury Comics, sold well.[32] Less likely items, such as Christmas ornaments (Kenny complete with detachable head), trading cards, inflatable furniture, and pinball machines, demonstrated that Comedy Central was willing to stretch the marketing bow as far as possible.[33] But Kenny, Cartman, and Chef condoms?[34]

In a reversal of product placement, foodstuffs such as Cartman's favorite snack food, "Cheesy Poofs," came from the screen to the Comedy Central shelves thanks to Matt Kavet's company, Boston America.[35] People were anxious to buy the product, sight unseen—or should I say, untasted. Also, it marked a licensed product that was most likely to be repurchased if the product filled a snack void. Clearly, the purchasers are not interested in the product as food item but as cultural product. Unopened boxes of Cheesy Poofs are often offered on eBay.

Despite the keen interest in the show's food, fast food chains would not pick up *South Park* giveaways because of the show's content. Millions of dollars of *South Park* stuff sold and not one kiddie meal in sight.

Most of the products were adult oriented. In the early days, Comedy Central espoused a this-show-is-not-for-children philosophy by rejecting any product that could be directly retailed to children. The vice president of new business development at Comedy Central explained, "We are an adult show and we only want products geared for adults."[36] This news was a surprise at the 1998 International Licensing Show, where attendees predicted *South Park* toys to be the next hot property. However, some plush dolls were released in 1998, and in 2000, McFarlane Toys signed a deal with Comedy Central to make a series of posable dolls. Each set included the four boys with a minor character.

South Park plush dolls[37] were not sold in kid-friendly stores like K-Mart, Wal-Mart, Toys R Us, or other big chains, though they did appear in specialty toy stores. Other rejected items include Mr. Hankey candy bars and Mr. Hat hand puppets and t-shirts in children's sizes.[38] Also declined was a Gamecube game idea. However, in 2002, Target carried *South Park* men's lounge pants, Towelie key chain included.

More appropriate for the series demographic are mobile phone products. Mobile phone users can have *South Park* ring tones (some fan sites have downloadable ones), wallpapers, a visual messaging service,[39] and mini-games[40]—all at a cost, of course.

In other countries, licensing companies produced novelty items not seen in America. One of the more unusual is the talking *South Park* TV Buddy:

> You place this on or near your TV & when you point the remote at TV & press it the sofa with the South Park kids on will talk back to you! says "I'm not fat I'm big boned" "Cartoons kick ass" "Dude, Dude, Sweet" "Lets go watch cartoons" "You're being totally immature" "Kick ass Dude" "I've really learned something today" "MMMM MMM MMMM MMM."[41]

http://www.toymania.com/toyfair2000/mcfarlane/southpark

TV Buddy

Another unusual product on eBay was a collection of French ceramic pieces that were to be baked inside a *galette des rois*—a cake baked for the Epiphany in January.

Another rather odd adult-only product is the *South Park* slot machine. Despite the fact that the idea was rejected when floated in 2003, the slot machine did eventually appear. Not surprisingly, the game seems to be remarkably bereft of rules. And while players don't get to kill Kenny, the machine is immediately recognizable to anyone who's watched the show because of its iconic *South Park* sign and characters.

Considering the *South Park* creators were known video/PC game enthusiasts, the arrival of Acclaim's *South Park* game in 1999 was no surprise. The press releases said creators helped develop the shoot-'em-up-style game, in which the four main characters protect *South Park* from enemies such as aliens and killer turkeys. Even though the press release claimed Matt Stone and Trey Parker and Isaac Hayes contributed voices, they later distanced themselves from it. What surprised the fans was the quality of the game: it was weak. Parker and Stone were disappointed and more than a little surprised at the $65 price tag.[42] A fan asked Stone about future plans for a *South Park* game:

Ceramic Pieces for *galette des rois*

> Q: Since Acclaim no longer makes *South Park* games, who does
>   and what type of games are we going to see in the future?
>
> Matt: We currently don't have a game developer. Acclaim did such
>   a good job of fucking up the games that now no one is really
>   that interested in the license. I will say this . . . Trey and I
>   had little to nothing to do with the first games, and if we do
>   another video game it will be R-rated. We wanted to do that
>   in the first place but everyone said it was impossible. Now
>   everyone is doing adult-theme games.

The game's failure appears to have had catastrophic effect on the company, as the Acclaim Web site is a dead one. Perhaps Comedy Central would have been better off enlisting the help of the fans like those at South Park Games Archive.

At first, the creators were "overwhelmed" by the *South Park* products; Parker reported, "Sometimes you'll pass stuff and say, 'What the hell is this thing?' Like a Stan piggybank.[43] But the dolls are really cool and the album, that was good. . . . The machine got so big we just couldn't do everything."[44] The creators continue to reject the overt commercialism of their show and created Towelie as a protest against aggressive merchandising. So too, fans became disgruntled, as many of the comments at Jump the Shark Web site demonstrate:

> As the merchandising machine began cranking out overpriced Cartman key
> chains, we'd only seen—what?—5 or 6 shows altogether?

> The only bad points about the show so far are the merchandise and the Jako-
> vasaurs episode.

> *South Park* is great but they really went overboard with all the crappy mer-
> chandise that was released. *South Park* golf balls, posters, t-shirts and key
> chains are just to name a few and all of which are overpriced anyway.[45]

Parker and Stone succumbed to marketing pressure in 2002 when it was
rumored that Comedy Central wanted to "make more Kenny merchandise."
Even though they'd intended Kenny to remain dead, Parker and Stone
revived him.[46]

The most accessible outlet for the *South Park* fan is, of course, the Internet. The Comedy Central online shop stocks DVDs and CDs, watches, dolls,
slippers, poker and chess games.[47] Prices range from $9 (baseball caps, mag-
nets) to $230 (boxed eight-season DVD set). The inclusion of poker sets ges-
tures to the recent rise in televised poker competitions and a fascination for
all things poker. One problem for fans, though: Comedy Central doesn't
deliver overseas. In the UK, Channel 4 used to offer merchandise on its *South
Park* micro-site, but no longer—instead fans go to Amazon.co.uk.[48] Amazon
specializes in new products while eBay caters more to the collector with its
recycled and esoteric items. In October 2006, the most expensive item was a
South Park pinball machine selling for $2,000; the previous November some-
one offered a set of fifteen $1 bills (supposedly legal tender) with *South Park*
characters instead of George Washington. But, of course, the ultimate animation item is a *South Park* cel:

> Comedy Central and South Park Studios offer a COMEDY CENTRAL
> SOUTH PARK ERIC CARTMAN STILL, from the original pilot. The bidding
> ends on December 12. The still goes for $10,100. Congrats to the winning
> bidder. :) December 2, 2002 –eBay

Other unusual items included a *South Park: Bigger, Longer and Uncut* song-
book, *South Park* navel rings, and hand-drawn sketches of characters (signed
by Trey Parker).

Non-Merchandising Income

Products are only one additional income from the show. One year after *South
Park*'s launch, Comedy Central's gross advertisement revenues had rocketed
from $89 million to $153 million. "Until then, we had been hitting mostly
singles and doubles," says CEO Tom Freston. "This was the defining show for
the network."[49] Within weeks of the first episodes, Comedy Central realized
its potential and wanted to integrate some brands into the content of the animated series because of the show's "cultish allure."[50] David Cole, vice president for advertising sales for Comedy Central, reported, "Six months ago our

highest-priced commercial was $7,500 . . . now for 'South Park' it's $30,000 and up."[51] Comedy Central more than tripled advertisement costs from $5,000–$10,000 for 30 seconds at launch to $30,000–$40,000 six months later.[52]

When the notorious April Fool's episode ("Not Without My Anus") aired, the advertisers were "thrilled," because the ones who signed early expected only a "0.9% share of the network's 43 million subscribers," but due to the episode's notorious ending, they realized "as much as a 7% share on Apr. 22," 1998. With ads attracting an average of $40,000 for 30 seconds, last-minute buyers paid up to $80,000 Show sponsors include Volkswagen, MCI, Snapple, New Line Cinema, MGM Home Video, and Rossignol in-line skates. Like retailers, not all advertisers are willing to be associated with the series, and some will advertise on other Comedy Central shows but avoid *South Park*.

Conclusion

South Park has become a marketing empire unto itself; over half a billion dollars in merchandise has been sold. Hamilton Projects reported that between August and December 1997, more than $50 million was made in the US and Canada.[53] In April 1998, Richard Huff reported that Comedy Central had "moved more than $100 million in licensed products."[54] That year, *South Park*'s "record-breaking sales" made licensing history.[55] At the end of 2002, *South Park* products had generated $500 million.[56] *South Park* was such a success that marketers were told to take note of the show in order to understand Generation Yers.[57]

Fans were credited with the phenomenal marketing success,[58] and with good reason—they were the major target for the products:

> The fan sites are amazing. . . . They often have more information about the shows and actors than the studio sites do. Fans are enthusiastic about linking to stores that sell products for their shows. eMerchandise.com gives them a way to make money doing what they were already doing.[59]

Fans not only purchase and critique the products, they suggest ones, too. Willie Westwood suggested the *South Park* Monopoly game (February 26, 2002). Other non-*South Park* items such as *Orgazmo* and *Cannibal! The Musical* are available at various *South Park*-friendly Web sites like Certified Renegade American Product (Crap TV www.craptv.com).

When did *South Park* jump the shark? When the ratio of "original South Park episodes" to "number of South Park T-Merchandises" exceeded "times 1,000." http://www.jumptheshark.com/

Favorite items: a Cartman doll that blows bubbles out of his ass; a pencil sharpener (guess where the pencil goes?).

Notes

1. "Comedy Central's Hit Series 'South Park' Spawns a Major Licensing Bonanza for Hamilton Projects," press release, June 9, 1998, http://press.comedycentral.com/press/press releases/release.jhtml?f=pr1496.xml, accessed November 20, 2005.

2. Melonee McKinney, "Licensees Do Cartwheels to Get a Piece of Cartman and 'South Park' Gang," *Daily News Record*, June 1, 1998, 18.

3. "How Do You Ride the Tail of a Comet, or What Can Cartman Learn from Beavis and Bart?" *Licensing Letter*, April 6, 1998.

4. Amy McMillan Tambint, "Targeted Teens Spend Lavishly," *Discount Store News*, June 7, 1999.

5. Ray Richmond, "Comedy Central Finally Parks Itself in the Black," *Variety*, October 6, 1997, 1.

6. Tambint, ibid.

7. "That's Not All, Folks," *The Australian*, December 29, 1997, 14.

8. Paula Span, "On the Cussing Edge: South Park Pushes the Taste Envelope," *Washington Post*, September 14, 1997, G8.

9. Ben Westhoff , "New Animated Comedy Is a Big Hit on Campus," *St. Louis Post-Dispatch*, November 5, 1997, E1.

10. "'South Park' Is Too Scary for Toytown," *Chicago Sun-Times*, June 11, 1998, 54.

11. Stephen Armstrong, "How to Make a Killing," *Sunday Times*, January 24, 1999.

12. Mike Snider, "Old TV shows never die. They grow more popular on DVD," *USA Today*, October 19, 2004.

13. Catherine Donaldson-Evans, "Networks Animate Prime Time," *Time*, June 3, 2004.

14. "South Park Timeline 2002," Willie Westwood's South Park Scriptorium, May 16, 2002.

15. "Judge" Bill Gibron, *DVD Verdict Review*, April 7, 2003. http://www.dvdverdict.com/reviews/southparkseason1.php, accessed October 22, 2006.

16. http://www.spscriptorium.com, accessed October 22, 2006.

17. Downloadable episodes weren't widely available until 1998. Joshua Quittner, "Free South Park," *Time*, February 23, 1998, 26. At one stage, people tried to "sell" downloadable links to episodes for a fee of $2.50 each for a two-day rental, $4.95 for outright purchase.

18. "Those Boys Are Back, as Timely as Ever," *New York Times*, October 19, 2005.

19. "Top-Selling TV Titles on DVD Year-to-Date," *Variety*, August 1, 2005, 8 .

20. Three versions were available.

21. Johnson, "Going Mainstream."

22. Alev Aktar, "Singing a New 'Toon," *Women's Wear Daily*, February 6, 1998, 4.

23. Johnson, "Going Mainstream."

24. "Target Gets Nod to Offer South Park Merchandise," *Brandweek*, November 16, 1998.

25. "Penney Kills South Park Merchandise," *Buffalo News*, April 28, 1999, A11.

26. "South Park: The Poisoning of Our Youth," http://web.archive.org/web/199812051 72336/http://www.cfnweb.com/Southpark/sptop.htm, accessed October 22, 2006.

27. McKinney, "Licensees Do Cartwheels."

28. Cobb, "'South Park'—It's a Gas."

29. Michael Mehle, "8-Year-Old with an Attitude," *Rocky Mountain News*, February 1, 1998, D12.

30. Cobb "'South Park'—It's a Gas."

31. McKinney, "Licensees Do Cartwheels."

32. Cobb, "'South Park'—It's a Gas," D1.

33. McKinney, "Licensees Do Cartwheels."

34. "*South Park* Lends a Lifestyle Touch to Condomania," *Marketing*, November 11, 1999, 3.

35. "Gross Effects," *Brandweek*, June 9, 1998, 38.

36. Associated Press Newswires, "Comedy Central Will Not License 'South Park' to Toy Manufacturers," June 11, 1998.

37. Characters include Tweek and Underpants Gnomes (2001), Jimmy and Ms. Choksondik (2002).

38. "'South Park' Is Too Scary for Toytown," *Tampa Tribune*, June 11, 1998, 54.

39. One of the characters "delivers" your message, "Vodafone D2 Turns SMS into MMS by Launching New 'Fun21' Visual Messaging Service," http://www.mobilemms.com/show_mmsnews.asp?id=1774, accessed November 20, 2005.

40. According to the Gamespot Web site, German mobile phone–game manufacture Infusio plans thirteen *South Park* mini-games for 2006, http://www.gamespot.com/pages/company/index.php?company=75545, accessed October 22, 2006.

41. Description from eBay. Information suppressed at seller's request.

42. Tom Ham, "Screen Shots," *USA Today*, January 15, 1999, 62. Acclaim also released Chef's Luv Shack (1999) and South Park Rally (2000).

43. If Parker had seen a Stan piggybank, then Comedy Central was marketing non-adult products.

44. Mike Snider, "'South Park' Spinoffs," *South China Morning Post*, January 22, 1999, E5.

45. "South Park," http://www.jumptheshark.com/s/southpark.htm, accessed October 22, 2006.

46. http://www.spscriptorium.com/SPinfo/SPTimeline2002.htm, accessed October 22, 2006.

47. http://shop.comedycentral.com/sm-south-park—ci-1080337.html, accessed October 22, 2006.

48. http://www.channel4.com/entertainment/tv/microsites/S/southpark, accessed November 20, 2005.

49. Tom Lowry, "Life beyond South Park," http://www.businessweek.com/magazine/content/01_22/b3734128.htm, accessed October 22, 2006.

50. T. L. Stanley, "Media: Sponsors, Licensees on Edge with South Park," *Brandweek*, August 18, 1997.

51. Bill Carter, "Comedy Central Makes the Most of an Irreverent, and Profitable, New Cartoon Hit," *New York Times*, November 10, 1997, D11.

52. Quoting Larry Divney in Michael Freeman and Jim Cooper, "Drawing in Viewers," *Mediaweek*, February 16, 1998.

53. McKinney, "Licensees Do Cartwheels."

54. Richard Huff, "'Park' Gets Multi-Season Deal," *New York Daily News*, April 28, 1998, 74.

55. Tambint, ibid.

56. "The Anatomy of a Cable Hit," *TV Guide*, February 24, 2003.

57. Neil Shoebridge, "Marketers and Agencies Tune In to the Y-Files," *Business Review Weekly*, March 9, 1998, 71.

58. Johnson, "Going Mainstream."

59. "Doesn't Stock *South Park*," *Business Wire*, October 24, 1998.

Part Two

You Killed Kenny!

Chapter 5

Warping Fragile Little Minds: The Show

The Culture in 1997

In 1997, *Titanic* made zillions with its bathetic story of doomed love wedded to schmaltzy songs; audiences knew the outcome and still they flocked to cinemas. Across the lobby, *Men in Black* poked fun at the FBI and made the threat of alien invasion funny. In the home, Mike Judge's *Beavis and Butthead* stopped their teenage snickering and made way for the suburban banality of small-town family life in America (*King of the Hill*). Buffy started kicking some vampire butt, and television said goodbye to the Bundys after a decade of dysfunctionality (*Married . . . With Children*). All of these shows altered the televisual landscape and created space for a new type of "family" show. Then came *South Park*. The show blended guffawing toilet humor, zany plotlines, and crude animation with biting social satire and taboo topics. The mix was confronting, humorous, offensive, and thoughtful.

What sets *South Park* apart is its ebullience. It doesn't just poke fun at society, it positively glories in upsetting the politically correct. It adopts a carnivalesque style in its depiction of the contemporary world.

Carnivals eschewed all that was correct. The wild revelries gave way to a joyous shucking of the normal roles and conventions. The subversive and anti-authoritarian carnival allowed, nay encouraged, the servant to be master and the master, servant. Bakhtin wrote of the duality of life in the Middle Ages, when servants lived a serious, gloomy life under strict control of lord, priest, and king. But during festival time, all hell broke loose; in the carnival

square, people swore, ridiculed, and parodied all that was rigid and controlling in their daily lives. But most of all they laughed. Admittedly, it was an
ambiguous laughter, no doubt soured by the reality of their lives. Bakhtin
describes the laughter:

> first of all, a festive laughter. Therefore it is not an individual reaction to
> some isolated "comic" event. Carnival laughter is the laughter of all the
> people. Second, it is universal in scope; it is directed at all and everyone,
> including the carnival's participants. The entire world is seen in its droll
> aspect, in its gay relativity. Third, this laughter is ambivalent: it is gay, tri-
> umphant, and at the same time mocking, deriding. It asserts and denies, it
> buries and revives.[1]

Humor and especially scatological humor ruled. Of particular focus was the
body, with its all-too-human needs: food, farting, feces, fouling, and fucking.
As Bakhtin explained, the genitals and belly, the "lower body strata," was the
opposite of the "higher body"—the rational, sane body with its love of control and order gave way to the naughty nether regions. In summary, the carnivalesque spirit is nonofficial, unruly, excessive, scatological, humorous, and
defiantly anti-authoritarian. Think Lucille Ball not Mary Tyler Moore,
Kramer not Jerry Seinfeld, Jerry Springer not Oprah Winfrey.

South Park delights in deliberately subverting conventions. It disregards
the strictures of institutions such as the family, politics, religion, and school.
The children rule, not the parents or the schools or the preachers. Naturally,
the show's excesses attracted criticism. These issues will be covered in detail
later. Suffice it to say, *South Park* embodies the spirit of the carnivalesque.

South Park as Animation

Cartooners delight in the carnivalesque by producing a zany world where
anything is possible. In the long ago of cartoon time, Bugs Bunny hammers
buck-toothed opponents with oversized mallets ("Nips the Nips," 1944),
kisses "males" Daffy Duck and Elmer Fudd, and cross-dresses[2] to fool the
enemy ("Herr Meets Hare," 1945). By today's standards, such cartoons were
gratuitously violent, ambivalently sexual, and overly racist.

South Park returns to the days of early cartoon mayhem with a knowing
wink to older audiences. It echoes the work of pioneering cartoonists Tex
Avery, Robert Clampett, and Chuck Jones, and likes to remind audiences of
its cartoon heritage by deploying cartoon characteristics such as the characters' unchanging wardrobe, static ages, tag lines ("You killed Kenny, you bastards"; "Screw you guys I'm going home"), and by the occasional visual gag
(Cartman eating a chocolate gun in "How to Eat with Your Butt"). Previously,

anthropomorphism allowed expression of and rejection of social norms. When the Goofy Gophers disrupt a factory's assembly line, they challenge the orthodoxy of mindless manufacturing, the unending repetition and grinding boredom of factory work ("I Gopher You," Fritz Freleng, 1954). In the 1940s, Tex Avery's Wolfie ogles, whistles, stamps his foot, and drools over Little Red Riding Hood ("Red Hot Riding Hood," 1943) in a way forbidden to a "real" person. When Wolfie howls his desire, he shows us "man" unmasked; literally and figuratively naked, he acts on impulse untempered by upper body logic. The cartoon's sense of the ridiculous, its topsy-turvy world, allows us to examine the uncivilized human.

In 1960, television released the first successful prime-time animation, Hanna-Barbera's *The Flintstones*.[3] *The Flintstones* proved that television audiences could enjoy "children's" fare and provided the template for the family sitcom: the not-so-bright but larger-than-life husband, the patient, understanding wife. It was cartoon Levittown. Fast forward almost thirty years to *The Simpsons* (1989). *The Simpsons* changed the television landscape forever. Suddenly, cartoons were cool again and a host of prime-time animated features followed. The most controversial of these was Mike Judge's *Beavis and Butt-head* (1993–97), which focused on slacker teens and challenged good taste; it was not family viewing, but MTV was not seeking that audience. Judge found prime-time acceptance when he switched to family and small-town America for *King of the Hill* (1997–).

Prime-time animation differs considerably from Saturday morning fare. As Mike Wolf summarizes it, prime time is "smarter animation."[4] Because it has to compete with live-action sitcoms, reality TV shows, and other "adult" fare, it needs better writing, adult topics, and moves "away from the over-the-top nature of cartoon acting and towards a more clever, insightful and witty, dialogue-driven show." *South Park* differs from live-action sitcoms in that it is predicated upon critiquing American society; it lacks the family sensibility of *The Simpsons* and *King of the Hill* and is more overtly politically motivated. It teeters awkwardly on generic cartoon boundaries. It blends the mayhem of yesteryear cartooning with boomer humor spliced with a healthy dose of cynicism. Like *Buffy*, *South Park* has become its own genre and those imitators that followed, *Bro' Town*, *Bromwell High*, and *Chilly Beach*, still lack a generic term. *South Park* doesn't merely reject the formulaic, it subverts it.

The Aesthetics of Crap

To say that *South Park* rejects what many see as traditional cartoon aesthetic is somewhat of an understatement. Critics pointed out its "grade-school,"[5] "cloddish"[6] style and, while there are pragmatic reasons for this (the creators' inability to draw[7]), the crappy style rejects the hyperrealism of Disney. In doing so, it eschews the institutionalization and conservatism[8] of the cartoon industry. In realism's place are the garish colors of *The Simpsons* and the minimalist form of *Peanuts*, only crappier. *South Park*'s acceptance was guaranteed by earlier animations like *Beavis and Butt-head*. The creators celebrate their self-titled "crappy" style. It's a cartoon for the new millennium, though it draws on animation form and content that have gone before.[9]

Crude animation style is not new. Around 1950, "limited animation," in which abstraction and symbolism are key elements, came to the fore. In limited animation, the background is reduced to simplistic, sometimes incomplete, drawings. Items in the background, palm trees or buildings, for example, are not fully realized, but are outlines sketched over the top of a single-color background. This shifts the focus to the characters. But even the characters are not "fully" animated. Limited animation has: "sets of mouths, eyes, noses, etc., which are placed on top of a head and photographed. In full animation, the whole head and all of its features would be redrawn. This allows the shape of the head to change depending on the expression, whereas in limited animation, the expressions will tend to look pasted-on."[10] The characters' heads do not change shape—only their mouths and eyes move. Limited animation means jerky rather than smooth movements; for example, the way the *South Park* boys walk. Pragmatically, limited animation is more easily drawn and more quickly produced, which therefore means cheaper cartoons. But *South Park*'s crappy aesthetic does not equate with low production techniques. Indeed, the opposite is true, South Park Studios utilizes the latest computer software; the crappy aesthetic is deliberate.

The low-tech graphics, rendered in primary colors, work at a symbolic level. As the simple visuals mask a complex technique, so too the simple *South Park* life masks the complexities of contemporary life. Politically, limited animation eschews the bourgeois love of "realism" and replaces it with avant-garde styles. The abstract form encourages viewers to engage with the content more thoughtfully—they are not distracted by "realism."

Characters come in three basic styles, crappy, crappier, and crappiest. The regular characters are rendered in crappy-style. The most obvious visual differences separate children from adults: children are small, round, and have no noses but enormous heads and eyes; the adults are taller and more angular, with noses and smaller heads. The eyes and mouths are the main carriers of meaning. The crappier celebrities come in two basic styles; either they have photographic heads atop *South Park* bodies (David Hasselhoff on Mr. Garrison's body) or they are caricatures (Jennifer Lopez, Paris Hilton, and Elton John). (These graphic representations invoke confusion about celebrities: are they "real" people or merely caricatures of people created by fame and publicity machines.) The crappiest characters are the Canadians—their cruder rendition differentiates them and suggests a more primitive "race." All in all, the iconography works—it differentiates children from adults, celebrities from ordinary folk, Canadians from Americans.

Mostly the characters face the viewer; they even drive looking at the camera and consequently, by default, the viewer.[11] So they address the audience directly; it's an old vaudeville technique that has been adapted for the cartoon world. The knowing look at the audience renders the "fourth wall" invisible and reminds the audience that this is artificial, a cartoon. It invites the viewer to wink with the characters as they desecrate many sacred cows. In theatrical terms, the creators utilize the "alienation" techniques of Bertolt Brecht, a fact the creators freely admit.[12] What seems to be a happy accident turns out to be more contrived and cleverly articulated than it appears on the surface. Characters do not *need* to look like anyone; they are representational ideograms.

Of course, cartoon characters are not meant to be "real"—that would limit their satiric and parody possibilities. Throughout the course of the series, the characters have done what live actors cannot: they have crapped out of their mouths, morphed into mechanized monsters, died and come back to life. Figuratively, they can do offensive things with relative impunity; crapping out of their mouths and cannibalism are potentially less offensive when done by a cartoon character. They can say and do the most outrageous things because they are, after all, only cartoon characters. The cruder the depiction, the less "human" they look, and the greater the comedic effect.

Over time, the animation has become increasingly glossy. To counter the increasingly high production values, the opening sequence has reinserted live-action hands assembling a character. The hands serve as visual reminders of the labor-intensive days when it took six months to create an episode. *South Park* doesn't want to sell out; it wishes to remain true to its homemade, crappy beginnings.

Format

South Park pretty much retains the sitcom format. Each twenty-two-minute episode follows roughly the same pattern: the show opens, a problem is presented, chaos ensues, the problem is solved, and order is reinstated.[13] In the earliest episodes, two and sometimes three storylines were intertwined, but from "Chef Goes Nanners," the shows have tended to focus on a single storyline. While the episodes have become simpler, the scripts have increased by roughly 50 percent, from thirty to more than forty-five pages.[14] When it comes to animation, apparently less is definitely more.

Each episode adopts the three-act play format common to most television sitcoms:

> Act I – Stan and Cartman smash into the beaver dam (rising action).
>
> Act II – South Park panics and people shelter in the Community Center and fight about how to help the people in Beaverton (conflict).
>
> Act III – Stan, Kyle, and Cartman return to Beaverton and the people are saved (resolution). "Two Days Before."

In two-plot episodes, both storylines follow the same sequence:

> Story 1 – Boys find out about the girls' fortune-telling device and plan.
>
> 1b – Butters a.k.a. Marjorine infiltrates the girls' slumber party.
>
> 1c – Butters returns home.
>
> Story 2 – Butters commits "suicide."
>
> 2b – His father reburies him in the Indian burial ground.
>
> 2c – Butters returns and is chained in the basement. "Marjorine."

The rising action presents the events that lead to the conflict: Stan and Cartman's wild boat ride, the girls' fortune-telling device, and Butters' death. The acts aren't always equally apportioned time-wise, but each episode follows the same basic pattern. Often the chaos comes from the deceptions or misunderstandings common to sitcoms. But unlike more traditional shows, the conflicts are often unresolved; Kenny's repeated deaths and the open endings of episodes such as "Marjorine" and "Kenny Dies" gesture to the postmodern tenor of the series as a whole.

Like the girl walking across the vaudeville stage with a sign announcing the next act, *South Park* starts with a text. The text undermines the show by demonstrating a consciousness of its own fictionality and positions the show as a parody:

> ALL CHARACTER AND EVENTS IN
> THIS SHOW—EVEN THOSE BASED
> ON REAL PEOPLE—ARE ENTIRELY

FICTIONAL. ALL CELEBRITY VOICES
ARE IMPERSONATED . . . POORLY.
THE FOLLOWING PROGRAM
CONTAINS COARSE LANGUAGE
AND DUE TO ITS CONTENT IT
SHOULD NOT BE VIEWED BY ANYONE.

Is the warning disingenuous? Yes. First, it's a parody of the preceding MA rating, which states: "This program is specifically designed to be viewed by adults and therefore may not be suitable for children under 17." The creators respond by deconstructing the restrictions of censorship; the "coarse language . . . and content" works as both a caution and a temptation. Tongue-in-cheek, viewers are told not to watch the show, thereby deliberately rejecting a television network's angst about ratings. The apology for poor impersonations operates on two levels. First, it is the literal truth—the impersonations are not even poor, they don't exist at all.[15] At another level, doing impersonations is the hallmark of shtick comedy and thus the show emphasizes its position at the lower rungs of comedy shows. The message also adopts legalese, as if daring celebrities to sue or puritanical viewers to complain. Overall, the message addresses a gullible and litigious audience, two qualities parodied in many episodes. After the silent warning, the hyper-energetic twenty-second opening sequence starts.[16]

Opening sequences position the show for the viewers. Most television shows have a visual narrative that anchors the show geographically: a graffiti-covered streetscape for *Aqua Hunger Teen Force*, the dull suburbia of *King of the Hill*. Over the past decade, *South Park* has developed three different openings, each of which mirrors a different aspect of the show. The first version follows the boys on their school bus ride through the township; the characters wave and smile at the audience while the lyrics celebrate the friendly town. This is a friendly and welcoming town. After "Fourth Grade," the high-tech computerized look and speedy font text demonstrate that the show is now "faster, cooler, [has] better animations, more explosions, [and is] smarter." And, in truth, it has developed a glossier, slicker look. In the third opening, human hands assemble characters over the short scenes clipped from recent episodes. The hands are historical reminders of the series' painstaking creative beginnings. In twenty seconds, some fifty images flash; the high-energy graphics recall pivotal moments from previous episodes while simultaneously reinforcing both the continuous and discontinuous nature of television. The MTV pacing mimics the "peek-a-boo" world of television.[17] Overarching the series are the background images of snowcapped mountains and Main Street—this is any small mountain town, USA—okay, any alien-abducting, cow-ruling town, that is.

Censorship

Controversial as *South Park* is, it still operates within a very controlling environment, the television network. Critics argue that the carnival is not a completely authority-free space; in fact, they convincingly observe that the misrule is, in reality, an officially sanctioned and therefore controlled madness.[18] Certainly, while the creators of *South Park* can indulge their love of celebrity bashing and iconoclasm, they must do so within officially sanctioned parameters—in other words, censorship guidelines.

In the United States, television "censorship" or standards are self-regulatory. Networks and cable stations, rather than a government body, are responsible for the on-air material they broadcast. Each network, and most of the cable networks, has its own standards and practices department that reviews potential content to ensure it conforms to that station's ideology; usually, guidelines (aside from the usual political and legal issues) are at pains to reflect "community standards."[19] If material aired does offend, the "Federal Communications Commission (FCC) will levy fines, *heavy* fines as CBS learned. CBS was fined $550,000 for showing 18 frames of Janet Jackson's breast (there are 30 frames to a video second)."[20] Nipplegate renewed debates about television standards and an FCC campaign against "indecency."[21] The FCC definition of "indecency" seems simple enough: "language or material that, in context, depicts or describes, in terms patently offensive as measured by contemporary community standards for the broadcast medium, sexual or excretory organs or activities," but as always, the crux of the matter is articulating what is "indecent" and who decides what is indecent.

Swearing is one of the most contentious areas of censorship. Standards have come a long way since *Gone with the Wind* had to receive special dispensation for Rhett Butler to utter, "Frankly, Scarlett, I don't give a damn." Today barely an episode of *South Park* goes by without at least one "goddamnit." Prime-time shows such as *NYPD Blue, Sex in the City, Homicide: Life on the Street*, and *South Park* contain words that "would have been unthinkable just a decade ago."[22] When "Shit Hits the Fan" aired, it was a catalyst for calls to overhaul the system of network self-censorship. L. Brent Bozell posted his response to the infamous "Shit Hits the Fan" episode invoking the slippery slope argument that the show would adopt stronger and stronger language.[23] Six months later, as the president of the Parents Television Council, he released a study that named *South Park* the most objectionable show on air because it averaged

126 instances of sex, violence, or foul language per half hour, "that's 4.2 per minute, even including commercials."[24] *Deadwood* has just as much swearing—it even has its own FPM Web site (fucks per minute).[25] Bozell might concede that the show "manifests real wit," but only when it agrees with his political leanings. He condemned it as "curdled, malodorous black hole of Comedy Central vomit"[26] in response to "Stupid Spoiled Whore." Still, when an episode contains "shit" repeated over 150 times and Mr. Slaves shoves Paris Hilton up his ass, one has to expect some media outrage.

Newspaper journalists scratched their heads. Paula Span was surprised the show hadn't been boycotted and wanted to know "where's the boycott? Where's William Bennett?"[27] Phillip Morris wondered why "there were no censors' beeps or any other effort made to mute the use of the profanity." He postulated that viewers had been "bludgeoned by profanity" and that this was an artifact of the coarsening of American society as a whole.[28] Comedy Central reported only four e-mails, all positive, after the episode aired. Naughty words on television are usually bleeped by the station, but the *South Park* staff has been amazed at how liberal Comedy Central has been.[29] They accepted (the s-word barrage) with "open arms."[30]

Naturally, a show as offensive as *South Park* has upset some groups, not the least being the Anti-Defamation League, which received complaints at the start of the series. But "now, we get only a handful of calls about it per season," reported the league's Amy Levy.[31] Religious groups have raised their hands from time to time. The Catholic League for Religious and Civil Rights objected to the fight between Jesus and Satan in their press release headlined "'South Park' Stoops to the Gutter";[32] four years later, the league condemned "Red Hot Catholic Love."[33] In season nine, "Bloody Mary" pushed the league's buttons again. It demanded that Viacom, Comedy Central's parent company, issue an apology to Roman Catholics and "a pledge that this episode be permanently retired and not be made available on DVD." It remains to be seen if the league will win this bout. Other than the league, there have been remarkably few complaints; a while ago, the Christian Family Network prepared a *South Park Education/Action Guide* to "help make people aware of *South Park* and its potential affect [*sic*] upon our youth."[34] In India, outraged Hindu and Muslim community leaders protested Mr. Garrison's politically incorrect "Merry Fucking Christmas,"[35] and in South Africa, *one* Catholic family protested local channel M-Net's airing of "Red Hot Catholic Love."[36] But in actuality, most of the early protests and outrage were a media myth perpetrated by Comedy Central. Matt Stone confesses, "No group has ever really protested *South Park*. That's the big lie that was sold to everyone way early on about the show. We kind of went with it cuz it was good for ratings, but the truth is that we've never been protested against in a serious way."[37] A search of media databases and the Internet in general reveals that Stone is correct. Since then, even the most offensive images, such as dog masturbation, drug ingestion, and a man tongue-kissing a llama have failed to attract media attention.

Before the show aired, critics sympathized with parents and teachers, "Parents and teachers, your latest headache arrives next week."[38] But not all parents found *South Park* objectionable. Barry S. Fagin, professor of computer science at the U.S. Air Force Academy and co-founder (with his wife) of Families Against Internet Censorship, uses *South Park* for lessons he can teach his kids.[39] Kathryn Montgomery of Media Education said parents need education, because it's not reasonable to expect all television to be child-appropriate.[40] Teachers found the marketing produced the most problems. Some grammar schools in New Jersey banned students from wearing *South Park* paraphernalia.[41] More often, the ban was not about text on t-shirts but about classroom disruption:

> Parents of the 520 students at Stormonth Elementary School . . . got a letter last week from Principal Linda Moore saying the clothing was causing a disruption in the classrooms and would not be allowed. Moore acknowledged seeing only one child wearing a "South Park" T-shirt on one day, but other children gathered around to look at it, and that took "a little bit of time away from the classroom." Moore banned Beanie Babies from school in 1996.[42]

The above incidents were isolated because "Most of the school principals contacted for this story had never heard of the show, and they said they were unaware of it causing any problems at school."[43] Newspaper reports seemed overeager to report anything that even resembled a controversy. However, the "outrage" about the show's toilet humor did have one positive outcome: it prompted the creators to develop censorship into a feature-length movie *Bigger, Longer and Uncut*.

While Comedy Central let the shit slide, it has harnessed some content. It wasn't too keen to upset sponsors, and "Subway Sandwiches" had to be changed to "Sub Sandwiches."[44] Garrison's oral application of a condom aired originally, but the 6–8 frames were subsequently removed ("Proper Condom Use"). Similarly, the creators were told they could not do an episode on the Nation of Islam—when the network refused to show depictions of Muhammad recently, the creators were incensed.[45] Comedy Central said a definite no to the racist ending of "Here Comes the Neighborhood." When *South Park* was sold for syndication, fifteen episodes had to be cleaned up, but nearly 200 passed.[46] The edited versions weren't terribly different: "asshole" became "ass"; "spooge," "goddamit," "Jesus Christ," and "ass rammer" were either cut or changed; "ass," "boner," "punk-ass bitch," "son of a bitch," and "buttholes" were okayed; and Kenny still dies.[47]

Conclusion

Into the postmodern TV-scape of the late 1990s stepped *South Park*. Younger viewers were used to "adult" cartoons and heavily ironic shows; after all, they had been watching *The Simpsons* for nearly a decade. They had grown up with shows rich in popular cultural references, shows that deconstructed the confused world in which they lived. Even better, *South Park* provided a non-sanctioned space to laugh at poo and fart jokes. *Beavis and Butt-head* had grown up—well, a little, anyway.

Little of what the show does in innovative. There had been cartoons about the disintegration of the American lifestyle before; there had been shows where kids were smarter than their parents. It wasn't the first show with toilet humor, nor was it the first iconoclastic comedy. Other comedies had been just as silly. But here was a show that exuberantly collapsed all of these and broached topics hitherto forbidden—where else could viewers see a satellite farted out of someone's arse or Jesus and Santa fighting? Who else had refused to kowtow to the strictures of political correctness and question contemporary politics? This indeed was television for the MTV generation.

> Gentlemen, we appreciate your concern. Here at HBC the general goal is providing the highest and most thought-provoking entertainment. How great it is that we live in a country where an artist can express himself freely. That's not only the American spirit, it's the HBC spirit which allows us to make great family programs like *Halo the Turtle*, and of course, everyone's favorite show, *Cop Drama*. We can't thank you enough for bringing your concerns to our network, for it is you, the loyal HBC viewer, who makes this great network, and indeed, the great country that it is. ("It Hits the Fan")
>
> STAN: You know, I think I've learned something today. It's really easy not to think of images on TV as real people. But they are. That's why it's easy to ignore those commercials, but, people on TV are just as real as you or I.
>
> KYLE: Yeah. And that means that MacGyver is a real person too.

> When Matt and Trey delivered the pilot to Comedy Central, they didn't have a "bumper" (that card at the end of the show that tells you who created it). Not having an appropriate company name or logo to use, they tossed in the logo of Braniff Airlines—a defunct airline. After the show aired, they were contacted by a company that owned the rights to the Braniff name and logo. An agreement was made to allow them the use of the logo on *South Park* broadcasts, but not on any other projects in the future.

Notes

1. Mikhail Bakhtin, *Rabelais and His World*, trans. Helene Iswolsky (Bloomington: Indiana University Press, 1984), p. 11.

2. Assuming Bugs is a male, of course.

3. A cartoon version of *The Honeymooners* (a popular sitcom starring Jackie Gleason), it was the first prime-time cartoon series.

4. Mike Wolf, "Animating in the Spotlight: Creating Prime Time," *Animation World Magazine*, March 12, 1998, http://www.awn.com/mag/issue2.12/2.12pages/2.12wolfpre.html, accessed October 25, 2006.

5. Frederic M. Biddle, "'South Park' Wickedly Makes the Grade," *Boston Globe*, August 13, 1997, D8.

6. Monica Collins, "Toons in the Hood," *Boston Herald*, October 28, 1997, 32.

7. Stone on *Jimmy Kimmel Live*, August 13, 1997.

8. Disney's conservatism has been discussed in many articles and books, such as Paul Wells's *Animation and America*.

9. Paradoxically, the earliest cartoonists did not seek realism. For more on this, read Esther Leslie, *Hollywood Flatlands: Animation, Critical Theory and the Avant-Garde* (London: Verso, 2002). Since the 1930s, though, the most realistic cartoons have achieved the highest critical praise and attention.

10. "Limited Animation," The GNU 3DLDF Animation Page, http://www.gnu.org/software/3dldf/animatn.html#Full_and_Limited_Animation, accessed November 8, 2005.

11. Chef did not even have a "side" view until much later in the series.

12. Studio FAQs, November 16, 2002. Q: I'm taking a dramatic studies course in which the ideas of Brecht and Artaud (among others) are taught. As I've been learning about these two schools of thought, I've constantly found myself applying their ideas to *South Park*. I may eventually write a paper for class illustrating such parallels. Have Trey or Matt been directly influenced by these dramatic theorists, or am I just trying to make *South Park* seem more intellectual than it actually is? A: A big fat affirmative to Brecht, but an equally fat negative to Artaud. Surrealism is for losers."

13. Two-parters include Cartman's search for his father in season one and season two; the season three trilogy "Cat Orgy," "Two Men in a Hot Tub," and "Jewbilee"; season four's "Do the Handicapped Go to Hell?" and "Probably"; and season ten's "Cartoon Wars."

14. *Rolling Stone* (Australia), January 1999.

15. The punctuation between impersonated and poorly serves a rhetorical purpose in that it interrupts the message for comedic effect. Rarely (if ever) do television shows suggest they do anything "poorly," let alone remind viewers each week that their shows are not quality shows. The flashing cursor symbolizes the contemporary computer screen—thus momentarily collapsing the television and the computer screen.

16. Cold openings are used for "Starvin' Marvin," "Probably," "Mr. Hankey's Christmas Classics," and "Butters' Very Own Episode." Cold openings alert fans/viewers that this is not a "normal" episode and the style of the opening hints at the content to come: the *Star Wars* opening of "Starvin' Marvin in Space," for example. And "Mr. Hankey's Christmas Classics" recalls Christmas variety shows, while "Butters' Very Own Episode" mirrors cheery family sitcoms.

17. Neil Postman, *Amusing Ourselves to Death* (New York: Penguin Books, 1986), chap. 5.

18. Terry Eagleton, *Walter Benjamin, Or, Towards a Revolutionary Criticism* (London: Verso, 1981); Chris Humphrey, *The Politics of Carnival: Festive Misrule in Medieval England*, Manchester: Manchester University Press, 2001.

19. Once upon a time all scripts were scrutinized; these days, the material is viewed after recording.

20. Joe Saltzman, "The FCC Gives Indecency a Bad Rap," *USA Today Magazine*, January 2005, 27.

21. Julie Hilden, "Jackson 'Nipplegate' Illustrates the Danger of Chilling Free Speech," CNN, February 20, 2004, http://www.cnn.com/2004/LAW/02/20/findlaw.analysis.hilden.jackson, accessed October 25, 2005.

22. Richard Huff "Frankly Speaking," *New York Daily News*, December 18, 1997, 117.

23. L. Brent Bozell, "Sleazy Sequels on South Park," Media Research Center, http://www.mediaresearch.org/BozellColumns/entertainmentcolumn/2001/col20010807.asp, August 7, 2001.

24. John M. Higgins, "Loose Standards Shock," *Broadcasting & Cable*, January 28, 2002, 16.

25. http://thewvsr.com/deadwood.htm, accessed October 23, 2006.

26. "Losers and Winners, 2004," Town Hall, http://www.townhall.com/columnists/Brent BozellIII/2005/01/03/winners_and_losers,_2004, accessed October 23, 2006.

27. Paula Span, "On the Cussing Edge: 'South Park' Pushes the Taste Envelope," *Washington Post*, September 14, 1997, G8.

28. Phillip Morris. "We're Bludgeoned by Profanity," *Cleveland Plain Dealer*, June 26, 2001, B9.

29. Stone, quoted in Span, "On the Cussing Edge."

30. Liane Bonin, "They Swear, It's True," *Entertainment Weekly*, June 20, 2001, http://www.ew.com/ew/report/0,6115,131459_3_0_,00.html, accessed October 25, 2006.

31. Donna Petrozzello, "'Park' and Ride: Aging 'Toon Still a Boon to Cable," *New York Daily News*, June 14, 2002, 150.

32. Tim Cuprisin, "*South Park* Isn't for Everyone," *Milwaukee Journal Sentinel*, February 9, 1998, 8.

33. "*South Park* Angers Catholic League," *Montreal Gazette*, July 14, 2002, A12.

34. The guide does not appear to be available on the Internet anymore.

35. Shyam Bhatia, "Outraging UK Muslims, Hindus," *Times of India*, September 24, 2000.

36. Giorgio, Lilia, Ornella, and Elio Pasqua, letter re: "Disgust at 'Red Hot Catholic Love,'" *The Star*, July 9, 2003, http://www.thestar.co.za/index.php?fSectionId=225&fArticleId=184465, accessed October 24, 2006.

37. South Park Studio, Staff Chat Page, November 25, 2005, http://www.southparkstudios.com/fans/staffchats.php?tab=40&sid=sid=ed18fe6991c05900b3825d13da67dadf, accessed October 24, 2006.

38. Jim Minge "Comedy Central's 'South Park' Pushes Lots of Parental Buttons," *Omaha World Herald*, August 7, 1997, 42; Jeff Simon, "Who's Really the Butt of All Cable Jokes," *Buffalo News*, August 3, 1997, TV2; Ann Hodges, "South Park for Adults Who Haven't Grown Up," *Houston Chronicle*, August 13, 1997, 2; Mark Lorando, "Cartoon Graziness," *New Orleans Times-Picayune*, October 29, 1997, E1.

39. "Goin' Down to South Park," *Reason Online*, April 25, 2000.

40. David Bauder, "Forbidden Fruit," *Chicago Sun-Times*, April 7, 1998, 39.

41. Petrozzello, "'Park' and Ride"; Rick Marin, "The Rude Tube," *Newsweek*, March 23, 1998, 56.

42. Jim Stingl, "They've Quashed Kenny!" *Milwaukee Journal Sentinel*, April 28, 1998, 1.

43. Ibid., 1.

44. Phil Rosenthal, "*South Park* vs. Subway," *Chicago Sun-Times*, March 6, 2002, 51.

45. Dennis Lim, "Television—Lowbrow and Proud of It," *The London Independent*, March 29, 1998, 26.

46. Yahoo News, "Syndication Means More Cuts," January 20, 2004.

47. Paige Albiniak and John M. Higgins, "Restraining Order," *Broadcasting & Cable*, March 15, 2004, http://www.broadcastingcable.com/article/CA403637.html?display=Top+of+the+Week &promocode=SUPP, accessed October 25, 2006.

Chapter 6

Ending Fart Sequence: Humor

Writing about humor is not funny. But writing a book about *South Park* and not writing about humor is like taking a shower without soap. Humor is the cleanser that washes away much of the distasteful *South Park* content (if indeed one finds the content distasteful). The serious subject matter of many episodes almost demands a humorous approach. Bakhtin devoted an entire chapter to Rabelais' place in the "history of laughter." He wrote:

> Laughter has a deep philosophical meaning, it is one of the essential forms of the truth concerning the world as a whole, concerning history and man; it is a peculiar point of view relative to the world; the world is seen anew, no less (and perhaps more) profoundly than when seen from the serious standpoint. Therefore, laughter is just as admissible in great literature, posing universal problems, as seriousness. Certain essential aspects of the world are accessible only to laughter.[1]

While laughter can be liberating, it can equally offend—jokes about farting might be okay, but jokes about Jesus are off limits. Laughter is also personal; what makes one person laugh does not necessarily make another laugh, and nothing is surer to spoil a joke than having to explain it. At the risk of spoiling some of the great *South Park* moments, it is worth exploring how humor is deployed within the series.

Basically, there are three theories of laughter: relief theory, superiority theory, and incongruity theory. Superiority theorists posit that we laugh at others' discomfort. Relief theorists think that laughter expels nervous energy and that we feel better when we laugh—the "laughter is the best medicine" school of thinking. Laughter relieves the tension of awkward and even dangerous situations; laughter releases fear. Incongruity theory claims that humor comes from the unexpected, the illogical, the inappropriate. As Pascal put it, "Nothing produces laughter more than a surprising disproportion between that which one expects and that which one sees." The superiority theory focuses on emotions involved in laughter, the relief theory addresses its biological/psychological function, and the incongruity theory considers the cognitive dimension of laughter.[2]

Television humor is, paradoxically, perennial and ever changing. Comedies such as *I Love Lucy* still manage to make viewers laugh and *Monty Python's Flying Circus* remains the benchmark of silliness. Some shows don't always retain their comedic appeal; *Benny Hill*'s eye-rolling double innuendos and sexist skits may look plain silly and even offensive to contemporary viewers, though they might be appreciated for their camp value. Certainly, *The Brady Bunch* is now read ironically by Gen Xers.[3] Many viewers who tuned in to the first *South Park* probably had either seen or heard of *The Spirit of Christmas* and were prepared for an over-the-top, irreverent show. They were ready to laugh at swearing children and Jesus and Santa duking it out. Even the most uncomplimentary critics found parts of *South Park* funny. But what parts?

Because of its multiple layers of meaning, *South Park* humor can be enjoyed at a variety of levels. Take, for instance, the scene where Father Maxi is caught having sex with Mrs. Donovan ("Do the Handicapped Go to Hell?"), the following are potential sites for amusement:

- a man having sex (bawdy humor),
- a priest having sex with a woman (taboo humor),
- a priest having sex with a married woman (committing a cardinal sin), and
- a priest having sex with a married woman in a church (parochial humor).

As it occurs in *South Park*, the scene is framed by the show's identity as a comedy rather than a desecration (though some might be offended). As John Fiske points out, genres orient readers and help them make "meanings in some ways rather than in others."[4] If the same scene occurred in a drama such as *Sex in the City*, perhaps it would not be as humorous.

The Father Maxi scene interweaves iconoclasm, irony, and ridicule—and the viewer can enter at whatever level his or her individual sense of humor decodes the "joke." Furthermore, the event is itself further marked by that which has gone before in the episode:

- Father Maxi having sex: his hypocrisy at committing a sin after warning the boys about sin;

- Father Maxi having sex in the confessional, where he's just laid hands on Cartman;
- Father Maxi having sex with Mrs. Donovan, an Irish woman, therefore insinuating she's a religious/Catholic parishioner (would it have been as amusing if she was a hooker?); and
- the boys catching Father Maxi—sex through the eyes of children; again, adults prove to be unreliable.

The situation is further exploited by Father Maxi's reaction: his "son of a bitch," his inarticulate "ahh—ahh—ahhh," his insincere prayer, and his accusation that it's all Mrs. Donovan's fault. Aesthetically, Father Maxi is rendered ridiculous by his goofy facial expressions and stuttering responses. When he falls to his knees and begs the boys for forgiveness, it's a parody of what he's been trying to get the boys to do. Obviously, not all of the humor relies on Father Maxi; the boys' response furthers the humor. Thus, the simple joke operates on multiple levels, not all of equal importance, and the viewer can be amused at any or all of the levels. Certainly deconstructing that small incident has managed to remove all the humor, hey?

Scatological Humor[5]

South Park embraces its toilet humor—fart and shit jokes abound. Scatological references are nothing new. Aristophanes' *The Clouds* (423 BC) opens with fart jokes. Jonathan Swift raised scatological standards to an art form in his writings. Francois Rabelais' Gargantua describes at length his experiments to find "a means to wipe my bum" and composes wee rhymes about such activities:

A Roundelay.
In shitting yes'day I did know
The sess I to my arse did owe:
The smell was such came from that slunk,
That I was with it all bestunk:
O had but then some brave Signor
Brought her to me I waited for,
In shitting!
I would have cleft her watergap,
And join'd it close to my flipflap,
Whilst she had with her fingers guarded
My foul nockandrow, all bemerded
In shitting.[6]

He names his lawyers "Kissarse" and "Bumfondle." So, given shit's rich cultural history, and, yes, there are books about shit,[7] what is the role of excrement in *South Park*?

"Lower body humor" is an essential ingredient of *South Park*'s misrule. Bawdy, smutty jokes and toilet humor are the provenance, apparently, of the working classes; they're part of folk culture. Working "blue" is "blue" collar. It is the opposite of cleansed, cerebral humor that is considered adult. *South Park* seems to be forever linked to toilet humor, which in turn pairs the show with adolescent boys. According to journalist Christy Boldenow, "[*Team America* has the] sort of low-brow humor that made the directors famous in *South Park*. It's also most appealing to adolescent boys."[8]

Toilet humor fascinates and repels because it focuses on the ejection of body waste and has taken on metaphors of uncleanliness (rather than metaphors of waste excess, which really it is). Uncleanliness means the great "unwashed," the common folk. Some theorists conjecture that poo jokes are often linked to lack of control. Bernadette Bucher claims, "what is decreed impure, [and] thus execrated and condemned by a culture, is an object out of place, a cause for disorder."[9] So toilet humor is distasteful because it deals with elimination; it is juvenile because it deals with the "lower body" rather than the upper body, and, because it is lower body, it appeals to the uneducated. As Scott the dick says, "You think farting is sooo funny! Well it isn't!! Fart jokes are the lowest form of comedy!" ("Terrance and Phillip").

From the very first episode, Cartman's body and its functions are sites of many of the scatological jokes. In "Anal Probe," two of the funniest scenes come from Cartman's ass: the visual gag of his flaming farts lighting Pip and Kitty, and his lament, "Why is it that everything today has to do with things either going in or coming out of my ass?" From here on, it only gets worse for Cartman; he is henceforth the ass man. Aside from the running gag about his big-boned ass, what goes in (alien probes and fingers) and what comes out (farts and excreta) are used for comic effect. He thinks rainbows are "those things that crawl up your leg and bite the inside of your ass" ("Weight Gain"); he jokes about shoving Pip's invitation up his ass ("Damien"); it's his ass that hurts after a drug search ("Ike's Wee Wee"); he persuades the boys to try The Chamber of Farts ("Cow Days"); Costa Rica and Kenny's house smell like ass ("Rainforest Schmainforest"); he sues Stan for talking about "having oral sex with my ass" ("Sexual Harassment Panda"); he thinks he's trapped in Helen Hunt's ass ("Cancelled"); it's his ass that is dressed as Stan's mom's boobs ("Preschool"); and his farts are legendary ("Osama Bin Laden Has Farty Pants"). He exhibits a predilection for Kyle doing things to his ass and presents his ass to Kyle whenever he can. Cartman's desire to fart on Kyle's face redresses what Cartman clearly feels is a power imbalance: to kiss someone's ass is to acknowledge his or her power. One of the most self-conscious scenes about farting and humor comes in "Cancelled." Cartman nominates Kyle to activate the intergalactic satellite in his ass; much farting ensues:

CARTMAN: Okay, okay. It's not funny anymore. [*Kyle tries again, Cartman farts.*] Oh yes it is!

CHEF: Eric, that's enough!

CARTMAN: Okay, okay. [*Kyle tries again, Cartman farts again and laughs.*] Ohh, double psych!

CHEF: It [*Cartman farting on Kyle*] stopped being funny forty seconds ago, boy! Let's just get this over with!

CARTMAN: But it was one of the best times I've ever had.

JEFF: Can I see this thing, please?

CARTMAN: Okay. [*Kyle tries again and Cartman farts.*] Ohhh! Goddamnit!

CHEF: Okay. Now it's funny again. ("Cancelled")

The scene combines repetition, scatology, and the ridiculous; it also demonstrates the creators' understanding of true comedic timing. Cartman's fascination with things that go in and out of his anus is more than just childlike fun. No one else exhibits the pleasure of shitting the way Cartman does. He even has a shitting song. Does this obsession hint at Cartman's homosexuality?

Aside from Cartman, the most overtly scatological character is Mr. Hankey. At first, the sight of the talking poo is confronting, especially when he jumps around leaving brown trails of shit behind ("Mr. Hankey, the Christmas Poo"). But he transcends his crappiness because he represents the Christmas spirit and is thus transformed into something benign, a chirpy Christmas poop. He sits by the fireside and introduces seasonal songs ("Mr. Hankey's Christmas Classic"); he saves the town ("Chef's Salty Balls"), and leads the boys to Santa in a shitty train ("Red Sleigh Down"). By the time we meet his crappy family, he is just another character. His son "simple" Simon has a peanut in his head—a masterful if slightly distasteful visual gag. His high-pitched voice, cheery "Howdy ho," and unfailing upbeat demeanor undo his fecality.

The most juvenile and consistent fart jokes come from the creators' alter egos, Terrance and Phillip. Terrance and Phillip are the creators' response to critics who think *South Park* is just about fart jokes. These one-joke ponies soon pall on the viewer, but the duo is much admired by the boys, especially by Cartman, who is in awe of their ability to keep their humor "fresh" ("Death"). Of course, they exist purely as ironic cartoon devices to demonstrate that farting jokes alone do not comedy make.

One episode in particular shows the viewer the political power of toilet humor and its role as marker of naughty boy rebellion. The counter tallying the iterations of the four-letter word in "Shit Hits the Fan" underscores the excesses of the episode. The political is hammered home in Ms. Choksondik's exegesis about shit grammar:

MS. CHOKSONDIK: Alright, children, in lieu of the common usage, I'm s'posed to clarify the school's position on the word, "shit."

STAN: Wow! We can say "shit" in school now?!

KYLE: This is ridiculous! Just because they say it on TV it's alright.

MS. CHOKSONDIK: Yes, but only in the figurative noun form or the adjective form.

CARTMAN: Huh?

MS. CHOKSONDIK: You can only use it in the nonliteral sense. For instance, "That's a shitty picture of me" is now fine. However, the literal noun form of "This is a picture of shit" is still naughty.

CARTMAN: I don't get it.

STAN: Me neither.

MS. CHOKSONDIK: The adjective form is now also acceptable. For example: "The weather outside is shitty." However, the literal adjective is NOT appropriate. For example: "My bad diarrhea made the inside of the toilet bowl shitty, and I had to clean it with a rag, which then also became shitty." That's right out!

    . . .

BUTTERS: Huh-uh, Ms. Choksondik, eh, can we say it in the expletive? Like, "Oh, shit," or, "shit on a shingle"?

MS. CHOKSONDIK: Yes, that's now fine.

Once shit is an acceptable and institutionally approved word (whether on television or in the classroom), it loses its power to shock. Furthermore, in case the subtlety of that bypasses the viewer (!), the point is belabored in the subplot: "shit" literally kills people. *South Park* responded to its critics and the show drew unwarranted criticism for the sheer abundance of times "shit" was repeated by people who obviously missed the point of the episode. The creators realized that the TV world has boundaries and, Lenny

Bruce style, it drew attention to those very boundaries. As Bakhtin wrote, "excrement is gay matter."[10]

Profanity and Ridicule as Humor

"Shit," "ass," and "fuck" are vulgar words, but they are not profane. Profanity is blasphemy, words that directly offend religious sensibilities. During the church festivals he wrote about, Bakhtin found that "language which mocks and insults the deity . . . was part of the ancient comic cults";[11] in sacred parody (the "parody of sacred texts and rites"), it was difficult to tell where the parody stopped and the ridicule began.[12] So it's nothing new to take the name of the Lord thy God in humorous vain. Jokes about God having a sense of humor are common; nineteenth-century writer G. K. Chesterton keenly felt Jesus's lack of humor, "there is one thing that was too great for God to show us when He walked upon our earth; and I have sometimes fancied that it was His mirth." *South Park* takes its religious mirth seriously too, because in debunking hypocrisy, religion comes in for some pretty hard blows.

The boys, Priest Maxi, and even Jesus use profanity. "God swearing," such as "goddamnit," "hell," and "Jesus tap-dancing Christ," is generally unacceptable; even more so when children do it. Why? The laughter signifies an "element of victory not only over supernatural awe, over the sacred, over death; it also means the defeat of power, of earthly kings, of the earthly upper classes, of all that oppresses and restricts.[13] Catholicism provides many of the laughs, and no wonder—it's a religion rich in medieval ritual and mystical lore and more recently has been at the center of some very unsavory scandals.

Priest Maxi is one of the most ridiculed people in the series.[14] Maxi embodies all that is contradictory, antiquated, and just plain bizarre about Roman Catholicism. As a priest, one of his sanctioned roles is to perform highly ritualized duties—ones of preordained order and set texts—in a dignified and appropriate manner. His language is typical carnivalesque parody when at a funeral he gravely intones the Colorado prayer:

PRIEST MAXI: Now, let us pray. Lord, though we have lost Neil Smith to free agency and Steve Atwater to the Jets, still, we hope our beloved Broncos can bring home another Super Bowl championship, and once again bathe in the glory of your light. Amen.

ALL: Amen.

PRIEST MAXI: Let's go

ALL: Let's go

PRIEST MAXI:	Broncos
ALL:	Broncos
PRIEST MAXI:	Let's go Broncos
ALL:	Broncos, let's go! ("Spontaneous Combustion")

Maxi's prayer undermines the ritualized seriousness of "prayer" in which one is supposed to ask God for more important things than winning football games. Supplication demands a level of circumspection and respect; the call-and-response style subtly demonstrates what is expected from God—a response. Maxi's prayers are filled with inappropriate phrases; his childlike or casual language demonstrates that prayers are not about "talking" to God, but serious occasions that demand a formalized style of language. For example, he says: "Well, on this blessed Friday let us give *thanks for stuff, and things.* Lord, is it so much to ask that you not let us suddenly burst into flame for no apparent reason? I mean, come on! Amen" ("Spontaneous Combustion"). Maxi's entreaty not only mirrors the boys' vernacular, and particularly Jimmy's stuttering vacuity in "Krazy Kripples," his request is simply ludicrous. In the genre "prayer," one is supposed to ask for forgiveness, peace on earth, and other lofty requests. Furthermore, asking "not to burst into flames" is risible because the concept itself is so outrageous. Semantics and appropriateness are often loci in the *South Park* irreverence; viewers hear Bakhtin's heteroglossia.

Boomer Humor: Parody, Satire, and Caricature

Cynicism, intertexual play, parody, and satire are hallmarks of boomer humor. Baby boomers, Gen Xers, and Gen Yers have come to expect more from comedy; straight sitcoms don't always satisfy their cultural needs. Comedies should not only be funny but they should also be embedded with cultural puzzles. Manifest buffoonery is best displayed through crossing generic boundaries (musical expositions about Mormons), pop-culture references (the more obscure the better), and a mocking awareness of the show's own shortcomings ("Cartoon Wars I"). In the post-*Simpsons* epoch, viewers expect more than clever one-liners or slapstick pratfalls;[15] if Web activity is any indication, viewers enjoy unpacking each episode according to their knowledge.

Humor expects, or demands, a level of intellectual engagement. Parody and satire are what *South Park* does best. Parody reproduces another item (music, painting, television show) almost exactly, but exaggerates parts of it to make a point; as Bakhtin explained, parody introduces another discourse that opposes the original, creating "an arena of battle between two voices."[16] Above all, carnivalesque parody is humorous, chaotic, subversive, and energetic.

Parody is a "type" of intertextuality; in 1997, Gerard Genette suggested the term "hypertextuality" to mean "a text or genre on which it is based but which it transforms, modifies, elaborates or extends (including parody, spoof, sequel, translation)."[17] For example, in "Red Hot Catholic Love," *The Catholic Boat* parodies the kitschy 1980s *The Love Boat*. It reproduces the opening scenes exactly but intersperses shots of beguiling priests (winking, lifting their shirts) with shots of anxious young boys (Butters and Tweek) while the background singer croons new lyrics:

> The Catholic Boat's
> gonna be headin' on out today.
> The Catholic Boat.
> Time to throw all of your cares away.
> Get some hot Christian action . . . ("Red-Hot Catholic Love")

Parody works best if the viewer is familiar with the original. Those familiar with *The Love Boat* know that in nearly every episode someone falls in love, hence the show's title. The *South Park* episode can be amusing without this knowledge; it just loses its parodic value. It can also work if the viewer does not know *The Love Boat* but knows about the Catholic sex abuse scandals. If the viewer knows about neither, then perhaps the inappropriateness of young boys and priests on a boat is likely to be amusing (if that is humorous).

Parody's first cousin is satire. While the essence of parody is humor, satire can be tragic. Satire focuses on the folly of human nature and has a social conscience. It takes political, social, or moral mores and examines them critically. Satire usually tells us what's wrong with the world with the idea that somehow we can cure it. Often the target is intensely personal. Leonard Feinberg points out that society's double standards are a fundamental source of satire.[18] Often satire focuses on the vulgar, indecent, and filthy; for example, Jonathan Swift's *Gulliver's Travels*. While parody tends to avoid exaggeration, the best satires embrace exaggeration. The hyperbole makes the focus of the attack more formidable, and the hallmark of satire is a persuasive rhetoric.

One of *South Park*'s main targets is the "celebrity." Most of the celebrity portraits are caricatures. Caricature is "the distortion of the face or figure for satiric purposes"[19]—such as Ben Affleck's "butt head"—and claims a long tradition in art. Thus, we have in *South Park* the fixed smile of Gary Condit, the colorful makeup of J-Lo, the wonky eyes of Paris Hilton—all images designed to reduce the celebrity to farcical anodyne.

Case Study: "How to Eat with Your Butt"

"How to Eat with Your Butt" captures the breadth of *South Park*'s humor; it has a scatological premise, one-liners, sight gags, contemporaneous references, and contains several examples of incongruity theory, both visual and verbal. It also considers the nature of humor as it explores what is it that makes Cartman laugh.

In this episode, for the class photo, Kenny puts his parka on so that his butt peeks through the hood—an illogical method of wearing his outfit— and a photo of Kenny's ass causes Cartman considerable amusement. When Ms. Choksondik returns the photos to the children, she is unimpressed by one photo:

Ms. CHOKSONDIK:	Alright, class, I have your school photos to hand out—
CARTMAN:	Yes, Yes.
Ms. CHOKSONDIK:	Most of them are very nice. But, apparently, one of you [*close up of Kenny looking worried*] thinks it's fun to spoil their school pictures, and thinks he's a comedian. That person will be spending the afternoon in the principal's office!
KENNY:	[*mumbles*] Aww, that's bullshit!
Ms. CHOKSONDIK:	School photos aren't for joking around, so you aren't getting your photo back . . . Butters!

The editing hints that Kenny is about to get into trouble.[20] When she shows the photo of a perfectly normal Butters, the incongruity of his getting into trouble while Kenny's ass photo is acceptable provides the joke. It sets up the episode's subplot and running gag, Butters' looks:

BUTTERS:	Ah-I'm grounded for lookin' stupid in my school picture.
	. . .
CAROL:	Butters can't come out and play, boys. He thinks it's funny to look like a jackass in his school pictures that I have to pay for!
BUTTERS:	Huh, but I told you mom: ah-I didn't mean to look . . . like a jackass, eh. It just happened.
CAROL:	You made a goofy face!
BUTTERS:	No! That's just what I look like. See?
CAROL:	. . . Don't you make that face at me, young man!
BUTTERS:	I'm not makin' a face, mom!
CAROL:	Stop it!

The Stotches become increasingly ridiculous in their perceptions of Butters; he's accused of making stupid faces and wearing makeup. At the end, Kyle sympathizes with Butters' predicament:

> KYLE: Dude, that poor kid.
>
> CLYDE: Yeah . . . we gotta remember to kick his ass tomorrow.

The verbal incongruity of Clyde's reply is amusing; instead of extending sympathy, as he should have done (which is the "right" response), he wants to kick Butters' ass.

The main comedic thrust of the episode is the Thompsons, a couple who have butts where their heads should be. The lower stratum joke becomes an upper stratum sight gag. Throughout the show, the Thompsons insist on explaining this to people:

> STEVEN: Martha and I actually have buttocks where our heads should be.
>
> PRESIDENT: Really?

It's obvious that the Thompsons have asses for heads, but everyone is too polite to comment or to laugh (well, almost everyone). The Thompsons continue to state the bleeding obvious, not once but several times, and everyone responds the same way, with a deadpan "really?" Their condition is even given a pseudo-medical name, torsonic polarity syndrome. Thus the joke is not merely a bawdy bum joke but a satire on political correctness. While the adults desperately try to be polite and ignore the Thompsons' condition, when the couple cry and blow their noses, the adults are appalled because it sounds like farting. Only the kids are truthful enough to laugh at people with buttocks for heads.

Cartman's love of scatological humor is indulged; he revels in providing a description of Kenny to the woman at the Dairy Gold Milk Company. He selects all the euphemistic words for ass that he can and mentions Kenny's "winking brown eye" and "rosy cheeks." Indeed, the humor is too much for Cartman; he loses his ability to laugh. He then seeks the advice of Mr. Mackey:

> MR. MACKEY: Well, I can't think of anything that would be THAT funny.
>
> CARTMAN: Two people with asses for heads. Ever since I saw them I can't laugh at anything.
>
> MR. MACKEY: Oh, I see, well . . . Well, what did you used to think was funny?
>
> CARTMAN: You know, all the usual stuff. Dirty jokes, funny movies, seeing someone die. This morning, I even saw a little girl get

> her fingers caught in a car door and I couldn't laugh. I mean
> I - I knew it was funny, but I couldn't laugh.

MR. MACKEY: Well, Eric, I suppose that, just like everything else, laughter
can be relative—in, in other words, sometimes people see
something so scary that nothing else scares them so the
same could be true for funny things.

CARTMAN: So does that mean I'll never laugh again?

MR. MACKEY: It's possible, hm'kay? But you know, if you have completely
lost your sense of humor, you can always become a writer
for the show *Friends*. Ohokahay.

CARTMAN: Ugh.

Mr. Mackey doesn't laugh at people with asses for heads but is amused at his own joke. Cartman finds Mackey's joke lame. Cartman explains his childish sense of humor; he loves "dirty jokes," tragic humor, and Jimmy's shtick. He also realizes that the ability to laugh is what keeps him same. He's driven to despair when he loses it:

> Dear Mom: I can no longer stand to be without a sense of humor. Without
> laughter, the world is a cold and sad place, and I can't go out to face it any-
> more. Please tell everyone why I won't be at school.

He stops and picks up a gun and places it in his mouth. Cartman is, to all intents and purposes, about to commit suicide, but he bites the end of the gun and resumes writing:

> And please buy me more chocolate guns. I'm starting to run out. Please get
> the kind with marshmallow inside. I don't like the peanut butter-filled ones.

Humor comes from the unexpected—the sad music, the heavy sighing, the words, and the gun all gesture to suicide. The joke is best understood if one knows the markers of "suicide."

The show ends when Ben Affleck steps forward as the Thompsons' lost son—Mr. Garrison can see the family "resemblance"—Affleck looks like an ass. Thus, the handsome Ben Affleck is considered as literally butt-ugly because he has a bum for a head. Cartman renames Affleck "Assleck," a childish pun that restores his ability to laugh at crude jokes. Toilet humor saves Cartman's humanity.

Stan and Kyle conjecture that Cartman's loss of humor is explained by maturity; he is losing his childlike ability to laugh at people's misfortune:

STAN: Wow, Cartman actually felt bad for somebody and couldn't
laugh at them.

KYLE: Our little man is growing up, Stan. He's growing up.

STAN: Yeah, I guess we all are. Maybe things are finally gonna start getting more sophisticated around here. [*close-up of the Thompsons kissing Ben Affleck*]

As Stan utters "more sophisticated," the farting noises start satisfying fans that the show will never take itself too seriously. The central premise of the episode is that substitution of the "lower body stratum" with the upper one is funny. Thus, the episode utilizes Bakhtin's theories about toilet humor, the grotesque body, and the carnivalesque.

Conclusion

Parody, satire, caricature, punning, ridicule, silliness, absurdity, irreverence, incongruity, and slapstick overlap and collide in the best *South Park* episodes. The popularity of the show indisputably lies in its unsparing joy in the destruction of cultural conventions and icons. Isn't that awful, fans giggle appreciatively, when Garrison demonstrates unusual condom application to kindergarteners, when a pig carcass dressed in Butters' clothing is thrown from a building, when the camera focuses on a slack-eyed O. J. Simpson's face as Mr. Stotch declaims "murderer." But teasing out specific comedic loci is well nigh impossible and futile—few of the moments are "pure"—and why bother? It's the promiscuous juxtaposition that delights fans. Outrageous statements overlay silly animation to the sounds of farting noises—it's a humor kaleidoscope. The humor is blissfully vulgar, scatological, and sacrilegious.

Creators Parker and Stone freely admit they indulge themselves; *South Park*'s jokes are often intensely personal:

> We have our own barometers about what is funny and how soon we should laugh . . . We're human beings. If we don't laugh at [a taboo subject], then it probably isn't funny. . . . It's not like we'd make fun of someone who died in something. That's not funny. But it's the job of people like us or Dave Barry to find humor [in] a situation so we can laugh again and get back to being human beings. I think a lot of mainstream comedy people are afraid of that, but that's their job.[21]

Of course, humor is a very dangerous thing. It makes the unpalatable palatable, for a second. Plato warned against laughter; it is too ego driven—we laugh when we feel superior. Thus, the laughter in *South Park* comes at some expense to our own beliefs, thoughts, and prejudices. Often, the jokes are on us.

MR. GARRISON: Eric, do you need to sit in the corner until your flaming gas is under control?

CARTMAN: No, Mr. Garrison, I'm fine. [Cartman farts fire, setting Pip alight.] ("Cartman Gets an Anal Probe")

CARTMAN: Okay, that does it! Now listen! Why is it that everything today has involved things either going in or coming out of my ass?! ("Cartman Gets an Anal Probe")

GENERAL: Heh—wait a minute, did, did that robot just fart?

BUTTERS: Hey, robots don't fart!

CARTMAN: Uh . . . now ending fart sequence.

GENERAL: Oh, and it, it smells, too!

CARTMAN: Smell sequence initiated. ("AWESOM-O")

The World is a comedy to those that think, a tragedy to those that feel. –Horace Walpole

Satire is a sort of glass, wherein beholders do generally discover everybody's face but their own. –Jonathan Swift, 1704

Lord Chesterfield to his son: "Having mentioned laughing, I must particularly warn you against it, and I could heartily wish that you may often be seen to smile, but never heard to laugh while you live. Frequent and loud laughter is the characteristic of folly and ill manners. In my mind, there is nothing so illiberal and so ill-bred as audible laughter."

Notes

1. Mikhail Bakhtin, *Rabelais and His World*, trans. Helene Iswolsky (Bloomington: Indiana University Press, 1984), p. 66.

2. Other theories include laughter as a form of controlled aggression; see Konrad Lorenz, *On Aggression*, 293–97; and Albert Rapp, *The Origins of Wit and Humor*, p. 21.

3. Mimi Marinucci, "Television, Generation X, and Third Wave Feminism: A Contextual Analysis of *The Brady Bunch*," *Journal of Popular Culture* 38, no. 3, 2005: 505–24.

4. John Fiske, *Television Culture* (London, New York: Methuen/Routledge: 1987), 108.

5. I have ignored vomiting, spitting, pissing, and other expulsion of bodily fluids, but they also occupy a space in humor and bodily function jokes.

6. Book 1, chap. 13.

7. Jeff Persels and Russell Ganim, *Fecal Matters in Early Modern Literature and Art* (Aldershot, England; Burlington, VT: Ashgate, 2004).

8. Christy Boldenow, "South Park Creators Vomit on American Politics," *Recount: A Magazine of American Politics*, November 9, 2004.

9. Bernadette Boucher, *Icon and Conquest* (Chicago: University of Chicago Press, 1981), 142.

10. Bakhtin, *Rabelais and His World*, 175.

11. Ibid., 16.

12. Ibid., 77.

13. Ibid., 12.

14. Douglas E. Cowan, "South Park, Ridicule and the Cultural Construction of Religious Rivalry," *Journal of Religion and Popular Culture* 10 (2005), http://www.usask.ca/relst/jrpc/art10-southpark.html.

15. Though of course one-liners are still valuable and validated throughout the series.

> Kyle: Do your impersonation of David Caruso's career! (101)
>
> Frank: Why, I haven't seen a beating like that since Rodney King. (104)
>
> Garrison: I thought we should learn something about the great horror writer, Jackie Collins. (107)
>
> Garrison: That's good, just use those mouth muscles like the girls in Beijing. (107)
>
> Cartman: Eh, too bad drinking scotch isn't a paying job, or else Kenny's dad would be a millionaire. (107)
>
> Cartman: I'm telling you, if you let this deal pass you by, you're making a fetal mistake. (513)

16. Mikhail Bakhtin, *Problems of Dostoevsky's Poetics*, ed. and trans. Caryl Emerson (Minneapolis: University of Minnesota Press, 1984), 193.

17. Quoted in Daniel Chandler, "Semiotics for Beginners," MCS [Media and Communications Studies Site], http://www.aber.ac.uk/media/Documents/S4B/sem09.html, accessed October 25, 2006.

18. Leonard Feinberg, *Introduction to Satire* (Ames: Iowa State University Press, 1967), 25.

19. Wendy Wick Reaves, *Celebrity Caricature* (New Haven: National Portrait Gallery, Smithsonian Institution in association with Yale University Press, 1998).

20. The camera juxtaposes shots of Kenny and Ms. Choksondik.

21. Terry Morrow, "What Will 'South Park' Writers Do for an Encore?" *The Record*, Hackensack, New Jersey, November 2, 2005, F7.

Chapter 7

Barnaby Jones as Cultural Text: Reference, Allusion, and Intertextuality

French theorist Julia Kristeva first introduced the term "intertextuality";[1] Kristeva developed the term from Bakhtin's ideas of language and literature. Basically, no text is an island. Each text, whether written, sung, painted, or performed, is influenced by that which has gone before; no text is unique. Reading, viewing, hearing a text requires knowledge of other texts we have viewed, read, and heard before to frame them and in some instances to make sense of them; as Kristeva wrote, "[E]very text is from the outset under the jurisdiction of other discourses which impose a universe on it."[2] Television is particularly intertextual because it is so heavily reliant on other filmic and visual forebears: Hollywood movie genres, painterly lighting techniques, and meaningful music. And that's just for original programs; the seemingly endless iteration of syndicated programs on free-to-air and cable stations present a continuous realignment of shows from those past with those present.[3] Often intertextuality is misused and invoked to mean overt referencing, allusion, influence—which intertextuality is not. However, the term has become pop-culture shorthand for exactly these things, so I have collapsed the three into this chapter.

Whether it be the printed word, a musical score, or a visual image, *South Park* melds texts from a variety of sources but is perhaps best known for its references to the most pervasive medium of the 1990s—film. Of the 139 episodes aired in the first nine seasons, there are visual and verbal references to nearly 100 different television programs and over 160 different movies—each episode references at least two other film sources. The series even cannibalizes itself. Getting an "inside" joke is particularly gratifying and adds *frisson* for viewers. Fans delight in recognizing the popular cultural referents and references; in fact, the episode "recaps" are predicated on their ability to pinpoint cultural references and subtle filmic nuances.[4]

Episodes are a mongrel mix, wanton in their jumbling references to movies, TV shows, and the actors therein; they also adopt and adapt musical styles, generic markers, popular culture, and cartoon techniques. Thus, an episode such as "Child Abduction Is Not Funny" combines the narrative of Charles Dickens's *A Christmas Carol* (1843) with tag lines from *Scooby-Doo* and movie quotes from *Scarface* (1983), while it parodies a contemporary product and satirizes moral panics about child abduction. It's a heady brew. Indeed, *South Park* is so referential that it has been accused of being a show of little content except the references. Such a pastiche of movie music, referent visual imagery, current culture critique, and textual verbal association is nothing new. Since the nineteenth century, printed texts and graphics referenced current events, visual and textual styles, making complex associations for readers.[5]

South Park creates a new television textuality by adopting/adapting traditional elements of film and television. These elements are used so often that viewers often forget they are filmic techniques. Flashbacks, laughter tracks, montage, and music are manipulated for varying effects. Usually, they parody their deployment in other film mediums. Take, for example, one scene from "Jakovasaurs":

ANNOUNCER: And now back to … Jakovasaurs! on Comedy Central. [*"Jakovasaurs" appears on screen. Then, Junjun appears in the living room with some of her children.*]

JAKOV: [*enters wearing a fedora and carrying a briefcase*] Hi, honey! I'm home! [*trips over the welcome mat and crashes into the sofa. Canned laughter is heard.*] Wooooo! [*gets up, rubbing his head*] Boy, it was rough at work today. I've never seen so much coffee.

JUNJUN: Booo-wooop?

JAKOV: No, in the boss's lap. [*canned laughter*]

BOY: Hello, dad.

JAKOV: Hello, son. How was your day?

BOY: Oh, not so good. Something really strange happened.

JAKOV: What? You mean MTV played a video that wasn't Will Smith? [*more laughter*]

BOY: Noho, dad. A man in a blue suit and a bag came to the door. He just left this li'l piece of paper with a stamp on it. [*brings out the letter*]

JAKOV: That's called a mailman. He takes care of mail.

BOY: Oh! He took care of mom, too. [*more laughter*]

JAKOV: You're a nut! Let me see that letter. [*opens it and reads the letter*] It's from a game show. The Mayor has invited me to compete. [*the front door opens*]

CARTMAN: Hi, Jakov. [*applause*] What the hell is that? [*laughter*] Who's laughing?

When Jakov trips over the welcome mat, he parodies the opening to a perennial family favorite, *The Dick Van Dyke Show* (1961–66). The "Hello, honey! I'm home" is a stock sitcom phrase, as are the corny jokes about the boss and the mailman;[6] the MTV joke caters to contemporary audiences, while the coffee joke recalls the propensity for programs such as *The Dick Van Dyke Show* to have actors drinking endless cups of coffee at work. Cartman's entry harkens back to the comedies when the nosy neighbor or wisecracking sidekick enters to start the narrative. Cartman's "What the hell is that?" draws attention to the artifice of studio applause and canned laughter, in his own inimitable swearing way. Overall, it's a pastiche of corny sitcom dialogue, events, and filmic techniques; what makes it *South Park* are the swearing and the layered referentiality to its comic forebears.

Self-Reflexivity

South Park demonstrates an awareness of its own culture and medium through its relentless parodies of other television shows and through its awareness of itself as a television show. When Cartman asks, "Who's laughing?" he might be asking the canned laughter track or his question might be directed to the *South Park* audience. At other moments, the method of address is to the other characters. When Kyle muses, "This is just startin' to look like another one of those times where it-it's gonna end up with the whole town turning out, it's a big showdown happening, and us havin' to talk about what we learned, and I say we just stop right now, and go play cards or something" ("Butt Out"), he deconstructs the *South Park* formula.[7] "Free Hat" also contains a mock interview with Parker and Stone in which they discuss a digital makeover, gesturing to the wider issues of filmmaking and ownership. In "Cancelled," the first episode is reenacted as a narrative device and the viewers learn that *South Park* is not really an animated show but an intergalactic reality TV show—a *Truman*-like show that parodies the fashion for reality TV programs. Because "Cancelled" was created around the time the series was due for renewal, it presents the possibility that *South Park* could be cancelled:

JOOZIAN 1:   Oh I'm sorry, Earthlings, but you have to realize the universe is a business.

JOOZIAN 2: You've made it to a hundred episodes, you should be proud!

JOOZIAN 1: Yeah, a show should never go past a hundred episodes, or else it starts to get stale with ridiculously stupid plotlines and settings. ("Cancelled")

It also gestures to the terminal nature of television shows. Every show must end at some time.

Over the seasons, episodes have parodied talk shows ("Freak Strike"), cop dramas ("Lil' Crime Stoppers"), cartoon styles ("Korn's Groovy Pirate Mystery," "Simpson's Already Did It"), and soap operas ("Cartman's Mom Is Still a Dirty Slut"). When a voice-over reviews the "story so far," his questions become increasingly bizarre:

ANNOUNCER: Previously on *South Park*: An air of sobriety fills the laboratory as the men of South Park gather to find out which one of them fathered this boy. . . . Who shot Mephesto? Was it the school counselor, or was it Ms. Crabtree, or was it . . . Who will the director cast first? Will it be Mr. Garrison, Officer Barbrady, Chef? . . . Who framed Roger Rabbit? Was it Jimbo, Mr. Garrison, Chef? . . . Who built the pyramids? Was it the Babylonians, Officer Barbrady, Samaritans?

Eventually, the viewer feels like Eric Cartman: "Forget it." "Kenny Dies" replicates hospital dramas when Cartman and a scientist banter in melodramatic ease:

CARTMAN: There's a pretty brave kid fighting for his life in the hospital right now, doctor. I'm gonna get him some bigger boxing gloves.

LARRY: Hey, kid . . . Give 'em hell. Give 'em hell.

CARTMAN: Oh, doctor. [*thumbs up*] Thanks. Thanks.

LARRY: Oh, hey, kid. [*returns thumbs up*] Good luck. Good luck.

CARTMAN: Oh, and doctor . . . Ah, never mind.

Bedside-scene clichés are deployed:

CARTMAN: We got you a present: it's a Gobo fighter.

KYLE: Heh, don't, don't tell him what it is, dude.

CARTMAN: Heh, sorry.

KYLE: Hey, uh - we were all just talkin' about how when you get better, we're all gonna go down to Stark's Pond again and go camping. Huh, Stan?

STAN: I -

KYLE: Stan? Stan, where are you going?

STAN: I can't, I just can't.

KYLE: Dude, he needs us right now.

STAN: I can't see him like that, Kyle. All those hoses and wires. He's a
            kid, dude. He's s'posed to be running around and laughing.

KYLE: I, I know it's tough but- Look at me! I know it's tough,
            okay?! I know! But we have to be tough right now!

STAN: And what are we supposed to do, huh?! Stand in that room
            and keep making small talk?! Make believe like everything's
            okay?! I CAN'T DO IT!

KYLE: Look, however hard you think it is for you, it's a lot harder
            for him!

STAN: Just leave me alone!

KYLE: Stan, you can't leave!

STAN: I'm not the one who's leaving, he is!

CARTMAN: . . . You know, it's funny, Kenny. Stan and Kyle have always
            been sort of two best friends, you know, and . . . well I-I
            don't know if I ever told you this, Kenny, but um . . . I kind
            of always thought you were my best f-friend. I don't know
            . . . Don't you worry, Kenny. I-I'm gonna find a cure for you.
            Everything's gonna be okay! ("Kenny Dies")

Of course Cartman's concern masks his real motivation, and thus the mock
melodrama is not merely played for humorous effect but also to highlight
Cartman's duplicity. He doesn't want stem cell research legislation overturned so Kenny can be cured, he wants to clone his favorite pizza restaurant.

South Park knows that the best way to deflect criticism is by beating critics to the punch through self-mockery; hence, their show-within-a-show,
The Terrance and Philip Show, highlights early accusations that the show
was all toilet humor. And to doubly upset parents (on both sides of the
screen), Terrance and Philip's monotonous farts continue to elicit gales of
laughter. An older audience might smirk that only eight-year-olds would
find lame fart jokes funny, but can they avoid laughing at a fart sequence in
"Cancelled"?

Since the early years of cartoons, anthropomorphic characters frequently
reminded audiences of the artifice of cartoons. Chuck Jones and Tex Avery
liked to include at least one self-referential moment, and Jones's surreal
"Duck Amuck" (1953)[8] is a masterpiece in cartoon-reflexivity. Part of *South
Park*'s textuality is its love of breaking down the fourth wall. It reminds viewers of the artifice of film by directing them to acknowledge it.

Filmic Techniques

Aside from the actual content/narrative, the filmic techniques employed are integral to creating intertextuality. Television shows and general feature movies are not the same filmic product. Though movies can be viewed on television, there are those that audiences know should or must be seen in a movie theatre, on a big screen—movies such as *Lord of the Rings*, *Harry Potter*, *Star Wars*, and *Star Trek*. These films offer spectacular viewing and require the movie theater experience—silence, darkness, largeness, and isolation—to fully appreciate them. They just don't transfer that well to the small screen. A television show differs. As well as deploying the cinematic apparatus, it must also take into account its small screen size and sporadic viewership. A television show is not created for undivided attention; indeed, television viewing is predicated upon its discontinuity. That's not to say that *South Park* episodes do not exhibit qualities that could translate to the big screen. Indeed, Parker and Stone have big-screen sensibilities (not to mention training) and capabilities, as *Bigger, Longer and Uncut* and *Team America* demonstrated. But in the TV series, big-screen effects are usually relegated to relatively minor roles such as background music and the montage.

Montage

One of the most often used cinematic devices is the "montage."[9] A montage is a film editing process that juxtaposes several shots to create a narrative whole. Most often, it is accompanied by suitable music. Montages can fulfill a variety of narrative needs: they document a change (Cartman's preparation for the Special Olympics, "Up the Down Steroid"), recall past events (Cartman reliving his dining experiences at Casa Bonita; calling Kyle a Jew sixteen times in "Casa Bonita"), or they can simply truncate events to provide an overview (clips of Butters for his "very own show"). With their fondness for montage, in "Asspen," the creators included a montage about montages. Sung to "Put It to the Limit" from *Scarface* (1983), the lyrics describe a montage:

> The day is approaching to give it your best
> You've got to reach your prime!
> That's when you need to put yourself to the test
> And show us the passage of time
> We're gonna need a montage
> A sports-training montage
> And just show a lot of things happenin' at once.
> Remind everyone of what's goin' on.

And with every shot, show a little improvement
To show it won't take too long
That's called a montage
Even Rocky had a montage
In any sport, if you want to go
From just a beginner to a pro
You'll need a montage
A simple little montage
Always fade out . . . into a montage
If you fade out it seems like a long time. ("Asspen")

The montage layers referentiality, both to the editing process and to its own narrative; it is a spoof within a spoof. When a version of this song was reworked for *Team America*, it added yet another layer of referentiality.

Parody in *Mise-en-Scene*—a Case Study

More than any other medium, animation yields "complete control over the *mise-en-scene*. The filmmaker can design and draw literally anything, whether it resembles something in the real world or comes strictly out of his or her imagination. Thus there is a vast range of possibilities for animated films."[10] And nowhere is this more obvious than in "Professor Chaos." At his home, Butters morphs into a new persona, Professor Chaos. It's a short, effective, and visually satisfying sequence, combining filmic techniques of horror movies and tropes from superhero lore. It relies on movie signifiers to ironic effect. It is one of *South Park*'s most filmic and aesthetically pleasing scenes.

The scene opens with long shot of Butters' house as thunderclouds gather, rain pelts, and lightning flashes. Inclement weather has long symbolized trouble. Shakespeare mastered it in his heath scene in *King Lear*; 250 years later, Frankenstein movies added lightning to the mix and voila—viewers know something traumatic and possibly sinister is about to happen. Jump-cut to Butters' bedroom and a back view of Butters; he stands on his bed looking out the window. The small, solitary figure, an outcast, clasps his hands behind his back and contemplates the stormy weather. The camera pans in slowly. Lightning flashes and Butters casts an ominous shadow (forecasting). The point of view changes to a frontal shot of Butters. The windowpane casts jail-like bars on his face. He is imprisoned and he's angry. From his frame within a frame, he delivers his soliloquy of the wrongs done to him: "The world isn't fair. I do everything people ask me to. I stand in the lunch line for them, I buy tampons at the store for them, I go on Maury Povich with balls on my chin for them." Butters' voice gets louder and louder the more incensed he becomes (and as the things he's done become sillier and sillier). Slowly, the camera focuses on his face through the driving rain. Another jump cut to Butters' bedroom; his face becomes increasingly shadowed and darker as he bemoans his fate. Somber music grows louder. Butters contemplates his shadow on the wall, which slowly morphs into a grotesque figure as he continues: "And yet, nobody accepts me. I am an outcast. A shadow of a man who can find no companionship. No love from others . . . ." As the music grows more dramatic, he jumps off the bed. "Fine! If I am to be an outcast, so be it!" He moves purposefully, walking towards the camera, indicating he's made up his mind. He stops and looks at the camera and tells us: "I'm through doin' what others tell me to do, and I am sick of this world and the stin-, and the stinky people in it!"

The camera moves left until Butters is almost out of frame; the background changes and static cartoon depictions of disasters flash as appropriate punctuation points to his speech: "[*nuclear blast*] From now on I will dedicate my life to bringing chaos to the world that has rejected me! [*killer bees swarm a town*] I will become the greatest super villain the world has ever seen! [*a tidal wave wreaks havoc*]." The camera moves Butters back to center screen and pans in as he threatens, "Where I go, destruction will follow!" He raises his hands and eyes heavenward as if addressing a divinity. Lighting flashes illuminate his body and the screen flickers—indicating the sequence's climax.

The camera switches to an outside shot of Butters' house and the raging storm; the shot recalls the decaying castle, the scientist's laboratory, and the haunted house. The very ordinariness of Butters' suburban home undermines traditional horror tropes. Back in his room, a very determined-looking Butters is creating something. The next few shots alternate between Butters working on his costume and the raging storm outside. Orchestra music continues staccato. As he sews, the dark gray material creeps up the screen and eventually engulfs the shot. There is about to be a revelation. The material turns black; as the camera pans out, it is the black of Butters' pupil and it continues to pan out, revealing the new Butters as he intones: "Prepare, O little town! Uh prepare for the greatest super villain you've ever seen!" He utters his dastardly threat to hammering percussion and clashing cymbals. The music stops and lightning flashes as he announces: "Professor Chaos!"

Silence. Then Mrs. Stotch's sing-song voice is heard: "Butters, time for bed." Butters is reduced to his little boy self and responds in his soft voice, "Uh okay, Mum." Even supervillains have their bosses. The music restarts and Butters picks up his narrative. Framed in the windowpane, he delivers his evil manifesto and warns the town: "Tomorrow, the chaos begins." Then he starts to laugh, a laugh that (in the best traditions of movie monomania) grows more and more maniacal. Another evil genius is born!

The entire sequence takes no longer than ninety seconds, but it is rich in meaning and nuance. It contains the markers of monster creation: an isolated house, a dark and rainy night, flashing lightning, a disgruntled human revealing despair. The music ebbs and flows to sustain the tension. Effective lighting positions Butters as a tormented creature at odds with the world but in tune with violent nature. The raging storm tells of the dissent in Butters' soul. The scene also plays on signifiers of superhero transformation in which some event changes a normal person into a person with super powers (Incredible Hulk, Spiderman). The irony comes from the very ordinariness of the suburban house, Butters' cheesy costume, and his mother's interruption. The music, camera angles and lighting, costuming, and location work to produce a meaning beyond the actual scene itself. This it is not a "typical" South Park scene, but it demonstrates the filmic eye of the creators.

Popular Culture Referents

Viewers who first tuned in to South Park in 1997 most likely had always known a life with television (and cable) and had probably watched hundreds of hours. They had probably been watching The Simpsons for nearly a decade. This savvy audience not only had the ability to decode complex cultural clues and the desire to decode them—they actively seem to need it. Carl Matheson labels these two elements as "quotational" and "hyper-ironic":

> First, today's comedies tend to be highly *quotational:* many of today's comedies essentially depend on the device of referring to or quoting other works of popular culture. Second, they are *hyper-ironic:* the flavor of humor offered by today's comedies is colder, based less on a shared sense of humanity than on a sense of world-weary cleverer-than-thou-ness. In this essay I would like to explore the way in which The Simpsons uses both quotationalism and hyper-ironism and relate these devices to currents in the contemporary history of ideas.[11]

South Park viewers are likely to be televisually literate, to reject the banality of the traditional sitcom, and are attuned to material that performs a wider cultural critique, shows such as *Beavis and Butt-head, The Tick,* and *Shrek.*

Star Trek: The Original Series and Star Wars are the new popular culture bibles.[12] Wikipedia, the popular Web site reference source, lists over twenty Star Trek references in various South Park episodes. Some entire episodes mirror the original television series ("City on the Edge of Forever" and

"Dagger of the Mind").[13] "Hooked on Monkey Fonics" contains a scene taken from *Star Trek*'s "The Gamesters of Triskelion," complete with similar incidental music. Others have multiple references: fans identified "three *Star Trek* episodes and two *Star Trek* movies" in "Spooky Fish":

"Mirror, Mirror" – Kirk, Spock, and others have warlike counterparts who are members of the Galactic Empire in the parallel universe.

"Assignment: Earth" – the portal found in the Indian Burial Ground Pet Store comes from this episode.

"Whom Gods Destroy" – Garth, once a famous starship captain, learns about shape shifting.

Star Trek: The Motion Picture – The vertical line separating the two Cartmans . . . is a manifestation of an entity called V'ger (the space probe Voyager), which takes Decker as its mate.

Star Trek VI: The Undiscovered Country – Kirk and a Kirk look-alike escape from the Rura Penthe and are confronted by Klingon guards. The lead guard has to choose which Kirk to kill.[14]

Often the references come in asides: Cartman says, "Well, captain, we've reached fag factor five" at the Cirque du Cheville ("Quintuplets"). Stan quotes *Star Trek* to Jesus:

> STAN: You know, somebody once said, "Don't try to be a great man, just be a man."
>
> JESUS: Who said that?
>
> STAN: You did, Jesus.
>
> JESUS: You're right, Stan. Thank you, boys! ("Damien")

And:

> KYLE: "The needs of the many outweigh the needs of the few?" That was *Wrath of Khan.*
>
> STAN: Uh, well, Bible, *Wrath of Khan*,[15] what's the difference? ("Spontaneous Combustion")

To complete the reference, Kyle gives Jesus a Vulcan salute.

References can be fairly oblique; for example, the Latin motto above the Planetarium's door reads "Beam me up, Scotty" ("Roger Ebert"), two nerds debate the number of original *Star Trek* episodes ("Probably"). Long bows are often drawn. Viewers have considered the use of number 47[16] and postulated that Kenny's death comes from *Star Trek* because in nearly every episode one of the ensigns is killed. Elements from *Star Trek*'s cinema cousin *Star Wars* include

Jar Jar Binks ("Jakovasaurs"); Chewbacca ("Chef Aid," "Korn's Groovy Pirate Ghost Mystery"); Jedi masters ("Cartmanland"); Jawas ("Osama Bin Laden Has Farty Pants"); and storm troopers ("The Return of the Fellowship"). A fusion of *Star Wars* and *Star Trek* informs the cold opening of "Starvin' Marvin in Space," inexorably linking the two. No matter how obscure, fans meticulously locate each reference. Like visitor spotting,[17] documenting *Wars* and *Trek* references offers fans additional active viewing opportunities.

The majority of the television references come from 1980s TV shows such as *A-Team* (1983–87), *She's the Sheriff* (1987–89), and *Full House* (1987–95). The mix is irreverent; no one genre is targeted, though generally the shows are an amalgam of American "popular" shows—especially the cheesiest ones. References anchor the narrative or action in the form of parodies: Garrison is rescued A-Team style ("Ike's Wee Wee"); Chef and the boys try a *Dukes of Hazzard* escape ("Cancelled"); *The Catholic Boat's* opening ("Red Hot Catholic Love"). These references gesture to an audience with similar viewing experiences—the overall effect is one of gentle nostalgia.

Media in *South Park*

What does it say about a town when the two most-watched public-access TV shows are *Jesus and Pals* and *Huntin' and Killin'*? Three main TV shows encapsulate South Park relationship's with television: *Jesus and Pals*, The *Terrance and Phillip* Show, and, of course, Channel 4's Live Action News.

In the rock opera *Jesus Christ Superstar* (1973), Judas is puzzled by Jesus's lack of planning. Now Jesus has returned to the mass communications of the twenty-first century. In this reincarnation, Jesus is part Dr. Phil and part Oprah Winfrey as he dispenses comfort and advice to his on-air callers. But let's be honest, Jesus isn't television material. He just isn't exciting enough, so his producer revamps the format: she adds a band (The Disciples) and long-forgotten TV personalities (Bob Denver) as guests ("Mexican Staring Frog"). When this late-night talk show format doesn't work, *Jesus and Pals* is further degraded into a sensational daytime show complete with controversial topics and a high-energy audience whose cliché-ridden trash talk captures the genre perfectly. No wonder Jesus is mistaken for Montel (Williams). While *Jesus and Pals* lampoons trash TV shows and their producers, it asks, "How would Jesus gather followers today?"

Jesus and Pal's ratings rival is Ned and Jimbo's *Huntin' and Killin'*, the perfect show to showcase the redneck penchant for guns, gun culture, and killing animals. It also pokes gentle fun at the gullibility of Jimbo, Ned, and their viewers. Clearly, anyone who thinks killing animals is okay will believe

Cartman in a dress and a rubber frog on a string. When the son of God can't compete with *Huntin' and Killin'*, the world is in bad shape.

"Is South Park Elementary about to explode from a methane gas leak?" asks news anchor Ric Cartman. Yes, it's the *South Park* version of nightly news. Bouffant Cartman, in three-quarter profile, taps his pencil and anchors a news show that lurches from the scantily clad girls to weather reports, school gossip, and the Panda Bear Madness Minute. In "Quest for Ratings," the team produces an extended examination of the current state of news reportage. And it's not a pleasant sight.

The boys know how to perform as television anchors—they've been watching Channel 4 News all their lives. *South Park* lampoons the buffed professionalism of the news team through its running gag of Channel 4's ridiculous on-the-spot reporters: a bikini-wearing midget ("Pink Eye"), a quadriplegic Swiss man ("Mecha-Stresiand"), "Creamy Goodness" ("Summer Sucks"), and an Asian Ricardo Montalban look-alike ("Roger Ebert"). The media, no longer serious, is given to editorializing ("Sick sonofabitch!" in "Cripple Fight"). Channel 4 News covers the major South Park events: the ATF mixup ("Two Guys Naked in a Hot Tub"), the Goobacks' arrival ("Goobacks"), and Cartman's run for the border ("Cartman's Silly Hate Crime"):

> Greg Nimins: [NEWS 4 LIVE!] Tom, it looks like the Go-Go Action Bronco is heading east on 285. Police officers are right behind him but as with any chase, they're keeping a safe distance to avoid any accidents here out on the highway. Tom, it looks like the fugitive is going to make a bold move off an exit off 285. He's going into a residential neighborhood now; this is where it could get dangerous, as there are pedestrians about.

The voice-over is urgent, the music dramatic, the "chase" as slow as the original. It is a classic *South Park* spoof. In its critique of the "news", the series questions the role of the media, is it there to entertain or to inform?

The American penchant for twenty-four-hours-a-day news is targeted in "Osama Bin Laden Has Farty Pants." Sharon Marsh has become addicted to SNN, and she lies on the couch covered by a blanket. Coffee cups, plates, and papers are scattered on the floor: She's clearly been there for some time. So long, in fact, she hasn't noticed that Stan's been missing for a couple of days, and when Randy asks if she's seen Stan, she says yes and points to the TV set. She is not alarmed or surprised because, at the moment, the TV world is her world.

News media products are limited in South Park. Radios broadcast sports and music ("Big Gay Al's Big Gay Boat Ride," "Korn's Groovy Pirate Ghost Mystery"). Newspapers are the product of a bygone era. They're something for "old" men, such as fathers. When nineteenth-century Joe makes a metal newspaper, Mrs. Joe mocks his creation. "What are we supposed to do with a metal newspaper?" ("Great Expectations"). Indeed, what use has South Park for newspapers when it has television? Garrison summarizes it best when he directs the children "Now, I want you all to read a newspaper, or better yet, watch television, and come up with something current in South Park to do a report on" ("Gnomes").

To "get" a parody, viewers have to be aware of both *South Park*'s style and the elements of the parodied text. Otherwise, there is no joke. All texts are multi-accentual: their meaning depends on how they are articulated to other signs and sign systems, and how they are articulated to social relations.[18] To poach from Bakhtin, each text "tastes of the . . . contexts in which it has lived its socially charged life."[19]

Conclusion

The creators of *South Park* cannot help themselves; they are parodying fools. They are shameless in their appropriation: cartoon characters, movies and TV programs, news, music—the texture is so dense at times it's difficult to unpick the layers of meaning. The show's use of other titles, genres, dialog, and music creates a different kind of textuality; a textuality that is often overshadowed by the show's controversial content. It is often too purposeful to be considered truly intertextual in the Kristeva/Bakhtinian sense, but it nevertheless presents the popular cultural intertextuality of television. Nearly every episode mentions TV, is about TV, or has TV shows in it (82 percent). Many episodes consider television ethics ("Freak Strike," "Jesus and Pals," "Cancelled"), advertising ("Weight Gain," "Starvin' Marvin," "Chinpokomon"), and censorship ("Death," "It Hits the Fan," "Cartoon Wars I," "Cartoon Wars II," and so on).

The audience wants such cultural cannibalism; the hyper-cynical twenty somethings (now possibly thirty somethings) expect to see their self-awareness on the television screen. They simultaneously snicker and wax nostalgically at the television of their youth. They don't want their favorite childhood movies digitized; they like the crappy special effects and the hyperbolic happiness of sitcom families. As *South Park* tears at the fabric of the contemporary television quilt, it succeeds best in the small touches. For example, when serial toilet-paperer Josh menaces Officer Barbrady:

> JOSH: Tell me something, officer: why is it that you police such a small town. You must have had larger inspirations. What happened to those . . . big-city dreams?
>
> OFFICER BARBRADY: Well, that's kind of personal.

JOSH: Quid pro quo, officer. Tell me what I want to know. And I'll help you catch whoever toilet-papered that house. ("Toilet Paper")

The scene recalls a familiar movie sequence and also posits a question to the audience at large: are their big-city dreams and larger inspirations being met?

CARTMAN: Do you have any idea what it's like? Everywhere I go: Hey, Cartman, you must like *Family Guy*, right? Hey, your sense of humor reminds me of *Family Guy*, Cartman! I am nothing like *Family Guy*! When I make jokes, they are inherent to a story! Deep situational and emotional jokes based on what is relevant and has a point, not just one random interchangeable joke after another! ("Cartoon Wars I")

TRUCKER: I mean, I know it's just joke after joke, but I like that. At least it doesn't get all preachy and up its own ass with messages, you know? ("Cartoon Wars II")

Notes

1. Julia Kristeva, "Word, Dialogue and Novel," *Desire in Language* (New York: Columbia University Press, 1980.), 65–66.

2. Quoted in Jonathan Culler, *The Pursuit of Signs: Semiotics, Literature, Deconstruction* (London: Routledge & Kegan Paul, 1981), 105.

3. Jim Collins, "Television and Postmodernism," in Robert C. Allen, ed., *Channels of Discourse* (Chapel Hill: University of North Carolina Press, 1992), 333–34.

4. The episode recap genre differs from more traditional movie/TV reviews. Yes, plot outlines and evaluative remarks are given, but of equal value is the locating of specific points of cultural reference. The best recaps also blend commentary on advertisements, the show's relation to other shows, and the episode's relation to the series as a whole and the show's place in the television pantheon. The author often writes tongue-in-cheek and with a strong eye to evaluating a show's place in popular culture. See Television Without Pity (TWoP), www.television withoutpity.com.

5. See J. F. Smith in *Victorian Print Media: A Reader*, ed. Andrew King and John Plunkett (Oxford: Oxford University Press, 2005).

6. Of course, the mailman joke wouldn't have been aired on 1960s television (the chronological reference point for this scene). The mailman/milkman joke is the hackneyed shtick of the "take my wife, please" vaudeville variety. Its adultery subtext is the antithesis of the harmony espoused in traditional family sitcoms such as *The Dick Van Dyke Show*.

7. Deconstructing other movie and television genres is commonly done too; for example, the first Christmas episode utilizes the familiar let's-put-on-a-play formula (à la summer stock, 1950), except in this case, the musical is a dismal failure and the play contains none of the musical numbers sung throughout the episode.

8. In "Duck Amuck," an unseen animator redraws, revoices, and recontextualizes Daffy. In doing this Jones directs the viewer to consider what it is the makes Daffy Duck, well, Daffy.

9. The theory of montage has been the subject of investigation by Soviet filmmakers and theorists such as Sergei Eisenstein and Lev Kuleshov. *South Park* has nearly two dozen montages.

10. D. Bordwell and K. Thompson, *Film Art: An Introduction* (New York; London; Sydney: McGraw-Hill, 1993), 417.

11. Carl Matheson, "The Simpsons, Hyper-Irony, and the Meaning of Life," *The Simpsons and Philosophy: The D'oh! of Homer* (Chicago: Open Court, 2001).

12. Sometimes the *Star Trek* quotes themselves are quotes; at the end of "Worldwide Recorder Concert," Mr. Garrison boards the bus and tells the bus driver, "Second star to the right . . . and straight on till morning"; fans trace this to a quote from Captain Kirk at the end of *Star Trek VI*; of course, the line originally comes from J. M. Barrie's *Peter Pan*.

13. Several episode titles reveal the cultural reference: "Red Sleigh Down" (*Black Hawk Down*, 2001); "Two Days before the Day after Tomorrow" (*Day After Tomorrow*, 2004); "Free Willzyx" (*Free Willy*, 1993).

14. "*Star Trek* in *South Park*," South Park Scriptorium. http://www.spscriptorium.com/SPinfo/SPStarTrek.htm, accessed October 25, 2006.

15. Approximately a dozen references are taken from *Star Trek* movies.

16. Fans claim that number 47 is apparently a key number in *Star Trek: The Next Generation*, *Deep Space Nine*, and *Voyager*, because it was a "script-writer's favorite number." For example, 47 is the court case number of "Everyone v. Everyone" (306); Kyle loses 47 game turns (406); the cyborg in "Trapper Keeper" is VSM471 (413); and in "Douche v. Turd," the school has been attacked by eco-terrorists for the 47th time (808).

17. Because the first episode celebrated the alien anal probe, the episode was replete with the ghost-like aliens called "visitors" (the oval-eyed extraterrestrials); discovering them became a popular fan pastime. Many fan sites have Web pages dedicated to visitor sightings. Animation director Eric (Butters) Stough apparently "puts them in at the last minute" (e-mail, March 27, 2002; quoted at http://www.spscriptorium.com/Sightings/Sightings.htm). In the opening credits they peek around the school and picnic in front of the stage; they have been spotted in pictures, in statues, on the notice boards, in crowds, and on signs.

18. V. N. Volosinov, *Marxism and Philosophy of Language* (Cambridge, MA.: Harvard University Press, 1986), 23.

19. "Discourse in the Novel" (1934–35), in Mikhail Bakhtin, *The Dialogic Imagination: Four Essays*, ed. Michael Holquist; trans. Caryl Emerson and Michael Holquist; (Austin: University of Texas Press, 1981), 293.

Chapter 8

Token, Give Me a Sweet Bass Line: Sounds of *South Park*

Τhe importance of sound in film and television is easily overlooked. It is just "there"; viewers often don't realize how much sound influences the narrative, characterization, and mood of a show. Paul Wells lists twelve types of sound in film.[1] Basically, three types of noise are heard: speech, sound effects, and music. Jeremy G. Butler suggests watching a show without sound and then without visuals in order to understand the role of sound in television;[2] Wells reports that playing a soundtrack alone can cue students to the narrative.[3] Speech, music, and sound effects add layers of meaning in ways viewers may not consciously realize. Speech provides narrative information; accents can potentially indicate ethnicity, class, gender, age, and geography; music adds mood and meaning and can drive the narrative;[4] sound effects enrich the visual action and can be humorous (farting, belching, and so on). Sound works liminally. It structures complex layers over the visual codes.

A major focus of Bakhtin's analyses was carnival language and particularly heteroglossia. Bakhtin uses the heteroglossia in a political way to describe the rhetoric of everyday speech acts (conversations, dialogue, and so on) rather than to describe the multiple voices of a society (polyphony). Heteroglossia embraces the inequality and subversiveness of speech acts, and certainly there is plenty of it in *South Park*—whether it be the use of politically incorrect terms or inappropriate speech in church, at school, or between friends. We live not simply in a world of words, but in a world of formal speech acts, even if they don't make sense, such as George W. Bush's speech to the United Nations, Father Maxi's football prayers, and songs celebrating Kyle's mother's bitchiness. The heteroglossia of *South Park* is not limited to speech acts; South Park is a cacophony of sounds, voices, songs, farting, crapping, and vomiting.

Speech

In animation, the "voice" is vital. Professional voice actors contribute considerably to the success of a character. Few viewers realized the importance of Mary Kay Bergman's voice work until she died. After her death in November 1999, the creators of *South Park* estimated it would take "four or five voiceover artists" to replace her,[5] and fans feel her replacements[6] have not matched Bergman's skill. Surprisingly, live-action actors do not perform voices well. Chris Turner notes the failures of some of *The Simpson*'s celebrity guest voices;[7] similarly, in *South Park*, Natasha Hendridge's Miss Ellen is lukewarm and Jennifer Aniston's choir leader is downright awkward.

Cartoonish voices are traditionally silly voices. The most memorable have distinctive features, such as Daffy Duck's lateral lisp, Elmer Fudd's "w" for "r" substitution, and Snagglepuss's exaggerated drawl. Such sound performances have little place in *South Park*—Jimmy's stutter is naturalized, though Slave's lisp and Gay Al's feminine intonation are part of "gender" performance. Women usually do boys' voices because boys, like women, have higher pitches. To overcome this, Parker and Stone (who do the majority of the boys' voices) increase the audio speed to achieve the right pitch. Other notable voices heard around South Park include Ike's baby talk (done by real children), Barbrady's loud voice (because of his deafness), and Towelie's ultra-high-pitched stoner voice. Sometimes voices are referenced to other roles: serial toilet-paperer Josh affects an "Anthony Hopkins as Hannibal Lecter" voice. When the jail warden asks if Josh is "doing the silly voice for the policeman again" ("Toilet Paper"), he ridicules the menace of the original.

Voices convey important cultural cues. Most of the characters have "neutral" Midwestern accents, though Cartman's voice changes when he takes up evangelical preaching. Sheila Broflovski's hypernasality and Connecticut Kyle's whining are "stereotypically" Jewish. Blackness presents in an array of different accents and speech patterns. Originally, the creators wanted to do Chef's voice, but Comedy Central was more racially sensitive and demanded a black voice artist. Isaac Hayes's Chef, many agree, was part of *South Park*'s charm, and nearly every media story about the first episodes made some mention of Hayes.[8] Even viewers who did not know Hayes soon learned of his importance as both a songwriter/performer and actor. Therefore, while many viewers possibly did not know the Hayes linked to a certain era and musical field, his chocolaty baritone voice still registered as that of a soulful black balladeer. Chef's parents present the most "Ebonic" speech (for example, "fitty-tree"); his father is a garrulous, long-winded storyteller in the Uncle Remus tradition ("Succubus"). Rapper Snoop Dog has two voices, his hip-hop "black" recording voice and another, less recognizable voice—one supposedly more middle class. Will Smith and his children have the same refined accent ("Here Comes the Neighborhood"). The OC coach speaks in rap rhyme: "Oh, so you're the father of the boy who's gonna get f'd in the a on Sat-tur-day?" ("You Got Fucked"). When Cartman performs black, he drops his g's at the end of words and stretches some words out and contracts others:

"I was just down in the SPC kickin' it with some G's on the Westsa-eed-eh. . . . You know what I'm sayin', G? Check you later—I'm gonna go chill with mide-my dad. . . . You know, jus' . . . layin' down some rhymes for G-folk, you know what I'm sayin'?" ("Cartman's Mom is a Dirty Slut").

Similarly Jimmy adopts gang speak when he joins the Crips: "Yo, don't be dissing my niggaz, dawg. They're my f . . . friends" ("Krazy Kripples").

Otherness is often portrayed through voice characterization. Chinese sports announcers ("Conjoined Fetus Lady") and City Wok's Tuong Lu Kim speak in predictable Chinese-speak; the boys love pranking Kim because of his accent:

CITY WOK OWNER:	Herro, Shitty Wok, take your order prease.
CARTMAN:	Hello, is this City Wok?
CITY WOK OWNER:	Yes, this Shitty Wok.
CARTMAN:	Uh, yes, we'd like one order of the City Beef.
CITY WOK OWNER:	Shitty Beef . . .
KYLE:	Aha, and I'll have the City Chicken.
CITY WOK OWNER:	[*writing*] Shitty Chicken . . . ("Jared Has Aides")

Native Americans speak in halting English, laugh in rhythm "*ha* hahaha *ha* hahaha" ("Red Man's Greed"), and show a marked preference for animal euphemisms:

CHIEF RUNNING WATER:	Kid, I hate to break this to you, but your mother is what we Native Americans refer to as, "Bear with Wii-ide Canyon."
CARTMAN:	Whadda ya mean?
CHIEF RUNNING WATER:	She is, "Doe who cannot keep legs together."
CARTMAN:	Huh??
CHIEF RUNNING WATER:	Your mom's a slut. ("Cartman's Mom is a Dirty Slut")

Hippies pepper sentences with "chill," "cool," and "man," linguistic hangovers from the 1960s, and tell people to "relax" and "take it easy" ("Die Hippie, Die"). Gayness is illustrated by lisps, singsong intonation, and a preference for feminine endings (an upward inflexion). Big Gay Al also adopts child-speak; for example, "all donesy wunsy" ("I'm a Little Bit Country").

Timmy demonstrates how animation can show and not tell. Timmy has the most limited vocabulary of the characters on the show, but his feelings and thoughts are portrayed in his facial expressions, actions, and intonational pattern. It is amazing how he communications without words. For example, when Timmy offers an olive branch to Jimmy in "Cripple Fight," Timmy smiles—he knows how to placate someone. Throughout their conversation (and many others), Jimmy does most of the talking. Timmy merely repeats his name:

> JIMMY: Oh, hey Timmy. I'm glad you called, very much. I've been detecting some a-animosity towards me lately, and I was hoping we could bury the hatchet.
>
> TIMMY: Timm—ay. [*falling intonation matches real-ly*]
>
> JIMMY: What's that?
>
> TIMMY: Hur-livin'-a-lah-Tim. [*smiling broadly as he hands Jimmy a gift*]
>
> JIMMY: A present? You got me a p-present?
>
> TIMMY: Timah! [*short as if "yes"*]
>
> JIMMY: Gee, you didn't have to do that. I mean, I understand why you've been jealous of my talent. If you work at it, maybe you could be as . . . handi-capable as I am, huh? Wow, a parka. You-you didn't have to do that, Tim-Tim.
>
> TIMMY: Tim-Timmay. [*intonational pattern mimics "that's okay"*]
>
> JIMMY: Oh, sure. I'll see if it fits. [*Timmy grins with pleasure as Jimmy dons the parka and looks like Kenny*] This is very warm. Thanks a lot, Tim-Tim. Well, I'll see you around. [*turns around to walk away*]
>
> TIMMY: Tim-may! [*intonational pattern for good-bye*] ("Cripple Fight")

Similarly, in "Up the Down Steroid," Timmy says little but Jimmy intuits Timmy's disapproval. The conversation makes sense in the same way Marklar speech makes sense.

Handicapable Jimmy has a "normal" vocabulary, but his speech is marred by his lack of fluency. In fact, his stuttering version of "The Twelve

Days of Christmas" frames a whole episode ("Red Sleigh Down"). People can be impatient with stutterers and try to finish their sentences, but few people make guesses as stupid as those proffered by the South Park parents:

RANDY: Jimmy! Jimmy! Where did the boys go with the porno tape??

JIMMY: They're taking it to the vi . . . the vi . . . the vi-i . . .

CHRIS: Come on Jimmy, we don't have a lot of time.

JIMMY: They took it back to the video s . . the video s . . .

RANDY: The video sandwich?

CHRIS: The video stockyard.

RANDY: What's a video stockyard, Jimmy?

JIMMY: No, the video suh . . . the video s . . .tih . . .

GERALD: Stinger?

CHRIS: Staples. They went to the video Staples. Where's that, Jimmy?

JIMMY: N-N-NO, you retards! the video s . . . tore! ("Return of the Fellowship")

The *South Park* world is a polyglot, a Babel of dissonant language, accents, speech acts, and sounds.

Original Music

Both Matt and Trey are musicians of some note. They have their own band, DVDA; Matt plays the bass guitar, guitar, and drums, and Trey is a very talented pianist/composer who has studied at the Berklee College of Music in Boston. The least crappy element of *South Park* is the original music, and *South Park* is saturated with music.[9] It could be argued that *Bigger, Longer and Uncut*, with over a dozen songs, is a musical. One of them, "Blame Canada," was nominated for an Academy Award. The creators' musical talents are reflected in the variety of musical styles heard throughout the TV series: opera, Christian rock, salsa, bubblegum, ballads, soft rock, thrash metal, and even a Jethro Tull-ish medieval sound. They have also proven to be adept at creating TV themes ("Butters' Very Own Episode"), musicals ("Helen Keller"), and Christmas carols.

The Christmas episodes are notable for their original Christmas songs. The first Christmas episode showcases a variety of musical styles, from the upbeat "Mr. Hankey the Christmas Poo" to Kyle's ballad, "Lonely Jew at

Christmas," Mr. Hankey's "Santa Claus Is on His Way," and the soon-to-be-loved "Kyle's Mom's a Bitch" (not a Christmas song *per se*) ("Mr. Hankey, the Christmas Poo"). The most tuneful Christmas episode, however, is "Mr. Hankey's Christmas Classics," which nestles newly arranged traditional tunes alongside original numbers with a *South Park* twist. The dreidl song has a memorable Marc Shaiman arrangement; Cartman warbles his way through a present-felt "O Holy Night"; and Adolf Hitler sobs "De Tannenbaum." Mr. Garrison's wonderfully offensive "Merry Fucking Xmas" is, of course, original. Santa and Jesus perform the best parody, a schmaltzy duet of Christmas classics, and their delivery comes complete with the bad comedy/performance shtick of the faded lounge act variety—Jesus even spins his halo on his finger and winks at the crowd. It's all too cringingly familiar.

The most consistent original music is the show's theme song. A theme song is a clarion call, and the lyrics often perform a narrative function. Most television viewers can sing how seven stranded castaways ended up on Gilligan's Island. Likewise, the *South Park* theme tells of bucolic bliss, small-town friendliness, and a laid-back lifestyle. The bluegrass banjo strumming recalls mountain folk, rednecks, and strange communities and has been employed in rural shows such as *Green Acres* and *The Beverley Hillbillies*. The *South Park* contemporary edge is realized through the cultural capital of alternative singer/songwriter Les Claypool (of Primus).

Most of the music is traditional—any of the *Bigger, Longer and Uncut* music could be heard in a Rogers and Hammerstein musical; the lyrics, however, are another matter. Many of the musical numbers are energetic, physical performances that disrupt (and potentially offend) traditional modes of address; for example, the catchy "Uncle Fucka" is a nonsensical song that piles scatological words upon scatological ideas accompanied by a rollicking tune. Further, "Uncle Fucka" drives the narrative in that its uptake by the boys starts Sheila Broflovski's anti-Canada campaign.

Musical interludes are important narrative devices in several episodes. Joseph Smith's story is told in music form and the "dum, dum, dum, dum, dum" refrain works at two levels; obviously, it is a nonsensical musical filler, but meaningfully, it reinforces what the creators think of Smith's history ("All About Mormons"). "There's Got to Be a Morning After" saves Chef from a disastrous marriage and, anecdotally, became addictive to staff members, who learned to sing it backwards. Thrash metal saves South Park from the dreaded hippies ("Die Hippie, Die"). With two musicians driving the series, music has always been used more overtly as a narrative device. Their ribald, folksy, and vulgar appropriations scream *South Park*. Of course, music does not exist in a vacuum, and the music industry comes under fire in several episodes.

Industrial Issues

South Park is not afraid to air the music industry's dirty laundry. "Chef Aid," "Fingerbang," and "Fat Butt and Pancake Head" expose the greed, banality, and machinations of the recording industry. Chef is sued for daring to oppose Capitalist Records (not very subtle), but his rock music friends help him. Rock musicians aren't always so generous; as Stan finds out in "Christian Hard Rock." J-Lo and Randy Marsh are dumped by their record companies when fresher talent appears ("Fat Butt" and "Fingerbang"). It's not just record companies and record producers who are the bad guys, agents don't fare too well either—apparently they receive 10 percent for doing "nothing" ("Wing"). To paraphrase Chef, the record industry is not about music—music is simply a product "created by corporations to make money" ("Fingerbang").

An auditorium crowded with screaming teen girls, explosive stage effects, and klieg lights focus on four similarly but not identically dressed figures—yes, it's Fingerbang. Wearing headsets and performing carefully choreographed routines, Cartman dreams of the South Park quartet performing a typical boy-band song: it's a mixture of repetitive love lyrics, conventional rhymes married to an appropriately catchy tune:

> Fingerbang! Bang-bang!
> Fingerbang-bang!
> Bangbangbang!
> I'm gonna fingerbang-bang you into my life
> Girl, you like to fingerbang, and it's alright.
> 'Cause I'm the king of fingerbang; let's not fight
> I'm goin' ta fingerbang-bang you every night

A mustached and goateed Cartman takes center stage to perform his solo bridge and then exposes his nipple to a frenzied audience of females, who scream their delight.

Cartman convinces the other boys that their lack of talent doesn't matter: boy bands are not about talent, they're about performance:

> STAN: Dude, we don't have any musical talent.
>
> CARTMAN: That didn't stop any of the other boy bands, dumbass! I've got prerecorded music we can sing to, just like they do. All we need to do is practice our choreography over and over and over!

Viewers learn that the standard number of participants in a boy band is five (they audition for a fifth member, Wendy); each member represents a "type" and is given an appropriate costume. Kyle is the "tough" one who has nose rings and facial hair. The boys are prepubescent children singing inappropriate words[10] and performing in a sexual way. Randy Marsh's morality tale is not only an exemplar for Stan, it documents the disposable nature of the boy-band industry. "Fingerbang" first aired in July 2000—on the cusp of reality TV-manufactured pop music shows such as MTV's *Making the Band* (2000),[11] New Zealand's *Popstars* (1999), and, of course, the various *Idol* series.

Three seasons later, Cartman targets Christian music. When the boys' garage band Moop argues over musical differences, Cartman suggests they try Christian music:

CARTMAN: Our band should play Christian rock!

KYLE: Christian rock?!

CARTMAN: Think about it! It's the easiest crappiest music in the world, right? If we just play songs about how much we love Jesus, all the Christians will buy our crap!

KYLE: That's a retarded idea, Cartman!

CARTMAN: It worked for Creed![12]

STAN: I don't wanna be in a stupid Christian rock band!

CARTMAN: You just start that way, Stan, then you cross over. It's genius! ("Christian Hard Rock")

Kyle is not convinced, so Cartman bets Kyle "ten bucks" that he can earn a platinum album first if he starts a Christian rock band. Why? Because "Christians have a built-in audience of over one hundred and eighty million Americans! If each one of them buys just one of our albums at twelve dollars and ninety-five cents that would be . . . Two billion, three hundred and thirty one million dollars" ("Christian Hard Rock").

Christian music is formulaic (like boy-band music). According to Cartman, all you have to do is "take regular old songs and add Jesus stuff to them . . . cross out words like 'baby' and 'darling' and replace them with Jeeeessssuuuss." Not surprisingly, the lyrics are a disturbing mixture of Christianity and erotic love:

I wanna get down on my knees and start pleasing Jesus!
I wanna feel his salvation all over my face!

The Body of Christ! Sleek swimmer's body, all muscled up and toned!
The Body of Christ! O, Lord Almighty, I wish I could call it my own!
. . . Oh I wish I could have the body of Christ!

Whenever I see Jesus up on that Cross
I can't help but think that he looks kinda hot . . .

The next key to success is the "flashy inspirational album cover"; Cartman outlines Christian cover aesthetic to Token and Butters:

> CARTMAN: . . . You're supposed to be standing in random places, look-ing away like you don't care!
>
> BUTTERS: Cheese!
>
> CARTMAN: No! Butters, you can't look happy on the album cover! That's not cool!
>
> BUTTERS: Oh . . .
>
> CARTMAN: Token, look away to the right. More. More!
>
> TOKEN: Why the hell would I be looking way over there??
>
> CARTMAN: So it looks like you're too cool to care that you're on an album cover, you black asshole! Now just hold it!

Soon Cartman's Christian band, Faith +1, has an album of songs such as "The Body of Christ," "A Night with the Lord," "Touch Me, Jesus," "I Found Jesus (With Someone Else)," "Christ, What a Day," "Three Times My Savior" (parodying Lionel Richie's "Three Times a Lady"), and "Jesus Touched Me." They set up a stall at Christfest 2003 and start selling albums. They end up on stage, land a recording contract, and start raking in the Christian dollars. Moop, on the other hand, is not doing so well.

Kyle, Stan, and Kenny are on strike. After being arrested for downloading music off the Internet and witnessing the "hardships" faced by musicians whose music is pirated, Moop refuses to play music until people stop down-loading music. The trouble is, no one notices or cares if Moop doesn't play. The artists who join Moop's strike are a veritable who's who of the music industry and accurately reflect these artists' stance on pirating.[13] When Kyle receives an invitation to Cartman's Faith +1 platinum award ceremony, he realizes that while he's been protesting, Cartman has been performing and selling albums. Kyle tries to stir his fellow strikers, but basically, they're about the money.

Characterization through Song and Music

As appearance and voice add depth to characterization, so, too, music adds another layer. A song such as "Kyle's Mother Is a Bitch" could only be a Cart-man song. Similarly, Chef's erotic crooning is integral to his characterization. His strong musical presence influences others, such as "James Taylor," who sings his own folksy sex song, "Prostitutes," when he visits Chef ("Fat Camp").

Others in the show are similarly linked to certain musical styles. Mr. Jefferson has magical fantasy songs to match his Peter Pan attitude toward life ("Jeffersons"). Russell Crowe chants a manly sea shanty theme ("New Terrance and Phillip Movie Trailer"). Whenever Mr. Tweek waxes lyrically about coffee, a soft guitar strums in the background ("Jakovasaurs"). In much the same way, Italian Mafioso-child Loogie is introduced with piano accordion music ("Tooth Fairy Tats"), and salsa music is associated with Hispanics ("Fat Butt"). Pip sings a "Hey Nonny Nonny"-type of medieval tune, marking him as thoroughly British:

Whippy-tippy tootoo, tralala-la.
Whippy-tippy tootoo, tralala-la.
Whippy-tippy tootoo, tralala-la.
Wickersham tally-ho. ("Two Guys Naked")

Jews have the dreidl song. Hip-hop tunes separate the trendy OCers from the country music-loving South Parkers ("You Get Fucked"). Stan learns the hippie antiestablishment anthem "Signs" ("Die Hippie, Die"). Cigarette factory workers chant an elf-like song:

With a hidey lidey lidey and a hidey lidey lay
We work and we make cigarettes all hidey lidey day
So folks can get a breaky from their stressful lidey lives
And relaxy with the cigarettes we make all day and night. ("Butt Out")

The song recalls the Disney penchant for happy workings songs, such as the seven dwarves' "Heigh Ho, Heigh Ho" and "Whistle While You Work."

Each of the boys is assigned a musical label: Stan claims to be "R&B"; Kyle is the "fusion guy," and, to his surprise, Kenny is "more Latin jazz," even though he wrapped his classically trained tonsils around various operatic arias a few seasons earlier ("Christian Hard Rock"). Muffled Kenny's operatic voice is, of course, heavily ironic. As a group, the boys have performed in musicals and choirs.

Several members of the cast have signature tunes. Though musically challenged, Kyle warbles a couple of songs, and he is best known for his Christmas lament, "A Lonely Jew on Christmas." Token is Kyle's musical opposite; unknowingly a talented and capable musician, he has pondered his life in South Park through song ("Here Comes the Neighborhood"), played with Cartman's Faith +1, and sings a mean pageant song ("Wing"). Butters' squeaky, hesitant voice is ideally suited to the nursery rhymes he favors and his celebratory songs match his upbeat outlook on life (*Butters' Show* theme song and "My Robot Friend"). Stan's most sustained singing achievement is the opening song in *Bigger, Longer and Uncut*. The boy with the most musical range (not necessarily talent) is Cartman.

Cartman's life is drenched in music. Mr. Jefferson thinks Cartman has a lovely voice ("Jeffersons"); well, Cartman did win the national search to sing the Cheesy Poof commercial. He has an extensive playlist in his head and has been heard humming songs such as "She Works Hard for the Money" ("Roger Ebert"), "Morning Train" and "Heat of the Moment" ("Kenny Dies"), and "You Picked a Fine Time to Leave Me, Lucille" ("Ginger Kids"); all in all, he favors 1980s songs. His nemesis song is Styx's "I'm Sailing Away," which he *has* to finish ("Cartman's Mom is Still a Dirty Slut"). He also has an impressive portfolio of original music, including "Kyle's Mom Is a Stupid Bitch" ("Mr. Hankey, the Christmas Poo" and *Bigger, Longer and Uncut*), a rapping "Fresh Cowboy from the Westside" ("Cat Orgy"), a rhapsody about third grade ("Fourth Grade"), "Sea People," which celebrates his new kingdom ("Simpsons Already Did It"), a song about a poo-train ride ("Red Sleigh Down"), and an upbeat Christian "Make it Right." He cannot even crap without singing:

> Poopin' outside,
> Makin' self-serve ice cream
> For my friends
> 'Specially Kenny. ("Jakovasaurs")

His range embraces energetic polkas ("Chef Aid"), laid-back calypso ("Free Hat"), soft Christian rock ("Christian Hard Rock"), Latino salsa ("Fatt Butt"), and ballads ("4th Grade"). Despite his prodigious and varied musical outpourings, Cartman is not driven by an artistic desire to produce music. He displays a cynical attitude toward the music business. In his quest to make a million bucks, Cartman has tried salsa and Christian music. And, while he might not know much about Christianity, he knows enough to exploit it.

Meaning through Music

Background music adds color and depth to the action. Romantic music, that is, softly played piano, harps, violins, and flutes, alerts viewers to the characters' emotions: when Ben Affleck first sees Hennifer Lopez ("Fat Butt"), when Wendy and Cartman develop a crush on each other ("Chef Goes Nanners"), and even while Garrison writes his erotic novel ("Cherokee Hair Tampons"). Seduction requires Chef's chocolaty bass voice crooning Barry White-esque songs. When Cartman visits the Ute Indian reservation, the background music is flutelike and haunting; his trip to Chef's place is accompanied by "black" music—drums and a smooth bass line. Europe is the center of operatic music ("Quintuplets"). The hedonism of Hell is underscored by the festive Hukilau and Hawaiian music ("Do the Handicapped Go to Hell"), while Heaven is a tinkle-y kind of place filled with wind chimes and choirs of heavenly voices ("Ladder to Heaven," "Best Friends Forever").

Happy music is upbeat; it is faster and tends to be higher in pitch. There's *Miami Vice*-type 1980s up-tempo music when Kenny plays his PSP ("Best Friends Forever"), the Christian pop song Cartman sings while performing good deeds to get into Heaven ("Death of Eric Cartman"), and the heavily ironic "Butters' Very Own Episode" theme. Lower-pitched, slower music can be sad music and indicates sorrow: when the boys learn there is no Tooth Fairy ("Tooth Fairy's TATS"), when Kenny is dying ("Kenny Dies"), and to mirror Kyle's despair when he is told he cannot play basketball ("Mr. Garrison's Fancy New Vagina").

Dramatic music underpins appropriate moments; it tends to be staccato and played with vigor, such as the drumming crescendo that accompanies Kenny's eating dog crap ("Fat Camp"). When the boys approach their art teacher's house to toilet-paper it, dramatic music becomes symphonic as Kyle throws his first roll and builds as more toilet rolls are thrown ("Toilet Paper"). The action slows, the boys' eyes close in pseudo ecstasy, and the scene becomes an eroticized prank; the romantic music contrasts with Kyle's dawning horror and later nightmares. Shuddering cymbals and measured sharp piano notes are used during Officer Barbrady's walk along the jail cellblock; the closer he gets to the serial toilet-paperer Josh, the louder the orchestration and the more insistent the choir voices ("Toilet Paper"). The music works best when it references movie moments. Haunting *Godfather II*-ish music is heard when Cartman takes Kyle out on Stark's Pond to Whiffle bat him to death ("Toilet Paper"); a *Psycho*-esque thumping tune accompanies Wendy's warning, "don't fuck with Wendy Testeburger" ("Tom's Rhinoplasty") and when Kyle goes after the *Queer Eye* guys ("South Park is Gay"). The boys thump their chests to music from *2001: A Space Odyssey* ("Bebe's Boobs Destroy Society"), signifying the dawning of their pubescence and, via the movie reference, to dawning of man. Signifying danger is the *Mission Impossible*-type tune associated with the break-in at Farmer Deet's ("Fun with Veal").

Well-known songs also add value. Cartman sings Elvis Presley's "Vicious Cycle" when he visits Kenny's place in the ghetto ("Chickenpox"). Stan mourns his lost love to "You Don't Know What You Got" by Cinderella and "All Out of Love" by Air Supply ("Raisins"). Butters sings Chicago's "If You Leave Me Now" when Cartman leaves him moldering in the bomb shelter ("Casa Bonita"); he sings the equally ironic "Sixteen Tons" while digging for coal ("Stupid Spoiled Whore"). Jimmy carries Nut Gobbler to the strains of "Love Lifts Us Up Where We Belong" from *An Officer and a Gentleman*, telling the viewers that Jimmy is about to consummate their "relationship" ("Erection Day").

Throughout the series, referential music indicates a heavy bias for 1980s music. Ace of Bases' "All That She Wants" is piped during "PreHistoric Ice Man" to reinforce his antiquity, and "musical force in the '70s and '80s" Ronnie James Dio plays at the Bay of Pigs Memorial Dance. Cartman's repertoire shows a marked preference for 1980s popular tunes. The Cure's *Disintegration* (1989) is the greatest album, ever. Like television programs, music is a vehicle for a potentially nostalgic audience.

Gendered and Political Music

"South Park Is Gay" is replete with musical symbolism. In the *South Park* parody of *Queer Eye for the Straight Guy*, techno-disco music is a signifier of homosexuality. Loud techno-disco music identifies Garrison and Slave's bar as "gay" bar; techno strains herald metrosexual Gerald Broflovski's entrance. And when the men shop at the mall, techno provides the background music. Another supposed musical marker of male homosexuality[14] is camp music, such as Marc's Ethel Merman-esque "Ooooh, I don't want her. You can have her. She's too fat for me" ("Cripple Fight").

At the opposite end of the musical tempo are the dramatic tunes that punctuate the melodrama. A soap opera-ish piano tune dramatizes scenes where the boys deny Kyle and his beating in the schoolyard; when he dejectedly returns home, the dramatic music is used as a counterpoint for the techno tune that introduces his newly metro father. Similar dramatic music also reinforces Kyle and Garrison's decision to kill the *Queer Eye* guys—but this time, the piano adopts a staccato thump, thump, thump in the vein of *Jaws*. Even the crab people have their own music—a primitive drumming for the repetitive "crab people, crab people." It has an industrial rhythm, a Fordist tune designed to help workers keep in time, and is perfect for brainwashing. The "crab people, crab people" refrain is imposed over the *Queer Eye* music when Kyle and Garrison are made over into crab people and underscores the theme of the episode, the mindless adoption of fads, and in this instance, the metrosexual fad.

Music also indicates political affiliation. In the one-hundredth episode, the war comes to South Park and the community is split in two: pro-war people who like country music and antiwar people who prefer rock music. The two sides sing their dissent in their versions of Donny and Marie Osmond's "I'm a Little Bit Country":

SKEETER: Well excuse me if . . . I'm a little bit country.

RANDY: Well I'm a little bit rock-n-roll!

SKEETER: I'm a little for supportin' our troops.

RANDY: And I'm a little for bringin' them home.

SKEETER: I believe freedom isn't free.

RANDY: No, but war shouldn't be our goal.

SKEETER: We must defend our country.

RANDY: If it means war, then we say NO!

SKEETER: Did you forget them towers in New York?
              Did you forget how it made you feel
              To see them towers come down?
              Were you like me? Did you think it weren't real?

RANDY: I like to rock, but I don't wanna rock Iraq!
              The only kind of rockin' America should do is the kind
                that we can all dance to, yeah!

SKEETER: We got GPS, ICBMs, and good old-fashioned lead.
              We're gonna show Saddam what America means; that
                son of a bitch will be dead.

RANDY: Why are we fightin' this war?
              There's a man in the office we didn't vote for.
              They didn't give me a choice.
              War is not my voice! Yeaaaaahhhh! ("I'm a Little Bit
              Country")

The alignment of musical preferences with political ideology is nothing new.

As *Country Music Goes to War* demonstrates, since the Civil War, country music has operated "as a symbolic discourse of nationalist feeling."[15] Country music sings in the voice of the white working class, which is metonymic for American identity; its fans are "conservative and patriotic," according to music journalist Chet Flippo.[16] Rock and roll music, on the other hand, is protest music and is especially associated with the anti-Vietnam movement. It is marked as "hippie" music and is typified in songs such as Country Joe and the Fish's "I-Feel-Like-I'm-Fixin'-to-Die-Rag" and Crosby, Stills, Nash and Young's "Ohio."

In "Ladder to Heaven," country singer Alan Jackson is accused of trying to "capitalize on people's emotions." *South Park* doesn't allow for maudlin

reminiscences; nope, they stretch Jackson's lyrics into banality as he celebrates every ladder moment:

> Where were you when they ran out of stuff to build the ladder to heaven? . . .
> Where were you when they saved that ladder to heaven? . . .
> Where were you when they decided heaven was a more intangible idea 'n
> you couldn't, you couldn't really get there? . . .

The banal and repetitive lyrics, like those of the boy-band songs, become
hallmarks of manufactured and, in this instance, insincere music. Schmaltzy
edu-tainment troops such as Getting Gay with Kids ("Rainforest Scmainfor-
est") and Butt Out! ("Butt Out") also suffer the same ridicule, not only for
their overt moral messages but also (and perhaps even more so) for their
patently manufactured song-and-dance routines.

Conclusion

South Park presents a multitude of aural opportunities. From the swearing of
the boys and ridiculous speeches of Priest Maxi to Token's musical lament,
South Park is no "quiet mountain town" (*Bigger, Longer and Uncut*). The heteroglossia encapsulates Bakhtin's notions about the complexity of language
and social intercourse. Listeners hear the conflict between "official" and
"unofficial" use of language in the children's naturalized swearing/abuse (and
their parents' disapproval), in their uptake and understanding of inappropriate language ("don't say pigfucker in front of Jesus," *The Spirit of Christmas*),
and in the duality of Snoop Dog's speech ("Here Comes the Neighborhood"). Language is not limited to words (think Timmy and Jimmy) but
includes other meaningful exchanges.

Language is not simply polyphonic, but is individualistic and political.
Speakers don't always have the same value or equality in speech acts. We hear
again from Bahktin:

> No member of a verbal community can ever find words in the language that
> are neutral, exempt from the aspirations and evaluations of the other, unin-
> habited by the other's voice. On the contrary, he receives the word by the
> other's voice and it remains filled with that voice. He intervenes in his own
> context from another context, already penetrated by the other's intentions.
> His own intention finds a word already lived in.[17]

South Park consistently challenges what is acceptable in the way of language
and language situations. Ms. Choksondik's exegesis on "shit" attempts to
institutionalize a hitherto unacceptable word—but still within linguistic constraints.

But speech is only one form of sound. Songs such as "Uncle Fucka" and "Merry Fucking Christmas" challenge socially acceptable norms; they disrupt lyrical expectations and challenge musical orthodoxy. However, radical melody experimentation such as Phil Glass's Christmas pageant is rejected (Mr. Hankey, the Christmas Poo")—it's just not folksy enough for South Park. Throughout the series, complex polyphony defines ethnicity (African American, Native American), moods (happy, menacing, dramatic), time (1980s pop, 1960s protest), and even politics (conservative, liberal). The show brims with musical sounds, styles, genres, and meaning.

CARTMAN:	You see Token, people really enjoy seeing African Americans on the news . . . *Seeing* African Americans on the news, not hearing them. That's why all African American newspeople learn to talk more . . . ho-how should I say . . . white. Token, all the great African American newspeople have learned to hide their Ebonic tribespeak with a more pure Caucasian dialect. There's no shame in it, and I think it'll really help our ratings.
KYLE:	He's smarter than you, fat boy!! I don't even know how you made it into fourth grade! I thought—
CARTMAN:	Trapper Keeper, I need to drown out my annoying friend. Please initiate music, country, high volume. ("Trapper Keeper")
BAND MEMBER 1:	We're the band Sanctified. We play metal and punk, but with lyrics that inspire faith in Christ.
BAND MEMBER 2:	Yeah. We proved that Christian music can be tough and hard core.
CARTMAN:	Yeah, you guys are real hard core.
SANCTIFIED BAND:	You bet your gosh-darned rear end we are! ("Christian Hard Rock")

Notes

1. Paul Wells, *Understanding Animation* (London: Routledge, 1998), 97–98.

2. Jeremy G. Butler, *Television Critical Methods and Applications* (Mahwah, NJ: Lawrence Erlbaum Associates, 2002), 143.

3. Wells, *Understanding Animation*, 99.

4. Music as a narrative is beyond this book; see Paul Wells, *Understanding Animation*; Lawrence Kramer, "'As if a Voice Were in Them': Music, Narrative, and Deconstruction," *Music as Cultural Practice, 1800–1900* (Berkeley: University of California Press, 1990).

5. South Park Scriptorium, www.spscriptorium.com, March 2, 2000.

6. Eliza Schneider took over until May 2004, then Gracie Lazar came to the show.

7. Chris Turner, *Planet Simpsons* (London: Ebury Press, 2004), 402-407.

8. Ernest Tucker, *Chicago Sun-Times*, August 11, 1997, 37; Caryn James, "Cartoons about Children Feature Grown-Up Jokes," *New York Times*, August 13, 1997, 14; Eric Deggans, "A Stroll in the Park with a Demented Muse," *St. Petersburg Times*, August 13, 1997, D1.

9. Most of the music is composed, written, and played in South Park Studios.

10. They don't know what fingerbang means, and when Kenny proffers an explanation, they reject it out of hand.

11. Created by boy-band manufacturer Lou Pearlman (Backstreet Boys and *NSYNC) in 1999.

12. Creed was formed in 1995 in Tallahassee, FL, by vocalist Scott Stapp and guitarist Mark Tremonti. Stapp and Tremonti wrote songs that "obliquely addressed themes of Christian spirituality"; bassist Brian Marshall and drummer Scott Phillips joined them. The band officially broke up in June 2004. For nearly a decade, the band sold over 30 million albums worldwide. Mark Tremonti, Scott Phillips, and Brian Marshall went on to form Alter Bridge with Myles Kennedy. There are plans for a Scott Stapp solo record, a collection of songs inspired by Mel Gibson's *The Passion of the Christ*. See http://www.mtv.com/bands/az/creed/bio.jhtml, accessed October 22, 2006.

13. Lars Ulrich, Britney Spears, Ozzie Osbourne, Metallica, Meat Loaf, Rick James, Missy Elliott, Blink 182, Rancid, and Alanis Morissette.

14. Apparently "lesbian" music is Indigo Girls ("Tom's Rhinoplasty").

15. Charles K. Wolfe and James E. Akenson, ed. *Country Music Goes to War.* (Lexington: University Press of Kentucky, 2005).

16. In response to the Dixie Chicks controversy, Flippo demonstrated clearly that while "the audience is tolerant of artists' mistakes and foibles . . . [they] will not tolerate an artist turning on them." "Nashville Skyline: Shut up and Sing?" Country Music Television, http://www.cmt.com/news/articles/1470672/03202003/dixie_chicks.jhtml, accessed October 22, 2006. Response from Bill C. Malone, "Guest Viewpoint on Chicks Controversy," Country Music Television, http://www.cmt.com/news/articles/1470798/03272003/id_0.jhtml, accessed October 22, 2006.

17. Mikhail Bakhtin, *Problems of Dostoevsky's Poetics*, ed. and trans. Caryl Emerson (Minneapolis: University of Minnesota Press, 1984), 131.

Chapter 9

No, Kitty, That's My Potpie:
Food and Drink

Food has long ceased to be about sustenance and nutrition. Alongside the calories come social, cultural, and symbolic meanings; food is "a highly condensed social fact."[1] The culinary world of *South Park* is rich with symbolic food and food practices. Exploring foods (imaginary and real) and dining practices uncovers food and drink as markers of family values, as political symbols, and as purveyors of class and even gender values in the South Park community.

Food is about moral choices. Over the centuries, food issues have evolved; Hub Zwart neatly summarizes the history of food ethics:

> Whereas ancient Greek food ethics concentrated on the problem of temperance, and ancient Jewish ethics on the distinction between legitimate and illicit food products, early Christian morality simply refused to attach any moral significance to food intake. Yet, during the middle ages food became one of the principle objects of monastic programs for moral exercise (*askesis*). During the seventeenth and eighteenth century, food ethics was transformed in terms of the increasing scientific interest in food intake, while in the nineteenth century the social dimension of food ethics was discovered, with the result that more and more attention was given to the production and distribution of food products.[2]

The Middle Ages' monastic obsession with control, abstinence, and fasting gave way to food revival during the Renaissance. In Rabelais' novel, readers find the big-bellied Friar John and the gigantic appetites of Gargantua and Pantagruel. "There is scarcely a single page in his book where food and drink do not figure ... These images are closely interwoven with those of the grotesque body. At times it is difficult to draw a line between them, so strong is their original tie," notes Bakhtin at the start of his chapter devoted to "banquet imagery."[3] Dividing the grotesque body into two categories is virtually impossible and, although it has been done in this book, it is a false division. The previous chapter on gender and sex concentrated on the genitals and anus as sites of copulation and identity, while virtually the same lower body area (this time including the mouth) is a site for exploration of more economic values.

Food is a culturally and spiritually powerful substance. It mediates human relationships and is often at the heart of familiar, romantic, and social interactions. Food also shapes the body. "Eating and drinking are one of the most significant manifestations of the grotesque body" and, through the mouth, man encounters the world—he literally takes it in through his body, makes it part of himself, and then expels it.[4] The grotesque body performs at least one very specific role: it reminds us that we are all creatures of the flesh, food, and feces.[5]

Food as Family Unit

During a meal, social messages about hierarchy, inclusion and exclusion, boundaries, and transactions are performed. The evening dinner meal is central to family ritual, a time for demonstrating the family as a social unit. When the Marshes, the Broflovskis, and the Stotches eat together, they reenact this cohesion. At the dinner table, the families come together to bond and to share their views and feelings. The Marshes have discussed the rights of the elderly ("Grey Dawn"), sex-change operations ("Mr. Garrison's Fancy New Vagina"), and voting ("Douch and Turd") at meal time, the one time of day that the family gathers as a group. It's at the dinner table that Randy asserts his position as the head of the family:

SHARON: Did you have fun at Eric's house today, Stanley?

STAN: Well, I guess.

SHARON: What did you do?

STAN: Well, Cartman wants to start a boy band, so we're gonna rehearse and then try to perform at the South Park Mall.

SHARON: Oh well, that sounds nice.

RANDY: No, it does not sound nice! Stanley, you are gonna have no part in that boy band!

STAN: Well, but, Dad, all my friends are doing it.

RANDY: If all your friends jumped off a cliff, would you do that too?

STAN: Cartman says we can make $10 million.

RANDY: YOU ARE NOT GOING TO BE IN A BOY BAND, STAN-
LEY! AND THAT IS FINAL!

SHELLEY: Geez, what's up Dad's ass? ("Fingerbang")

When Wall*Mart inserts its insidious fingers into the Marsh household, the routine is disrupted. They no longer gather at the dinner table, but eat in front of the television on newly acquired, separate TV tray/tables. The final straw comes when Randy interrupts a family dinner to visit Wall*Mart to purchase a replacement drinking glass. Wall*Mart has ripped the delicate fabric of family life ("Something Wall*Mart").

Aside from the ritual of eating, dinnertime is also regulated by what is eaten. What constitutes a "proper meal" is well documented in food sociology: it is a physical event that takes place in a certain location (such as at the dinner table), it must be prepared (cooked), and it is eaten in a particular manner. When Randy prepares a solitary breakfast, complete with beer, he burps and farts; his drink and behavior genders his meal as "masculine" and, because he's eating alone, it's okay. He might be upsetting notions of the traditional family breakfast, but for a single male, it's acceptable ("Losing Edge").

What is served is governed by strictures about what is "proper"—takeouts and barbecues are not as proper as a roasted meal of meat and two vegetables. There are even strictures about the order in which food is served: soup before the main meal, desserts last. Standardized rituals such as the Sunday lunch and the evening meal are markers of "properness." Regulation can even extend to repetition; for example, Monday night is stew night, turkey for Thanksgiving, oatmeal for breakfast. The Marshes usually eat quite traditional food; they enjoy ham and turkey, tacos, meat, and two veggies ("Fingerbang," "My Future Self," "Grey Dawn"). During Wall*Mart's evil influence, Randy purchases bulk ramen noodles. No longer will the family eat "proper" meals. No longer is Sharon Marsh necessary as the preparer of food; anyone can prepare the simplistic, prepackaged noodles. Ramen becomes a complex symbol of foreignness (Asian-esque food), overindulgence, and the disintegration of traditional family roles. The Broflovskis' dinner table indicates difference. Kyle laments that "instead of eating ham I have to eat kosher latke" ("Mr. Hankey") and gefilte fish ("Tooth Fairy"). When Kyle's cousin visits, his inability to consume Kyle's favorite meal disrupts the meal and further highlights the differences between the two:

KYLE: Ah-Ah-ah what is this?

KYLE TWO: Mom's special stew. She makes it every Monday and I love it.

KYLE: Oh, is, is this beef?

KYLE TWO: Yeah, dude, it's great!

KYLE: Ah-ah actually, I, I can't eat beef. I have a degenerative problem with my intestinal lining, and beef really gives me gaass.

SHEILA: Oh, I'm so sorry, Kyle. What else can I fix you?

KYLE: Oh no, I d- I don't want to be a bother, I uh-

SHEILA: Nonsense. Can't I make you some nice pasta? Or a frozen fish fillet?

KYLE: We-ull, some fish would be great if it isn't too much trouble. ("Entity")

The meal table, usually a place of bonding, is disrupted as Sheila leaves to prepare another meal. (In *South Park*, we most often see the consumption and not the production of food.) Connecticut Kyle is divided from the Broflovski family and its lifestyle.

Sharing a meal is not only a family activity; it can also be a social event. At the carnival ("carne vale" or "farewell meat"), banqueting was the central event. When South Park gathers to eat, naturally it has a diabolical flavor. When the *America's Most Wanted* crew is trapped with the locals, the first concern is food ("Cartman's Mom is Still a Dirty Slut"). And the immediate solution is cannibalism. Similarly, when they gather for a chili festival, Scott Tenorman is served his parents ("Scott Tenorman"). Cannibalism is one of the most fundamental human food taboos—and the South Parkers' willingness to break the taboo demonstrates that it is the stuff of legends. And, of course, the creators have evidenced a certain fascination with cannibalism, namely, their musical based on the story of Alferd Packer (1996). Their fascination with food and dining extends to cannibalism, because it is the ultimate grotesque image of consuming and transcending the body.[6]

If someone in South Park invites you to his or her home, that's another matter. A dinner party welcomes someone into the community. Breaking bread together in South Park is a way to consolidate friendships:

The Stotches have the Marshes and Broflovskis over so they can become friends. ("Asspen")

Sheila has a dinner party for Nurse Gollum because she feels "It is up to us to make her feel comfortable and welcome in our town." ("Conjoined Fetus Lady")

Newcomer Mr. Jefferson is invited to dinner. ("Jeffersons")

Children are excluded from the dinner table because they are adult-bonding and not family-bonding events. Noticeably absent from these dinner parties is Liane Cartman.

At the Cartman house, meals are considerably different. Cartman and his mother are rarely seen eating in the socially acceptable family way, at a table.[7] Their exclusion from the Jefferson dinner party indicates to Cartman that not only is he an outsider, but (to his mind) that he is deliberately being slighted so that the others can curry favor with Mr. Jefferson. Both Cartman and Blanket have similar, unconventional diets. Blanket's life is dominated by fun food (cotton candy and popcorn machines replace a dining table in his house), and Liane feeds Cartman a steady diet of snack foods. The families' dysfunctionality is highlighted by their paucity of proper meals.

A proper meal is tightly bound by social rules. All participants sit down at the same time, sometimes in set places, and perform in certain ways.[8] Table manners are strictly codified, a fact Pip acknowledges when he asks Pocket to instruct him in the ways of a gentleman: "And now I might mention, Pip, that in London it is not the custom to put the knife in the mouth. . . . a dinner napkin should never be placed into the tumbler. . . . one should never pass gas at the dinner table. . . . one should never pull out the wee wee and check it for scabs whilst at the table" ("Great Expectations").

South Park has images and rituals of traditional, proper meals—but the show is best known for its nontraditional consumption and preparation of food.

Dining Out

Meals are not always prepared and eaten in the home, of course. South Park has a cross-section of dining-out places where the community goes, usually to celebrate something: Happy Burger, Pizza Shack, Whistlin' Willy's, Crust E. Krotch's Pizza, and, of course, City Wok. Perhaps the most popular are the all-you-can-eat buffets: KC's All You Can Eat, King Jimmy's Buffet, Mel's Buffet, Country Kitchen Buffet. Buffets are particularly popular with the elderly; they offer value for less money, and people on limited budgets can afford them (except, of course, the McCormicks). Eating food prepared by other people is nothing new, but it is relatively new to the televisual world. It subverts the 1950s images of the family meal prepared by mother and gestures to the changing world where to eat out is merely another part of American culture.

Cartman's favorite restaurant is Denver's Casa Bonita, a Mexican restaurant that offers the complete dining experience: "cliff jumpers and Black Bart's Cave and all kinds of stuff!" ("Casa Bonita"). He is so enthralled with the restaurant that he will do anything to go there. He kidnaps Butters and holds him hostage, panics the entire town, loses his friends, and goes to Juvenile Hall—but, it was totally worth it. Cartman doesn't merely want to consume food; he, greedy consumer that he is, also wants to consume a performance. Eating in a restaurant has a performative aspect, as Erving Goffman noted in his *Presentation of the Self in Everyday Life*. Food service in restaurants is a type of theatre, a ballet of food. Special as Casa Bonita's is, it does not hold a candle to Butters' reverence for Bennigan's. Bennigan's, for Butters, represents family cohesion and happiness. The Stotch's trips to Bennigan's are so ritualized that Butters can outline their visit:

> Have you ever been to Bennigan's, Mister? Oh, it sure is great. I'm goin' to Bennigan's tomorrow night with my family. Oh, I can just see it now. We'll walk in the front doors and the nice Bennigan's hostess lady will take us to our cozy booth. Then we'll order some mozzarella sticks, for appetizers. Dad will open his present, and Mom will open hers. Uh, then the Bennigan's wait staff will sing "Happy, Happy Anniversary" . . . ("Butters' Very Own")

What Butters describes is a highly developed set of social practices. The thought of which sustains him through his arduous trip back home. When he arrives home and learns his family's dreaded secrets, his belief in the family unit is shaken:

> BUTTERS: I really wish I didn't know that stuff. I guess I learned that sometimes, lying can be for the best. Yup. Oh well, when I [*get?*] a chipotle bleu cheese bacon burger at Bennigan's, I'll forget all about my dad bein' queer and my mom tryin' to kill me. I'm gonna be okay.
>
> STAN: Really?
>
> BUTTERS: No, I'm lyin'. ("Butters' Very Own")

His faith in the recuperative powers of Bennigan's is shaken.

Gendered Food

Food is gendered. Apparently, men barbeque and women bake. Masculinity is linked with meat; not eating meat turns you into a pussy, literally ("Fun with Veal"). Vegetarians are not manly men:

> SADDAM: . . . What the hell is this crap we're eating, anyway?
>
> SATAN: It's all vegetarian, Saddam. Chris was a nutritionist before he died.
>
> SADDAM: Oh, isn't that fascinating. So, tell me, Chris. How is it that you died?

CHRIS: Oh, well I, I actually slipped down an escalator, in a mall.
           Those things can be pretty sketchy.

SADDAM: An escalator? What kind of pussy way of dying is that?!
           ("Do the Handicapped")

Women provide feminine food, salads and desserts. It is no accident that
Liane Cartman is, in the opening credits, shown holding a plate of cookies.
She might be a crack ho', but she is defined by her baking. She has a reputa-
tion as an excellent cook:

STAN: Oh, sweet! Your mom's giving you a big party again this
           year?

CARTMAN: That's right! Cause it's my birthday.

KYLE: Kick ass, dude! Cartman's mom throws the best birthday
           parties ever.

CARTMAN: That's right!

STAN: Yeah, if my mom could cook like Cartman's mom, I'd be a
           big fat-ass too.

CARTMAN: That's right . . . HEY! ("Damien")

Liane generally feeds Cartman "female" fare: toasty chocolate nummers,
powdered doughnut pancake surprise. Her mega-comfort food underscores
her incapacity to regulate her role as a traditional mother. She overcompen-
sates with gastronomical overindulgence. Similarly, the feminized Mr. Jefferson provides carnival food such as cotton candy and popcorn for Blanket. It
appears that Blanket hasn't even had the ubiquitous standby meal, the TV
dinner. Both children are loved, but the love is not tempered with guidance
and discipline; their strange eating habits become signifiers of neglect and
their parents' sexual ambiguity.

A Panopticon of Snacks

If there's one form of food that is a signifier for *South Park*, it's the show's
snack foods. Over thirty fictional food products[9] surface throughout the
series, which indicates the role and importance of food in the creation of an
imaginary Midwest town. Products such as Cheesy Poofs, Snacky Cakes, and
Happy Tarts add a *frisson* of recognition because they're fusions of real snack
foods. In fact, viewers wanted to know where they could buy Cheesy Poofs,
and soon they were part of the *South Park* merchandise,[10] thus proving that
product placement does work.

Snacks are inexorably linked with popular entertainment. They are an integral part of going to see a movie. The social practice of eating as part of viewing experience is highlighted when Cartman sits on a deck chair outside the Stotch's place—the sounds of Butters' punishment is accompanied by the sounds of Cartman slurping his drink and munching his popcorn ("Jared Has Aides"). Snacks are also the antithesis of proper meals. They don't require parents to prepare them and they become powerful, important symbols of rejection of parental control. When the parents are away, the children resort to snacks as their primary food source—houses become littered with discarded snack wrappers ("Wacky Molestation Adventure"). The boys stock up on "chips, cookies, popcorn, Cheesy Poofs, snacky cakes, and doughnuts" for the *Terrence and Philip Movie* trailer. As they trek across the town, the food goes with them. Snack food consumption is not limited to children, though; parents also consume Cheesy Poofs and popcorn while they watch television.

Food as Personal Identity

The most overt consumer of food is Cartman. Food dominates his life and defines him. His signature phrase is food related: "No, Kitty, that's my potpie." He wants a bris just so he can have "lots of food" ("Ike's Wee Wee"). He equates food with love: he falls in love with Wendy Testaburger over a plate of double-stuffed Oreos ("Chef Goes Nanners"); his romantic offering to Miss Ellen is a chocolate pie (which of course he eats, "Tom's Rhinoplasty"); and he advises Jimmy that to woo a girl he needs to take her on a date with plenty of Italian food ("Erection Day"). While the other boys turn their attention to the girls at Raisins, Cartman suspends his judgment until he's eaten; once he's tried the "zingy tangy wings, mozzarella tasty tarts and the bite-size pizzazzas," only then can he proclaim Raisins the "greatest place in the world" ("Raisins"). When Cartman wins money, he buys food ("Fat Butt"); his "psychic" trances focus on food items ("Cartman's Incredible Gift"); he has stem-cell legislation overturned so that he can clone a Shakey's pizza ("Kenny Dies"). He goes through the Marsh's trashcan because he's seen a jelly doughnut ("Towelie"). He consumed Kenny's ashes thinking it was chocolate drink mix ("Ladder to Heaven"). Food even "kills" him ("Death of Eric Cartman"). Basically, Cartman has lied, deceived, kidnapped, and even "died" for the sake of food.

Cartman's gluttony marks him as selfish and uncaring. He not only keeps food from Starvin' Marvin, but also he takes Marvin's dessert. He is the only one at Rancher Bob's not disgusted by the sight of the chained calves ("Fun with Veal"); in fact, the shackled calves make him feel hungry. At fat camp, he exploits the campers' weakness for food and profits from them ("Fat Camp"). While the boys might rib him about his fat ass, they cannot accept a slim Cartman, either. When he is not fat, he can no longer be the butt of their jokes.

A fat body indicates a person who lacks control, and success is linked to control. When future Cartman visits, he's slim and successful; he tells Cartman that when he stops eating junk food, he starts to study harder and to reject drugs. Thus, overindulgence in food is part of Cartman's inability to control his life—naturally, he rejects it: "Go have sex with yourself, asshole! I'm not that stupid! Just for that, I'm gonna spend my whole childhood eating what I want, and doin' drugs when I want! Whatevuh! I'll do what I want!" ("My Future Self"). His rejection is the rejection of moderation.

Politics of the Body

During the carnival excesses, control that is normally exercised is abandoned. Feasting and celebration is not a time for religious abstinence but a time for secular indulgence. At the center of feasting and eating is the consuming body. As the body grows in girth, the concentration is on the open mouth, the defecating anus, and increasing belly. It is therefore a grotesque body of orifices that ingest and eject. The grotesque body is the exact opposite of the closed, clean, and nonfunctioning body of classical art (Michelangelo's *David*, for example). In medieval times, the bodies of the carnival denied the control imposed by the church, as in Lenten fasting and the Deadly Sin of gluttony. It is the body of the common people, the popular body we all possess. However liberating gorging can be, it is also repulsive. *South Park* revitalizes the grotesque body of Friar John.

Sally Struthers's monstrous shape symbolizes the greed of the American people and is used as a contrast to the lack, and particularly the starving, of third world countries. Her body size is closely aligned with selfishness and meanness; she does not share her stockpiled food. Both she and Cartman are fictional cousins of Mr. Cresote, Monty Python's *Meaning of Life* gargantuan, who explodes in one of the most grotesque and vomitous scenes in movie history. Mr. Cresote's superior attitude and Struthers' indifference represent selfishness and gluttony. All of these people possess, in carnival terms, grotesque bodies. Fat people have two symbolic and somewhat ambiguous roles: they represent lack of control and yet they can express energy and voluptuousness. This energy can be associated with ambition (Cartman's various money-making schemes, for example). He might huff and puff, but he does so on his way to making a million dollars.

Cartman's body size is directly related to his diet. In the earliest shows, Cartman asserts that he is big boned; so distorted is his body image that in "Weight Gain," he "bulks up" in order to appear at his best on television. He realizes that to be "seen," he requires a larger-than-life body. His mother consistently encourages him in his distorted body image. However, she is not completely delusional; she giggles at the boys' obesity jibes ("Korn's Groovy") and eventually confesses to that she's lied to him—he is fat ("Fat Camp"). The contradictory body in society is exemplified in Cartman's time at Hopeful Hills Children's Weight Management Center. The pain of weight loss comes in the form of Chad, who sobs his despair:

> CHAD: I'm always gonna be fat. I don't wanna eat no sweets, but I
>   can't control myself when they're right in front of me like
>   this. All my life I've been fat. I've been-I've been to seven
>   camps and I swore to my momma that I'd lose the weight. I
>   want to, but I can't help myself
>
> CARTMAN: Hey, Chad you know what you need? You need a friend.
>
> CHAD: I'd, I do?
>
> CARTMAN: Yes. A chocolate friend. Mr. Candy Bar doesn't judge you,
>   Chad. Mr. Candy Bar likes you just the way you are. Look at
>   how yummy and sweet he is. . . . There you go. That'll just
>   be four dollars. . . . There you go. ("Fat Camp")

Cartman's exploitation of Chad is appallingly insensitive (even by Cartman standards) and reflects the media at large, which sends out conflicting body-image messages. Obesity and weight issues are news in a media that jeers at overweight celebrities and delights in their weight-loss stories. In "Jared has Aides," Stan comments that only in America can one become famous by going from being a fat ass to not being a fat ass.

Food as Difference

Food also represents difference. When the Hollywood crowd invades South Park, they want foods foreign to South Park. When two outsiders ask Chef if he has "tofu or steamed celery," he doesn't understand them—this is not traditional South Park fare. The outsiders' diet consists of roughage that backs up the sewage system. Mr. Hankey becomes ill because the new people "eat nothin' but couscous, tofu, and raw vegetables," a diet that destroys Hankey's environment. Their diet eventually flushes them out of South Park forever.

Of course, they're not the only ones with strange eating habits: Mormons eat "Rice Crispy squares . . . with chocolate frosting ("All About Mormons") and Canadians eat Kroff Dinner. The community is constituted by its consumption of similar foods; these people, with their strange eating habits, are clearly not South Parkers.

Food is also a marker of money. Token's lunch box contains "crab cakes and lobster tail." The others have "cut-up hot dogs for lunch" and, while at school, they buy school lunches ("Here Comes the Neighborhood").[11] Seafood is synonymous with wealth and, by association, sophistication. Naturally, it is Cartman who notices Token's diet. Token believes eating macaroni and cheese for dinner will help him fit in. Though not possessing the same wealth as Token, Mr. Mackey serves crab soufflé at his meteor party. Crab soufflé requires more than expensive ingredients, it requires sophisticated cooking skills. And sure enough, he has hired help, Juanita ("Two Naked Men").

At the other end of the social scale is Kenny. Kenny's family exists on food stamps and frozen waffles. Stuart McCormick's grace drips with irony: "Lord . . . we thank you for this staggering payload of frozen waffles that you have bestowed upon us. And since we have been faithful to you, we know that you will send us some good fortune one of these days, even though you sure as hell seem to be taking your sweet time. Amen" ("Chickenpox"). Stan, Kyle, and Cartman are appalled at waffles for dinner. Cartman is particularly concerned, not only about the fare but also by the quantity:

KENNY'S BROTHER: That one's [*waffle*] mine! That one's mine!

    CARTMAN: What kind of side dishes will we be enjoying this evening with our frozen waffles? [*silence*]

    CARTMAN: Am I to understand there will be no side dishes?

    KEVIN: My waffle's done, my waffle's done!

MRS. MCCORMICK: Now, Kevin, we ain't got enough for everybody. You have to split that with your brother.

    CARTMAN: Oh Jesus, are you fucking kidding me? ("Chickenpox")

Stuart McCormick and Gerald Broflovski came from the same socioeconomic sphere; but Gerald has succeeded because, according to Mrs. McCormick, he sought a life beyond frozen waffles ("Chickenpox"). Stuart, however, does not blame his lack of incentive, but his wife's inability to cook. It's not the waffles, but that she doesn't know "how to use spices and stuff" ("Chickenpox"). Again, food is gendered: men should provide the fare that women then prepare.

Kenny's family is the focus of the annual Thanksgiving canned food drive. South Park families contribute tins of creamed corn and green beans; in other words, the dross of kitchen pantries. Even this fare is grudgingly given and Kenny has to "earn" it in the humiliating and painful GRAB-O-RAMA. Again, Stuart's grace is replete with irony:

KENNY'S DAD: Lord, on this day of thanks, we would like to extend our deepest gratitude for this incredible bounty of green beans you have bestowed upon us. And though for some reason you found it necessary to take our son from us, and though you for some reason find pleasure in watching us suffer, still, we give thanks. Amen.

KENNY'S MOM: Amen.

KENNY'S MOM: Does anybody have a can opener?

KENNY'S DAD: Goddamnit. ("Starvin' Marvin")

Ironically, of course, Thanksgiving celebrates food and plenty; it is "the one time of year you're supposed to care about people who can't eat" ("Stavin Marvin"). The McCormicks' plight contrasts with the plenitude of the other residents and mimics that of the starving Ethiopians.

Politicized Food

America's insensitivity is not limited to its own poor and hungry. In the Starvin' Marvin Thanksgiving episodes, *South Park* explores issues of famine and America's contribution to alleviating starvation in third world countries. Cartman and Struthers are disinterested and uninterested in those who don't have enough food. When Cartman withholds food from Starvin' Marvin, he demonstrates not only his greed but that of the nation; on Struthers's body is inscribed the hypocrisy of the nation.

The boys eat Cheesy Poofs while listening to Sally Struthers's advertisement to save children from starvation: "Here in the heart of Africa children are dying. Not from disease or war, but from hunger" ("Starvin' Marvin"). While they are unmoved by the plight of the children, they *are* motivated by the sports watch. But they get more than they bargain for when Marvin arrives.

Marvin is indoctrinated into the American way of life via a visit to an all-you-can-eat buffet. The buffet exemplifies the plentiful, ready, and cheap supply of American food. Marvin is awed by the excessive amount of food and doesn't eat while the others stuff themselves. Marvin and Cartman symbolize the world's food imbalance. Marvin has a small plate with one item; Cartman has a platter filled with numerous items. Marvin is the starving famine of African nations; Cartman, the plenty of the Western nations.

Cartman gets his comeuppance when he is accidentally sent to Ethiopia. He spends a biblical forty days in the desert, searching for food. There is none from the Red Cross, because the money has run out. There is no food but plenty of watches; too few people have donated money. Cartman eventually finds a warehouse marked "no admittance." Inside the warehouse, Struthers has stockpiled Cheesy Poofs, Snacky Cakes, Boogie Bars, and Veal Roll-Ups. Reclining on a chaise lounge, she gorges while being fanned by Ethiopians. She is thus the epitome of insensitive America; she eats while those around her starve. Marvin therefore is the food counterpoint of Cartman and Struthers. In Marvin's emaciated body, brown, shriveled, and unclothed, resides a physical reminder of the starving "other." He reminds viewers of the failure to feed the world despite the promises of Band Aid, Live Aid, and various charities.

Drink

Like food, drink too acts as a marker of personal and social identity. Beer seems to be the alcohol of choice among the South Park males, especially the local brew, Dude Beer, "for those who like their beers big and strong" ("Damien"). It is the drink of seduction and primes Liane Cartman for her drunken night ("Elephant Fucks a Pig," "Cartman's Mom Is a Dirty Slut"). Like food, beer creates a community, as groups gather round Randy Marsh's "Friday night kegger" ("The Mormons"). The scoutmaster, Mr. Grazier, bonds with the boys' fathers when he suggests they go to pound back brews ("Cripple Fight"). Alcohol also tends to create gendered groups. When the men go on a s'more-flavored schnapps-fueled trip across the US, no women join them ("Red Badge"); nor are women seen drinking in bars. Richers who try to imbibe at the local bar are directed to the bar across the road:

KOBE BRYANT: 'Scuse me, can we get a couple of beers here?

SKEETER: They've got nice expensive beers for you across the street at the new Wolfgang Puck's.

KOBE BRYANT: That's alright, we just want some cheap beer tonight.

BARKEEP: . . . Maybe you didn't see the sign out front: This bar is for people livin' below their means ONLY! ("Here Comes the Neighborhood")

Beer is therefore also a marker of class. Gerald Broflovski's preference for Aspen micro beers highlights the divide between him and Stuart McCormick. The only thing worse than drinking expensive beer is not drinking beer at all, as Mr. Cotswolds finds out. Mr. Cotswolds refuses a beer because he likes "wine coolers," so Jimbo and the others decide to duct tape him to a bench in the bar ("Hooked on Monkey Fonics"). Not all drinks are alcoholic, and minor references are made to soft drinks such as Zoop ("Anal Probe"); yes, even drinks have cultural meaning.

Conclusion

Banquets are an integral part of the carnivalesque, and Bakhtin's study drew attention to the centrality of feasting. When people ate and drank together, they were freer to be merry.[12] Medieval banquets provided the opportunity for people to eat and drink together without formalities and to enjoy free conversation and laughter and, "Wherever men [sic] laugh and curse, particularly in a familiar environment, their speech is filled with bodily images."[13]

Food therefore becomes a communal product, and around its consumption a community takes shape. In *South Park*, however, the feasting has turned to gorging. The contemporary stomach is distended. It is filled with fatty, nonnutritious food and probably with alcohol—at least the rich American bellies are. Others don't fare so well. The excess is most obvious on the grotesque bodies of Cartman and Struthers, but there is more to the grotesque bodies than accumulated weight—their bodies are political and performative:

> In Rabelais' fiction, the human body is a theater of transformation. His art ignores the body's smooth surface and focuses on its excrescences and its orifices: the gaping mouth, loins and anus. The grotesque body is constantly active, exceeding its margins: a body in the act of becoming. It is never finished, never completed: it is continually built, created, and builds and creates another body . . . eating, drinking, defecation and other elimination (sweating, blowing of the nose, sneezing), . . . copulation, pregnancy, dismemberment, swallowing up by another body—all these acts are performed on the confines of the body and the outer world, or on the confines of the old and new body. In all events, the beginning and end of life are closely linked and interwoven.[14]

Rabelais' Gargantua would have been proud of Mr. Hankey's "Circle of Poo Song." Food is so much more complex than nutrition; its manufacture, distribution, and consumption embed, in simple sustenance, complex political, gendered, and social tropes.

> "The world begins at a kitchen table. No matter what, we must eat to live." –Poet Joy Harjo, "Maybe the World Ends Here"

Notes

1. Arjun Appadurai, quoted in David Bell and Bill Valentine, *Consuming Geographies* (London: Routledge, 1997), 3.

2. Hub Zwart, "A Short History of Food Ethics," *Journal of Agricultural and Environmental Ethics* 12 (2000): 113–26, http://www.filosofie.science.ru.nl/cv/food%20ethics.pdf, accessed October 24, 2006.

3. Mikhail Bakhtin, *Rabelais and His World,* trans. Helene Iswolsky (Indiana University Press, 1984), 279.

4. Ibid., 281.

5. Ibid., 175.

6. Cannibalism continues to fascinate and repel through a myriad of texts, from the Grimm fairy tales, Lewis Carroll's *Alice in Wonderland,* and Jonathan Swift's "Modest Proposal," to *Silence of the Lambs* and Shakespeare's *Titus Andronicus.*

7. Though in the earliest manifestation of the show, when Cartman had a father, there was a scene in which the family was seated at a table eating. The still is available at http://www.fortunecity.com/underworld/sonic/87/cartmansfather.html, accessed October 24, 2006.

8. Bell and Valentine, *Consuming Geographies,* 61.

9. Powdered Donut Pancake Surprise, Chocolate Chicken Potpies, Cheesy Poofs, Happy Tarts, Snacky Cakes, Sweetie Pops, Chocolate-Peanut Butter Cream Puffies, Tootie Bars, Poofy Pies, Veal Roll-Ups, Boogie Bars, Freezy Pops, Snacky Candy, Cookie Dings, Beefy Logs, Super Chocolaty Chunky Funk Chip Surprise Ice Cream, Chocolate Noogies, Nilla Crunchies, Crispy Yum-Yums, Nilla Yum-Yums, Berry Bars, Choco-Numbers, Snacky S'mores, Chocolate Yum Yum Bars, Coo Coo Chips (*South Park: Bigger, Longer and Uncut*).

10. "'South Park'—It's a Gas," *Boston Globe*, January 28, 1998, D1.

11. School dinners were "initially provided as a way of countering the poverty of many children's diets at home"; school lunches are therefore another marker of poverty, or at least of reduced income. Bell and Valentine, *Consuming Geographies.*

12. Ibid., 284–85.

13. Ibid., 319.

14. Ibid., 317.

Chapter 10

Pissant American Town: The Community

Okay, so it's not really Small Town, USA, but it plays one on television. Small towns are supposed to be friendly, caring communities, an ideal setting to raise a family. They're safe, quiet, have little traffic and even less crime;[1] they're the kind of place where you hear birds chirp and a flag unfurl. Right? Small town values are those of friendliness, neighborliness, and community spirit, the idealized televisual world of Andy Griffith and the Waltons and parodied in *Green Acres*. *South Park*'s theme song celebrates its small-town values. It's just a pity that the humble folk in South Park suffer many temptations and sometimes aren't so friendly; sometimes South Park is the antithesis of the idyllic small town because, well, it's South Park, UFO-sighting capital of the world.

The boys know what constitutes a town. When Butters believes himself to be the only survivor, he articulates his new "society": "I'm rebuilding society. Here, take a look. This is the library and over here is the bank. That over there I'm thinking into a P. F. Chang's or a Bennigan's. And this is a memorial to Eric Cartman, the person who gave his life so that I could rebuild society. Well, ma'am, I guess we should start repopulatin the earth, huh? I'm ready whenever you are" ("Casa Bonita"). Society is synonymous, in the first instance, with buildings: a library (strangely enough), a bank, restaurants, and, most important, a monument. Butters plans a town of learning (or at least of reading), food, and finance. Then he can get on with the third "f." His memorial to Cartman reflects a founding-father spirit—homages to pioneers figure prominently as reminders of historicity, no matter how ludicrous. Indeed, the more ridiculous the story of foundation, the more revered the

151

founder. The story of a town's founding is part of its lore, and South Park's story is typical of the expansion of the mid-nineteenth century:

> BEBE: This is the story of South Park. It begins over a hundred years ago. When the noble and hearty Ute Indians lived on the land . . . Then, from the east, came the great white pioneers. [*Pioneers beat up the Indians*] The pioneers met with the Indians, and negotiated for their fertile lands. [*Pioneers continue to fight the Indians*] ("Weight Gain 4000")

South Park Topography

Topographically, South Park consists of a handful of streets. At its center both geographically and economically is Main Street. Main Street is, of course, a bearer of multiple layers of meaning for the inhabitants of South Park and for the US in general; Main Street bears cultural meanings of nostalgia and community and has, over time, been romanticized—think Disneyland. Richard Francaviglia has studied the concept of Main Street and finds that

> "Main Street" has come to symbolize a place close to the people, people who have few pretenses and honest aspirations; and because it fuses images of place and time, it also symbolizes their past. Small wonder, then, that Main Street is easily romanticized and has become one of America's most cherished images. As both a place and a concept, Main Street is ubiquitous and characteristically American. . . . There are several thousand small towns in the United States, and, by definition, as many Main Streets. As the heart of the small town, Main Street serves many purposes, perhaps the most important of which is retailing—the marketing or sale of items or services to the public.[2]

The South Park shops have suitably homespun names that underscore their friendliness and gesture to the nostalgia of a place where everyone knows your name: Tweek's Barn, Luau's Toys, and Mis-Information's New Age Shop. Of course, in typical *South Park* style, the shops are not the "usual" countrified shops—Tom's Rhinoplasty and Jimbo's Guns add extra meaning, telling viewers that this is a redneck twenty-first-century town. Behind the shops' facades resides the dignity of small-town America as articulated by Mr Tweek:

> The answer is still no, Mr. Postem. You see, when my father opened this store thirty years ago, he cared about only one thing: making a great cup of coffee. Sure, we may take a little longer to brew a cup, and we may not call it fancy names, but I guess we just care a little more. And that's why Tweek Coffee is still home-brewed from the finest beans we can muster. Yes, Tweek Coffee is a simpler cup, for a simpler America. ("Gnomes")

And nothing is simpler than the South Park community.

The antithesis of Main Street retailing is the mall. The mall is basically a horizontally challenged Main Street, right? With the vertical structure comes a different type of consumerism, more codified shopping regulations, and ultimately different meanings. In his mesmerizing film on Small Town, USA, David Byrne noted that shopping "has become the activity that brings people together" (*True Stories*, 1986). And thus the mall serves as both the new town square and the new marketplace. The products are not simply those needed for survival; essential to the mall are the frivolous and the faddish—one metro-shops at the mall and not on Main Street. As Stephen Harper points out, "Romero [in *Dawn of the Dead*] certainly recognized the dramatic potential of the mall, which may be regarded as both the epitome of corporate capitalism and—for the same reason—a potential site of resistance to the forces that regulate consumerism."[3] But it's the new millennium marketplace of horror[4]: there is the obligatory Orange Julius stand where one might potentially meet Charlie Manson ("Merry Christmas Charlie Manson!"), the try-hard mall entertainers ("Fingerbang"), the ridiculous new concept shops ("Stupid Spoiled Whore"), and, of course, the potential for death ("Spirit of Christmas"). Stan learns of the evils of consumerism from arch-capitalists, hippies: "[T]he mall is a way for the corporate fat cats to imprison you into a life of servitude."[5] Servitude also translates into literal control. Mall control is demonstrated by the overzealous mall cops and twitchy mall managers, because although the mall is supposedly a democratic space, mall visitors have to observe fairly rigid rules of conduct. It is too controlled for the carnivalesque activities of the town square. One can stroll up and down Main Street in relative autonomy. Not so in the mall. The South Park Mall is a contemporary Panopticon where people are observed and ordered to "move along." The mall is rarely a happy place. Or a benign one. The mall is central to the American lifestyle; Cartman explains that America is a place of "log rides," "bacon double-cheeseburgers," "sheep-shearing contests," and "shopping malls" ("Quintuplets").

In its extended critique of consumerism, *South Park* also turns its attention to the mega-store; the mall is so 1980s. When "Something This Wall*Mart Comes," shopping is no longer a benign consumer activity—it becomes eternally destructive. Not only is the title of the episode taken from a horror novel, throughout the episode, horror images are superimposed over consumerism. *South Park* pulls out all the horror clichés: Main Street turns into a ghost town, Butters plays monsters, Randy Marsh becomes a zombie, and terrified managers whisper paranoid warnings. Like zombies and vampires, Wall*Mart refuses to die; it continues to resurrect unless properly killed. Vampiric Wall*Mart feeds on people's consumerist desires like the zombie consumers of *Dawn of the Dead* (1978); horror is overshopping. Mega-corporation Wall*Mart destroys South Park; as Main Street crumbles, so too does the family unit. (Strangely enough, the mall is unaffected by Wall*Mart because malls represent not family-run businesses but are corporate marketplaces.) The effects of rampant consumerism are devastating, family life disintegrates, and only death can rejuvenate the town. The zombification of Randy Marsh mirrors the deadening of the human spirit by consumerism. Of course, South Park people never go gently into that dark night; dying people eliminate their body waste, they crap themselves, much to Cartman's fascination. The juxtaposition of elimination, death, and rebirth is another aspect of lower body humor and grotesque realism as Bakhtin observes:

> To degrade also means to concern oneself with the lower stratum of the body, the life of the belly and the reproductive organs; it therefore relates to acts of defecation and copulation, conception, pregnancy, and birth. Degradation digs a bodily grave for a new birth; it has not only a destructive, negative aspect, but also a regenerating one. . . . Grotesque realism knows no other level; it is the fruitful earth and the womb. It is always conceiving . . .[6]

Before South Park's Main Street (and families) can be reborn, it therefore must eliminate its old wastes and excesses.

South Park has an uneasy relationship with retailing. While the episode recognizes the harm of consumerism, the boys, especially Cartman, eagerly take up the latest fads such as MegaMan ("Damien"), Chinpokomon ("Chinpokomon"), Osaka Gamesphere ("Towelie"), and PSP ("Best Friends Forever"). As the boys know, part of being one of the crowd is keeping up with the others, and that often means buying the latest toys. Kyle patiently explains the playground realities to his parents:

KYLE: Mom, Dad, can I have money to buy Chinpokomon?

SHEILA: What's a Chinpokomon?

KYLE: I'm not sure.

SHEILA: Well, why do you need one?

KYLE: I don't know.

SHEILA: . . . Well then, the answer is no, Kyle. You just got money to buy your Cyborg Bill doll.

KYLE: Yeah, but Cyborg Bill is totally gay now. Please Mom? Everybody else has Chinpokomon.

GERALD: Well, Kyle, that's not a reason to buy something. . . . You see, son, fads come and go. And this Chin-po-ko-mon is obviously nothing more than a fad. You don't have to be a part of it. In fact, you can make an even stronger statement by saying to your peers, "I'm not going to be a part of this fad, because I'm an individual." Do you understand?

KYLE: Yes. Yes, I do, Dad. Now, let me tell you how it works in the real world. In the real world, I can either get a Chinpokomon, or I can be the only kid without one, which singles me out and causes the other kids to make fun of me and kick my ass. ("Chinpokomon")

Owning the latest toy is linked to self-worth; Cartman always wants to be the first with new toys and is peeved when Kenny is first in line ("Best Friends Forever"). Santa and Jesus come to blows over the meaning of Christmas:

JESUS: Christmas is for celebrating my birth!

SANTA: Christmas is for giving!

Stan and Kyle reconcile Jesus and Santa by explaining how interdependent they are:

STAN: Hey, Jesus! You have to understand that Santa is keeping the spirit of your birthday alive by bringing happiness and joy.

KYLE: Yeah. And Santa, you need to remember that if it weren't for Jesus, this day wouldn't even exist! (*The Spirit of Christmas*)

Apparently, to bring "happiness and joy," one must give presents. The presents-as-essential-to-Christmas theme is explored through several Christmas episodes. In "A Very Crappy Christmas," the lack of Christmas spirit depresses Mr. Hankey and the retail trade. So it's up to the boys to teach the town a very important lesson: that Christmas is about presents.

Main Street, besides being a shopping precinct, is also a place for the community to gather. As Francaviglia observes, the distinction between the economic and social functions of Main Street is often blurred: "[It] is also the location of government and its services,"[7] thus the city hall, the library, and the courthouse occupy the same geographical location as the retail shops. The townsfolk gather there to celebrate Kathie Lee Gifford, to raise the town's flag, to fight, to protest. Divided as the crowd might be, they still share a physical space of "collectively shared or experienced assumptions, designs, and myths."[8] When politics divides the town, as in "I'm a Little Bit Country," the topography of South Park shows that the community needs each other:

SKEETER: There! All finished. From now on, this is the pro-war side of town, and that's the unpatriotic side.

RANDY: How about we call this the rational side of town, and that the redneck side?!

PROTESTERS: Hahahaha, yeah.

JIMBO: You just keep all your flag burnin' and your hippie-rock protest songs on your side o' the town!

PROTESTER: Hey, wait a minute, your side of town has the post office.

STUART: Well, your side has the grocery store.

JIMBO: Well, you can come to our side of town to use the post office and we can go to your side to use the grocery store.

GERALD: Aaah, can we cross the line to take our kids to school?

JIMBO: W-hell, naturally you could cross the line for that. Just like . . . we could cross the line for hardware, supplies, gas, and pharmaceutical needs.

Because it's such a small town, there are simply not enough resources to share. However divided the town becomes, the community always reaches a compromise.

Main Street dissects the city and is used as a thoroughfare for the opening credits. The boys' ride to school in the opening sequences provides glimpses of the townscape; past the drive-in, in the background, Mt. Evanston dominates. The shops' façades gesture to stereotype. The town's flat layout aligns with the *South Park* animation aesthetic and gestures to the one-dimensionality of town life and the narrowness of small-town mentality. Other town features include the town square, later the Kenny McCormick Memorial Talent Square, where crowds gather to celebrate celebrity visits. It's the town's carnival space, where "all free and familiar contact" reigns.[9] In the public town square, rational discourse is supposed to happen; of course, it becomes mayhem in *South Park* fashion when the townsfolk gather there to celebrate celebrity visits, fight over political divisions, and so on. *South Park* succeeds in the small touches: where else does an elaborately columned city hall nestle beside a gun shop, or a plastic surgeon's office take pride of place on Main Street?

South Park reflects the rural heritage of the pre-nineteenth-century USA—a rural heritage that was challenged in the industrial nineteenth century and in the suburban twentieth. Small towns were often supplanted by larger cities. But more recently, small towns are being "rediscovered" for their perceived values, country charm, and less stressful lifestyles—which explains Robert Redford's interest. However, as "Red Man's Greed" demonstrates, small towns are still expendable, especially where economics are concerned.

But the small-town communities of the twenty-first century can fight back; South Park shows that small towns can fight back. As Wendy Testaburger would say, "Don't fuck with South Park."

The community spirit comes to the fore when others, usually outsiders, threaten the town. Robert Redford and the Californian movie crowd are so full of shit, they ruin the town's delicate ecosystem and are flushed out as a result; Streisand's monstrous ego threatens the town's safety, but she is dispatched by a combination of entertainment smarts and South Park determination. Ben Affleck and Jennifer Lopez don't fare well; neither does Paris Hilton, Puff Daddy, Rob Reiner, Tom Cruise, Michael Jefferson, or the "richers," Will Smith, Oprah Winfrey, and Kobe Bryant. The message is clear: this is not a town for celebrities or wealthy folk; it's a town for working-class "ordinary" people. Newbies to the community only survive if they are fully integrated family units, no matter how much they might deviate from the "norm": the challenged Swansons, the Mormon Harrisons, and even the insular Cotswolds. Groups that won't assimilate are the Jakovasaurs, who are just too annoying and too fecund, or the Goobacks, who are too poor. Such episodes highlight the problems of small towns as outlined by Gary Mattson: "Successful economic development efforts and subsequent population growth often bring racial and ethnic diversity into smaller communities, increase pressure on local real estate markets, and create conflicts over local housing policies."[10] Even more dangerous than the overachieving richers and the hardworking Goobacks are the pestilent hippies.

Previously, the town faced destruction, demolition, and cultural imperialism, but the hippies will "end life" as South Park knows it ("Die Hippie, Die"). The do-nothing hippies smoke weed, play drums, listen to music, but little else; they don't contribute financially (as Mayor McDaniels had imagined) because they have no money. They do not perform any seemingly worthwhile function—a fact underscored by Stan's frustration at the music festival. They present the antithesis of the hard-working American lifestyle. Cartman, adopting a Cartmanesque metaphor, fears the town will be "consumed" by them ("Die Hippie, Die").

South Park must dispel influxes of large numbers of people; otherwise, it cannot sustain its laid-back mountain lifestyle. But in order to accomplish this, the townspeople have to work together to thwart the outside invasion; as the adults are usually ineffectual, it's up to the boys. Only they are clear-sighted and clever enough to save South Park; they have stood in front of bulldozers, battled mechamonsters, and prevented intergalactic annihilation. As the next generation, it is clearly up to them to protect their town.

Signification of Buildings

They appear to be visual white noise, but the buildings of South Park are iconic displays of their inhabitants and their functions. The art-deco sounding Bijou Theater is very Small Town, USA. Most towns have multi-cineplexes, so South Park's one movie theatre denotes its small-town status. When it comes to places of worship, the Roman Catholic Church is imposing, but only half the size of the synagogue. The public buildings differ quite markedly in architecture; the school is utilitarian, whereas the library, the courthouse, and the city hall are classically designed. However, the most important buildings in the town are the family houses.

The most often seen buildings are the family houses. The dominance of detached, owner-occupied houses set on individual lots embodies the national values of private property rights and the American dream of home ownership. The houses look remarkably similar at first glance, declaring visually that this is a community of people with similar incomes and values. But subtle visual cues proclaim the differences of the inhabitants. There's the economically significant architecture: the multiple-level mansions of the Blacks and other "richers,"[11] the two-story houses of the Broflovskis, Cartmans, Marshes, and Stotches, the single-story bungalow of the McCormicks. Hardly surprisingly, the houses differentiate income and class. Houses change as fortunes do. The Broflovskis' house grows with Gerald's increased income ("Sexual Harassment Panda"); their newer home has double doors, five stories, massive front doors, and the ultimate South Park sign of money, a water fountain.[12] Everything at the new Broflovski house is bigger, even the icicles. The Marshes' kitchen has been recently renovated, too ("Death of Eric Cartman"). The barred windows on the Cotswolds' house symbolically show that they do not want people coming in; they also keep the occupants from going out ("Hooked on Monkey Fonics"). Naturally, the Hankeys live in the town's sewerage system; their brightly colored house is a collage of the town's refuse: discarded cans, cartons, and wrappings constructed as a house and covered in fairy lights. The Hankeys are clearly no ordinary family, but their house certainly mirrors those of the rest of the town, except for its exceedingly cheery exterior.

Darkish, neutral-colored houses are the norm; brightly colored houses are the hallmark of fussy old ladies ("Die Hippie, Die") and gayness; Garrison's purple house signaled his sexuality long before he came out of the closet ("Cherokee Hair Tampons"). With the upbeat color scheme comes neatly tended gardens and blooming flowers. The houses become outer garments that cloak a lifestyle and a political/economic unit, the family. If the camera pans out, it incorporates the outlying areas and shows that the Tokens live on a much larger block, an estate, on the outskirts of the town, as do the Native Americans. Thus, these groups are physically marginalized, but for different reasons.

Even the interiors are remarkably similar—functionally furnished, they are neat and uncluttered. The marginalized characters have different interiors. Chef's house has the accoutrements of seduction 1970s style: a tiger-skin rug, a lava lamp, a record player, and incense stick holders ("Mecha-Streisand"); Big Al's place is campy, with its theatrical bed, polished floors, and lime green furniture. Token's house contains the ultimate marker of money, high culture in the form of original artwork, paintings done by a European artist, Van Gogh ("Here Comes the Neighborhood").

The McCormick house is metonymic for "white trash." Signifiers of "white trash" are the front yard detritus of car repairs: an empty oilcan, discarded tires, and a car with front wheels on blocks; furthermore, the yard contains a broken refrigerator and a sofa and the garage door is skewed and seemingly broken. The inside completes the "white trash" picture: the living room boasts a neon beer sign, cinder blocks prop up a makeshift coffee table, a car seat stands in for a couch. The kitchen cupboard doors hang off their hinges and Kenny's room has a hole in the ceiling, a frameless mattress, and ripped curtains. The hallmarks of "white trash" are dirtiness and untidiness. Empty liquor bottles, oilcans, and a car engine litter the living room. The coffee table shows un-mopped spills. Kenny's clothes are scattered on the floor of his bedroom. Rats roam freely. The walls are cracked, and the house leaks when it rains. It smells like a cow's ass, according to Cartman ("Prehistoric Ice Man"). Outside, the sofa on the lawn indicates a disregard for the conventions of middle-class furniture. The white trash house rejects control and orderliness. It is the traditional TV house undone.

Conclusion

Generally, TV towns are harmless towns, such as Mayberry and Dawson's Creek; occasionally, they're more interesting, as in Twin Peaks and Cicely, Alaska. But the satirical fun begins when the small town is turned upside down and shaken. The wonderfully zany towns of Hooterville, Springfield, and South Park reveal plenty about the surreal state of Small Town, USA.

As a physical entity, South Park contains what one expects from a "small" town—with the usual satiric twists. First, there is the main street where Tom's Rhinoplasty and Jimbo's Gun Shop flank city hall. Then there are the "ticky tack"[13] houses reminiscent of Tim Burton's *Edward Scissorhands* (1990). But behind the front doors, some dark secrets molder. It's a town of limited geography, and equally limited cultural-scapes.

Then there is the town's propensity for disaster and destruction: hurricanes, shit storms, and mechanized monsters threaten its very existence. When Stan contemplates the "great times" of South Park, the montage is a testament to the destructive nature of the town:

> zombies destroy the town
>
> Trapper Keeper grabs and eats a phone booth
>
> townsfolk clobber the mutant turkeys
>
> Christopher Reeve throws a truck at people, and they duck out of the way
>
> giant fireworks snake demolishes the town
>
> a pirate ghost ship fires a cannonball, killing people
>
> pro-war and anti-war factions fight
>
> the town reenacts the Civil War
>
> people drown in a crap-slide
>
> Mecha-Streisand threatens the town

It's a cliché, but in times of adversity, no matter how devastating, South Park triumphs—the community pulls together.

The town's one claim to fame is that it has the most UFO sightings in America. Naturally, therefore, from the first episode, South Park embraces aliens. Aliens, unlike celebrities, are not threatening. They are simply observers or, in *South Park* lingo, visitors.

South Park is not a town, it's a state of mind.

Tom
[TV reporter]: I'm here live in South Park, Colorado, where citizens from Los Angeles are arriving in droves for the town's first annual film festival. This is just a small, quiet mountain community where nothing out of the ordinary ever really happens, except for the occasional complete destruction of the entire town. ("Chef's Salty Balls")

Newscaster: The people of South Park are humble and friendly. But now, a ticking time bomb of hot lava waits to engulf these people and end their miserable lives with one last fleeting moment of excruciatingly painful burning agony.

Crowd: Yeahhh.

Individual in
crowd: Hey, I'm on TV, I'm on TV. ("Volcano")

Newscaster: So, just weeks after the devastating attack of mutant genetic creatures, zombies, and Thanksgiving turkeys, the town of South Park has managed to rebuild itself, once again, be ... [Screech. Mecha-Streisand begins her destructive rampage].

Newscaster: Oh, goddamnit, not again!

Notes

1. See Gary Mattson, "Redefining the American Small Town: Community Governance," *Journal of Rural Studies* 13, no. 1 (1997): 121–30.

2. Richard Francaviglia, *Main Street Revisited: Time, Space, and Image Building in Small Town America* (Iowa City: University of Iowa Press, 1996), xxii.

3. Stephen Harper, "Zombies, Malls, and the Consumerism Debate: George Romero's Dawn of the Dead," *Americana: The Journal of American Popular Culture* 1, no. 2 (Fall 2002), http://www.americanpopularculture.com/journal/articles/fall_2002/harper.htm, accessed October 22, 2006.

4. William Kowinski, *The Malling of America* (New York: William Morrow, 1985).

5. Harper, "Zombies, Malls, and the Consumerism Debate," http://www.americanpopular culture.com/journal/articles/fall_2002/harper.htm, accessed October 22, 2006.

6. Mikhail Bakhtin, *Rabelais and His World*, trans. Helene Iswolsky (Bloomington: Indiana University Press, 1984), 21.

7. Francaviglia, *Main Street Revisited*, ibid., xxii.

8. Ibid., xii.

9. Bakhtin, *Rabelais and His World*, 10.

10. G. A. Mattson, "Redefining the American Small Town," ibid., 127.

11. Token's mansion is not in town but on the outskirts; his ostracism is complete, so Token laments in song:

> Why can't I be like all the other kids?
> They all have three-bedroom homes, broken trucks on their lawns.

12. Token Black's house, the boy's talent agency.

13. Malvina Reynolds's 1962 song "Little Boxes."

Chapter 11

Kick the Baby: The Characters

Prime-time animation is largely character driven; thus, the family of *The Simpsons* and the boys of *South Park* are central to the show's success. Stan, Kyle, Kenny, and Cartman *are South Park*—they've become as iconic as Charlie Brown. In their roles, they play somewhat naïve fools who look at the town in which they live and shake their heads; they do not understand their parents, their schoolteachers, or the events that shape their lives. It is through their investigation of contemporary society that its foibles are critiqued.

Childhood, Philippe Aries argues, is a relatively modern invention.[1] He shows how children were treated as little adults until the Middle Ages: they dressed, worked, and played with adults. Thus, he posits that childhood is a social construct. It is also an important marketing category too, as any Happy Meal purchaser can testify. Stone and Parker believe their portrayal of the boys is not far from the truth—kids are "selfish little bastards," they agreed during a *Nightline* interview.[2] In television land, children have long been objects of contention; the wise-cracking kid is as much a stereotype as the nosy neighbor. In a study of children on television, Amy Jordan concluded that TV children are manipulative and more mature than their adult counterparts.[3] Enter *South Park*, a world where the children are adults.

South Park is viewed through the eyes of the disenfranchised. The boys, like the disenfranchised classes of the carnival, view the world through fresh eyes. They are "liberated from the prevailing point of view of the world, from conventions and established truths . . . from all that is humdrum and universally accepted."[4] Like Shakespeare's naïve fools, they speak the "truth." They see the naked emperor and aren't afraid to shout it to the community and to the world at large.

Throughout the series, the children cope with life at a school of abusive teachers and ineffectual counselors. At home, they have to contend with murderous, censorious, and stupid parents. Society presents them with philosophical conundrums: Is euthanasia right? What about homosexuality, stem cell research, and war? Such issues are usually, in television land, part of the adult experience, but by filtering these problems through children, the world and its hypocrisies are exposed.

Stan Marsh

Voice: Trey Parker
DOB: October 19
Catch Phrases: Dude! Aw, crap! Cartman, you asshole. Shut up, Butters.
Talent: To see through the crap
Family: Mother Sharon (receptionist at Tom's Rhinoplasty), father Randy (geologist), sister Shelley (bully)
Defining Characteristics: Confident group leader
Most Endearing Quality: Heroic potential; social conscience; heart
Anime Role: To fight evil

Stan is the "hero" of the quartet. Every television show needs a hero, and every hero needs a quest. He quests against that which is wrong. While his deeds might not seem the stuff of superheroes, Stan doesn't tilt at windmills; he takes on the baddies: farmers who kill calves ("Fun with Veal"), Blainetologists ("Superbest Friends"), a political system that offers "lame" candidates ("Douche and Turds"). He makes his stand and leads others to fight the good fight. No wonder his anime aim is "to fight evil."

He is also the most romantic character, in both senses of the word. He is the only boy to have a steady relationship and is heartbroken at its failure, just as he is despondent to think he cannot raise an egg. But more noteworthy is his romantic idealism. Stan is a sucker for a good cause, but he is not unthinking. He likes the hippie ideology, but close examination uncovers its flaws; the Mormon lifestyle appeals, but their bizarre dogma alienates him; and Scientology—well, it was good to be the leader for a while, but Stan just can't lie.

He tries to lead an Aristotelian "good life." He believes in the golden mean and he tries to become moral and more virtuous person and to do the "best thing." Stan realizes that being a moral person involves practice, and he tries every day to improve. Sometimes he stumbles, but he stands for what he believes in and articulates the lessons he has learned: "You know, I learned something today. . . ."

Stan is the group's middle-body stratum: he rules with his heart. He is the archetypal cartoon kid; he is not as bad as Bart Simpson, Beavis, or Butt-head but he has more spine than Charlie Brown and David Hill. He is an eight-year-old Ferris Bueller. He is everyboy, a white, Midwest, eight-year-old American; he is a "good" boy and everyone's friend. Like all heroes, he is flawed, but not fatally.

Kyle Broflovski[5]

Voice: Matt Stone
DOB: May 26
Catch Phrases: You know, I've learned something today. He responds to Stan's "Oh my God, they killed Kenny" with "you bastards."
Talents: Certainly not dancing
Family: Mother Sheila (homemaker), father Gerald (lawyer), younger brother Ike (genius, Canadian)
Defining Characteristics: Jewishness, diabetes, Cartman's kidney
Most Endearing Quality: Angst about the world and his place in it
Anime Role: To protect those in need

Kyle is the group "thinker." He's reportedly the smartest and is prone to anxiety and worry. He is ruled by the upper body stratum—his head. When his father reveals that the tooth fairy is not real, Kyle questions "reality" and intellectualizes it. He reads *Space-Time and Quantum Theory* ("Dude, *this* book says there could be infinite alternate realities to every reality"); *Taoism and Zen Philosophy* ("Oh my God, *this* book says that negative and positive are the same thing; that real and not real are one"); and Descartes ("Dude, *this* book says I don't exist unless I think I do") ("Tooth Fairy"). Kyle exhibits a penchant for Cartesian rationality. He reasons through people's feelings; he explains to Cartman that Cartman didn't blow a funny fuse but that he couldn't laugh because of remorse ("Eat with Your Butt"); he sees past the materialist trappings of Blanket Jefferson's life and pities him ("Goo backs"); he realizes it's the club that's changed Chef's personality ("Return of Chef"). The difference between Kyle and Stan is best demonstrated in the exchange about the manbearpig; when confronted with the concept of a manbearpig, Kyle thinks the concept is not rational, Stan reacts emotionally:

> KYLE: That doesn't make any sense.
>
> STAN: He could be half bear, half manpig.
>
> RANDY: Boys, there's no such thing as a manbearpig. The vice president is just desperate for attention.

STAN: But I feel kind of bad for him, Dad. I don't think he has any
        friends. ("Manbearpig")

Like Stan, Kyle is basically a good kid, so good that his parents don't hire a
future self to scare him; it's why he can't be the bad boy of Fingerbang
("Fingerbang"). He is the group's conscience. He tells Cartman that he does-
n't think putting Kenny's butt on a milk carton is funny ("Eat with Your
Butt") and confronts Cartman about the ethics of entering the Special
Olympics ("Up the down Steroid"). Of all the boys, he's the most disturbed
after toilet-papering the art teacher's house ("Toilet Paper"), and it's Kyle
who Cartman fears will crack.

Kyle's nemesis is, of course, Cartman, and though they have traded insults
for seasons, recently, their animosity has escalated. Twice Kyle has bloodied
Cartman's nose ("Christmas in Canada," "Jeffersons"), and Kyle has encouraged Cartman to jump off the roof ("Cartman's Incredible Gift"). Yet the two
seem inexorably linked, even if only because they disagree—what Kyle likes
(*Family Guy*), Cartman hates ("Cartoon Wars 1"). Kyle develops a painful
hemorrhoid when Cartman inherits a million dollars and, as Cartman's fortunes grow, so does Kyle's pain. The injustice calls into question his faith:

KYLE: . . . all my life I was raised to believe in Jehovah! To believe
        that we should all behave a certain way and good things will
        come to us. I make mistakes, but every week I try to better
        myself. I'm always saying, "You know, I learned something
        today . . ." and what does this so-called God give me in
        return? A hemorrhoid. He doesn't make sense! [*to God*]
        What is your logic?! . . . I finally figured it out. You see, if
        someone like Cartman can get a million dollars and his own
        theme park, then there is no God. There's no God, dude. . . .
        There is no justice! There is no God! Do you hear me?! I
        renounce my faith! ("Cartmanland")

It's not the first time Kyle has renounced his faith ("Probably").

Kyle is confused as to exactly what being Jewish means; he apparently
understands little about his faith. He constantly seeks advice as to the role of
Judaism and its beliefs. He embraces Blainetology because it gives him a sense
of belonging "for the first time in his life" ("SuperBest Friends"). His status as
"Jew" marks Kyle as an outsider—a state he laments in his signature song,
"Lonely Jew." He attends a different scout group and a synagogue instead of a
church; he celebrates different rituals and is never quite up with the latest
fads, whether Chinpokomon or metrosexuality.

Ideologically, Kyle is a contemporary Jewish figure, and he has nothing but distain for his archetypal whiney cousin: "I spent five years in this town making a good name for Jews and this . . . this . . . stereotype shows up and wrecks it all! You know what my biggest fear is? That I'll become him. That somehow his mannerisms will start rubbing off on me, and I'll become a stereotype. I mean, I'm a Jew and he's making me hate Jews" ("Entity"). Kyle strenuously denies Cartman's Jewish stereotyping, but Cartman is correct: Kyle wears a bag of Jew gold ("Two Days Before") and cannot throw away the weapons he's just bought ("Good Times").

Kyle and Stan are almost indistinguishable, and even the creators recognize this fact and blame themselves. So much so that they decided to kill Kyle in an episode ("Kenny Dies") but changed their minds. The world is too much with Kyle.

Theodore Eric Cartman

Voice: Trey Parker
DOB: July 1
Catch Phrases: Screw you guys, I'm going home. I hate you guys. Respect my authoritay. No, Kitty, that's my potpie.
Talents: Money-making schemes
Family: Mother and father Liane (whore)
Defining Characteristic: Fat ass
Most Endearing Quality: Curmudgeonly approach to life
Anime Role: To eradicate hippies from the world

Cartman has been voted number ten in *TV Guide*'s top fifty cartoon characters and is the second scariest television character (behind Mr. Burns of *The Simpsons*).[6] He's also the only character to have a TV marathon of his twenty-five greatest TV moments (October 14–16, 2005) on Comedy Central. He might be Stan's nemesis and the rudest kid on television, but Cartman is the darling of the viewers. Why?

When viewers respond to Cartman, they're responding to a centuries-old stereotype. He exhibits many of the characteristics of one of the oldest comic stereotypes, the *Commedia dell'Arte* character, Harlequin (Arlecchino).

> Arlecchino is childlike, "lazy but energetic, stupid but clever, insolent, clownish, and ribald." Arlecchino lives in the present, forgets what is out of sight. His first attention is to food: how to get it, how to savor it, how to preserve it for later. He relishes his adroitness at getting out of difficult situations and seldom considers the consequences until it is too late. He is ignorant yet clever; his actions and moods can change in an instant.[7]

While viewers might not be familiar with Harlequin, they probably know his more recent incarnations: Fred Flintstone, Homer Simpson, and Peter Griffin. It's no coincidence that Cartman is the same larger-than-life size.

Cartman is the show's bad boy, a role he adroitly summarizes in his talent show speech:[8] "D'you know what you are? You're all a bunch of fucking cockroaches! You need people like me! You need people like me so you can point your fucking finger and say, 'That's the bad guy!'" ("Election Day"). Despite the speech, he doesn't really think he's bad:

> BUTTERS: Did you ever do anything really bad?
>
> CARTMAN: [*thinks*] Not really . . . [*In Butters' bedroom, later*]
>
> CARTMAN: Let's see. Oh, and I broke Mr. Anderson's fence and never told him about it.
>
> BUTTERS: [*writing*] Broke fence . . .
>
> CARTMAN: I took a crap in the principal's purse . . . seven times. Then there was the time I convinced a woman to have an abortion so I could build my own Shakey's Pizza. I pretended to be retarded and joined the Special Olympics. I tried to have all the Jews exterminated last spring. Uuh, oh yeah, and there's this one kid whose parents I had killed and then made into chili which I fed to the kid. ("Trapped in the Closet")

Part of Cartman's problem or charm is his amorality. He honestly doesn't understand the difference between right and wrong. He is genuinely confused when the boys are concerned that Butters has confessed to their crime:

> CARTMAN: You see, guys, it all worked itself out. Tadow, tadow, how you like me now? Feel a little silly now, Kyle? Tadow, how you like me now?
>
> KYLE: I still feel bad, Cartman.
>
> CARTMAN: What? Hu- How can you feel bad? Somebody else is gonna pay for our crime.
>
> KYLE: Yeah. That makes it even worse.
>
> CARTMAN: Bu . . . eh . . . Kyle, you don't seem to understand. We're- we're not gonna get punished for this. Ever.
>
> KYLE: I know.
>
> CARTMAN: So . . . so then, how can you feel bad?
>
> STAN: He feels guilty for doing it and for letting someone else pay for it.

CARTMAN: . . . But he's not gonna get in trouble.

STAN: It doesn't matter if you get in trouble or not, you can still feel bad. [*to Kyle*] I think you're right, Kyle. Maybe we should confess.

KENNY: (Yeah, maybe we should.)

CARTMAN: What?? Eh . . . [*tries to be upbeat*] hey, you guys! There's nothing to feel bad about! We're, we're off scot-free!

KYLE: We feel bad for other people.

CARTMAN: [*looks in disbelief*] For oth-er . . . Uh. Oww . . . Ih . . . Ih, ih, is it that . . . you think you might get in trouble later? ("Toilet Paper")

His badness is manifest in his bigotry, his rudeness, his vitriol,[9] his selfishness, and his greed. His acts are malicious and only serve to further him or his desires; he loves to be in "authoritay," not merely because he's a natural bully but because he wishes to exercise some control in his crazy world. Like his television precursor, Archie Bunker, he certainly does not go quietly into that dark night. The boy is a twenty-first-century angry young man.

Cartman's misogyny is legendary. From his mouth tumbles words of political incorrectness, he provides a manifesto for misogynistic behavior:

> I would never let a woman kick my ass. If she tried anything, I'd be like: hey, you get your bitch ass back in the kitchen and make me some pie! . . . Be a man, Stan. Say, "Heyy woman, ee, ee, you shut your mouth and make babies." . . . If a woman ever gave me crap, I'd say, "Hey, you go do my laundry and . . ." . . . Yeah, if some sissy chick tried to kick my ass, I'd be all like, "Hey, listen, missy, eh, why don't you go knit me sweater before I slap you in the face!" ("Elephant Fucks a Pig")

He is the mouthpiece of the disenfranchised male. He embodies the masculine crisis of identity.

As the only child of an overindulgent mother, Cartman is selfish. He cannot share his potpie with Kitty or food with Starvin' Marvin. He schemes to get what he wants, whether it's getting even with Scott Tenorman or going to Casa Bonita. He is a "mercilessly bully,"[10] orders his mum around, and wants everything he sees. Even the son of Satan, Damien, sees that Cartman has "emotional" problems. His solitary play indicates his loneliness and his wish for acceptance and praise:

CARTMAN
[*As Peter Panda*]: I like you Eric, you are the coolest guy in the world. This is tremendous tea.

CARTMAN: Why thank you, Peter Panda. It's a distinctive Earl Gray.

CARTMAN
[*As Polly
Prissypants*]:   Eric is the best.

CARTMAN
[*As Clyde Frog*]:   Hooray for Eric.

CARTMAN
[*As Peter Panda*]:   Eric kicks ass. ("Cartman's Mother is a Dirty Slut")

The other boys have siblings; Cartman has his dolls and fantasies. When the others say goodbye to their loved ones, he says goodbye to Clyde Frog. His loneliness is not the cultural separation Kyle experiences or Kenny's economic deprivation, his is an emotional isolation.

As the only fatherless boy in the group, Cartman searches for his father with disastrous results. When he learns his mother is his father, it only serves to increase his "difference." Knowing that he cannot find a "real" father, he seeks adult male companionship. Mr. Jefferson is his ideal father figure, a person who provides plenty of material things but lacks emotional stability. Because he always feels he is a nobody, Cartman strives to be successful; when he dreams of Fingerbang, he tosses in bed, smiling and joyfully repeating, "Yes! Yes! Yes! I'm a star, I'm a star, I'm"—but when he wakes he is peeved. "Aaawww, I'm nobody! God damnit!" ("Fingerbang") Cartman's dream "since I was th-three years old" has been to have "at least one million dollars" ("Cartmanland"). Cartman wants to write his own Horatio Alger story and he dreams up hosts of get-rich-quick schemes. It's not a new concept; Fred Flintstone did it four decades earlier. But while Fred's plans generally involved inventing a new product, Cartman's ideas reflect his postindustrial world. He sues Stan for sexual harassment ("Sexual Harassment Panda"), makes music ("Christian Hard Rock," "Fat Butt"), develops his own religion ("Probably"), negotiates a lucrative City Wok endorsement deal ("Jared Has Aides"), and manages a successful talent agency ("Wing"). Cartman's schemes are to a large extent predatory; he preys on people's gullibility by selling them dreams, ideas rather than products. The lessons are all too human and are part of Cartman's appeal. Obnoxious, rude, and overbearing as he is, he is not ground down by the system and represents the indomitable human spirit, no matter how misguided or ill informed. Cartman wants to be affluent but simply ends up being effluent.

Cartman is the human embodiment of American consumerism; he is greedy, self-serving, and misogynistic. While Stan and Kyle are everyboy(s), Cartman is everyman.

Kenny McCormick

DOB: March 22
Quotes: Mmmmmmm.
Talents: PSP
Family: Father Stuart (unemployed), unnamed mother, brother
Defining Characteristic: Muffled speech and propensity for dying
Most Endearing Quality: His honesty and his wide grasp of sexual terminology
Anime Role: Indecipherable

The po' white kid with the wide sexual knowledge, Kenny says little but still manages to have a personality. He lives on the wrong side of the tracks in relative squalor with his family. His muffled speech has been interpreted as the silencing of the non-working class, the voiceless of America. And certainly, while the creators might pooh-pooh this reading of Kenny, it's difficult to deny its veracity; why, of all the boys, did they silence the poorest one? Perhaps it can best be understood in cartoon heritage terms. Cartoon characters frequently die, only to return a few minutes later: think Wylie Coyote. He also harkens back to the silent Zeppo in the *South Park* version of the "unseen" or "missing" character.[11] Kenny's death mirrors what Bakhtin considered part of the cycle of redemption and creation. In philosophical terms, the death and redemption of Kenny gestures to the hopeful and accepting world of children. Fans responded to Kenny's silencing with a plethora of Web sites. The boy's acceptance of Kenny's deaths and resurrections indicates their acceptance of things they really don't understand, and no matter how often he dies, they know that one day he'll return.

Butters Leopold Stotch a.k.a. Professor Chaos

DOB: September 11
Catch Phrases: No! I'll get grounded, Ohhhh, it's all sticky, Oh Sweet Jesus
Talents: Tap dancing, drumming, mathematics
Family: Father Chris, Mother Linda
Defining Characteristic: Naïve honesty
Most Endearing Quality: Loyalty

While he's not strictly one of the boys, Butters has commanded considerable air time (since season four he's appeared in nearly every episode) and for a few episodes he replaced Kenny. He is the most childlike, and it is this quality that has made him one of the most popular characters, especially with fans.

He is the perennial victim and thus is the butt of many of the boy's jokes ("AWESOM-O"). He is given all the crappy jobs. He is volunteered to appear with chinballitis ("Freak Strike"), to gain/lose weight ("Jared Has Aides"), to dress as a greeting card to cheer Kyle ("Cherokee Hair Tampons"), to do the cardboard cutouts ("Crappy Christmas"), and even agrees to give handjobs to the bar patrons ("New Terrance and Phillip Trailer"), but perhaps the biggest sacrifice he was prepared to make was to "take one for the team":

CARTMAN: Well, look. Those perverts aren't going to rest until they've made love to one of us. Right? So somebody's just gonna have to go out there and and-take one for the team. And I think, in all fairness, it should be Butters.

BUTTERS: Huh?? Uh-uh well, huh, why me?

CARTMAN: Now, are you a team player or not?!

BUTTERS: Well, sure, u-uh I'm a team player-uh, I guess.

CARTMAN: Well, Butters, there is no "i" in "team."

BUTTERS: Huh-you mean to expect me to go out there and let all those . . . huhu-horny old men have their way with my fragile person?? Well just what team is this anyway?!

CARTMAN: Just go, Butters. We're running out of time.
          Well uuh-uuh-alright then.

CARTMAN: Heh, he's such a dumba-a-ass. ("NAMBLA")

Though Butters helps Cartman make amends ("Death of Cartman") when Kyle moves, Cartman transfers his anti-Semitic remarks to Butters:

STAN: You know, Cartman, you may be stoked now, but I bet you're gonna find that without Kyle around to rip on, your life is empty, and hollow.

CARTMAN: Psh! Whatever dude. I don't need Kyle to rip on, I've got Butters. Come on, Butters, you stupid Jew!

BUTTERS: Yeah! I'm a dumb Jew. ("Smug Alert")

Butters' ready acceptance of the boys' ribbing marks him the perennial victim. He has been Hitlered ("Asspen"), kidnapped ("Casa Bonita"), and maimed ("Good Times with Weapons"). However, he isn't a total wuss; after Faith +1 fails he farts on Cartman ("Christian Hard Rock") and refuses to wallow in self-pity like a "faggy" goth kid when Lexus dumps him ("Raisins").

Despite his naïveté, he is sexually quite mature. He has some strange fantasies about slapping women's "titties" ("Very Crappy Christmas"), enjoys porno videos ("Two Towers"), and is the first to successfully masturbate ("Lil'

Crime Stoppers"). He has been sexually abused by his Uncle Bud ("Return of Chef"). He knows what a fruitbowl is ("Fourth Grade") but doesn't know what a hummer is ("Fat Camp"). He's the goodie goodie that they love to hate and he knows he's a pussy ("Krazy Kripples").

Butters has undergone several harrowing experiences—his tap shoe has killed several people ("You Get Fucked Up the Ass"), his mother tried to kill him ("Butters' Very Own Show"), and his parents chained him in the basement ("Marjorine"). He lacks Stan's smarts, Kyle's angst, Kenny's indifference, and Cartman's insensitivity. His birth date succinctly summarizes Butters' angst-ridden life.

Other Boys and Girls

Secondary characters come and go throughout the series. Some have greater impact and social significance. Jimmy and Timmy are important for the diversity they bring to the show. Token's name encapsulates his role. One of the most popular characters is Towelie, the stoner towel who bores the boys but delights the fans with his lameness. Twitching Tweek, the French boy Pip, devil-spawn Damien, finger flippin' Craig, whiney cousin Kyle, Starvin' Marvin, Trent Boyett, and Scott Tenorman have all impacted on the show but remain secondary characters.

The girls have particularly been prone to disappearance. The creators acknowledge the paucity of female leads, "I guess there could be a show about girls, but this isn't it."[12] Wendy Testeburger was one of the original characters in *The Spirit of Christmas*, but since the first two seasons, she has gradually faded into the background. In the beginning, she seemed set to be the smart girl. But since then, she's become increasingly annoying. Females are usually presented as foils to the boys' burgeoning curiosity about the opposite gender. In "Bebe's Boobs Destroy Society," Bebe becomes smarter, cooler, and much more interesting when her breasts develop. That boys do not understand girls is clear in "Marjorine," in which Butters is given a brief glimpse into that strange tribe, female. In Home Ec, the girls are taught to expect money and security from marriage and from men in particular. A subtly misogynistic show, *South Park* generally portrays the girls as bitchy, controlling, and materialistic.

The Adults

Generally, the adults have shown themselves to be incapable, unreliable, and generally poor role models. The boys learn not to rely on authority figures, with good reason. The parents have threatened their physical well-being—

parents are prone to chop off their penises, give them diseases, and let them die.

Thank goodness for Chef.

Chef

He believes in aliens and Mr. Hankey, has parents who conduct voodoo-ish ceremonies, and watches *Sanford and Son*. He drives a green Town and Country station wagon with wood panels, dresses as Evel Knievel for Halloween, and has sparred with Jesus. He calls the children "crackers" and was sent to intolerance camp because he called Garrison a sick queer. His real name is Jerome McEroy, but the town knows him better as Chef.

Chef's major role is as the boys' mentor. He is their *de facto* parent and answers their most difficult questions: "Dag-nabbit children! How come every time you come in here you gotta be askin' me questions that I shouldn't be answering?! 'Chef, what's the clitoris?' 'What's a lesbian, Chef?' 'How come they call it a rim job, Chef?' For once, can't just come in here and say, 'Hi Chef. Nice day, isn't it?'" ("Fat Camp"). Sometimes his advice is controversial. "Look, children, this is all I'm going to say about drugs. Stay away from them, there's a time and a place for everything and it's called college. Do you understand?" ("Ike's Wee Wee"). But generally, he talks plainly to the boys and gets sick of their parents shirking their responsibilities. He thinks the parents should provide sex education (not the school) and thinks that parents are too eager to drug their children and label them ADD, "Damnit, children, you don't need drugs to make you pay attention in school! In my day, if we didn't pay attention we got a belt to the bottom! Now they're tryin' to cure everything with drugs!" ("Timmy"). During his time in South Park, he was the town's voice of reason; at times, it seems that he is the only sensible adult in the community.

But he's not just a talker; he's also a man of action. He rallies the city to fight the mutant turkeys, mobilizes the fight against Mecha-Stresiand, and takes the children to see John Edwards when Cartman's channeling Kenny ("Biggest Douche"). He has taken a stand against the racist flag and even sacrifices himself during the hippie eradication ("Die Hippie Die"). He contributes to the community in a meaningful way and serves on the town's council as public safety officer.

Chef is most noted for his libido—and for his libidinous songs. His attitude toward sex is pre-AIDS and he tends to be chauvinistic:

> CARTMAN: I don't think my pig would want to make love to that stupid elephant.

CHEF: Sure they would. But you're gonna have to get 'em in the mood.

STAN: So how do we do that?

CHEF: Do what I do, get 'em goood and drunk.

CHEF: Ohh, children, you just can't stick a drunk pig with a drunk elephant, and, and, expect them to do the mattress mambo. You need to set the mood. Let me show you boys what I'm talking about. . . .

KYLE: Aren't they ever gonna wake up?

CHEF: Oh, they will. It's gonna be one ugly sight.

KYLE: I thought you said the wonder of Mother Nature was a beautiful thing.

STAN: Yeh, when does Mother Nature go from beautiful to ugly?

CHEF: Usually about 9:30 in the morning, children. ("Elephant Fucks a Pig")

He explains to the boys that one pays a prostitute to leave, so she doesn't hang around after sex and "talk and talk and talk and talk" ("Fat Camp"). He likes his women young and attractive; he doesn't find Ms. Choksondik attractive, even though she has large breasts. Similarly, he thinks all women get fat after they "trap" a man:

CHEF: Well, if you want him to get really fat as fast as possible, one of you will have to marry him.

STAN: Marry him?

CHEF: It definitely worked for every woman I ever met. ("Jared Has Aides")

Chef likes to seduce but not to be intimate with women. His energies go into making love but not being in love.

Chef is to be much envied; he has led an exciting life filled with famous people and sexual encounters, he holds a stress-free job, he has the respect of the community and the joys of children without the responsibilities. He is an antidote to the ineffectual, bored married men and the lonely, love-starved single ones. Clearly, he is to be much admired. He is full bodied and the show focuses on his lower body; he focuses on his genitals and sexual satisfaction.

Unfortunately, the voice of Chef, Isaac Hayes, left the series after the controversial Scientology episode. However, Chef had been appearing less and less since the first season.

Chef is currently in *South Park* limbo.

Season and number of episodes	Number of appearances by Chef	Percentage
Season 1, 13	13	100
Season 2, 18	12	66
Season 3, 17	11	64
Season 4, 17	7	41
Season 5, 14	8	57
Season 6, 16	7	43
Season 7, 15	6	40
Season 8, 14	4	28
Season 9, 7	2	28

Mr. Garrison

Catch Phrase: Imagine that!

Words we thought we'd never hear from Mr. Garrison: Damn this beautiful face of mine, damn it to hell.

Most Endearing Quality: Mr. Slave

Named for William Lloyd Garrison, a radical antislavery activist.

As every viewer and TV critic knows, Mr. Garrison is mentally unstable;[13] he's ill-informed, impatient, rude, racist, and bigoted. He tried to kill Kathie Lee Gifford, stole Mr. Mackey's marijuana, wrote an award-winning homoerotic book, and has pedophile tendencies. He's the worst person to put in charge of children, so in *South Park,* of course, he's a grade-school teacher.

In the earliest seasons, Garrison was mostly defined by his unusual teaching methods. His lessons demonstrated an obsession with popular culture. He uses television shows such as *Love Boat* and *Medical Center* as teaching tools, and teaches *Barnaby Jones* as cultural text:

> MR. GARRISON: Okay, children, what do you think Barnaby Jones meant when he said, "This is not a victimless crime"? Anybody? Children, were you paying attention?!
>
> KYLE: Mr. Garrison, we've been watching *Barnaby Jones* repeats for eight days now. It's hard to keep paying attention.
>
> MR. GARRISON: Oh, well excuse me, Kyle! Why don't you just *forget* what Barnaby Jones has to say?! Why don't you *not* pay attention to Barnaby Jones and then let's see how far *you* get in society?! Okay, Stanley, why don't you tell us how Barnaby Jones knew the poison was in the milk? ("Roger Ebert")

In this way, the show parodies cultural studies as legitimate texts for study (such as this book). Yet, sometimes Mr. Garrison's cultural lessons are socially spot on: "Children, since today is Halloween, I thought we should learn something about the great horror writer Jackie Collins" ("Pink Eye"), and certainly Collins's sex and shopping fictional world is a horrifying one. He also presents an amalgam of bizarre historical "facts," such as "Christopher Columbus discovered America and was the Indian's best friend. He helped the Indians win their war against Fredrick Douglass and freed the Hebrews from Napoleon and discovered France" ("Anal Probe"). Aligning the Christopher Columbus fact with the subsequent ridiculous statements questions the veracity of historical "fact" and brings into question Garrison's own education. Could part of his inadequate education be that he has a master's degree in engineering from Denver Community College? On the other hand, engineering helped him invent a mode of transport that he and roughly 10 percent of the population find particularly enjoyable ("Entity"). He is a product and therefore a critique of the educational system in America.

Eventually, his nontraditional teaching methods are brought to the attention of the school board:

CHAIRMAN: Mr. Garrison, after very careful review the school board believes that you should take a . . . hiatus from teaching. Indefinitely.

MR. GARRISON: What??

BOARD MEMBER: Frankly, your conduct has been somewhat disconcerting.

CHAIRMAN: Did you know that not one of your students knew who Sam Adams was?

MR. GARRISON: Well, who cares about a guy that makes beer?! Jesus Christ, I'm trying to teach history! ("Cherokee Hair Tampons")

The school board decides Garrison should have break while the "child molestation thing dies down a bit" ("Cherokee Hair Tampons"). Garrison's hiatus from teaching gives him the space to finally come to terms with his sexuality.

He is the antithesis of the nurturing, patient teacher. He is remarkably dismissive and disinterested in the boys' welfare:

MR. GARRISON: Uh, uh, Stanley, can I talk to you for a minute?

STAN: Okay.

MR. GARRISON: I couldn't help but notice that black eye you have. Are there problems at home?

STAN: Yes.

MR. GARRISON:	Oh dear. Here, Stanley, sit down, have some cocoa, and tell your friend Mr. Hat all about it.
MR. HAT:	I'm your friend, Mr. Hat, Stan. You can tell me anything. Now, who hits you, is it your father or your mother?
STAN:	Oh, neither. It's my sister.
MR. GARRISON:	Your sister?!? Oh for Pete's sake, don't be such a little wuss. Stop wasting Mr. Hat's time with pansy little foo-foo problems, and give me back my cocoa! ("Elephant Fucks a Pig")

He is quick to point out the boys' faults: "Noo, that's a caesarian section, Eric, but that's okay, remember, there are no stupid questions, just stupid people" ("Starvin' Marvin"). And he ridicules everyone. He calls Officer Barbrady a "dumbass" and a "retard" ("Chicklover") and Cartman a "butt-for-brains" ("Hooked on Monkey Fonics"). When Mark Cotswolds joins the class and impresses Garrison with his knowledge, his praise of Mark comes at the expense of the rest of the class:

MR. GARRISON:	. . . Yes, Mark?
MARK:	The answer is 1492. However, the Americas had already been discovered by many before him, including the Vikings and the Native Americans. And therefore, your question is a charade. . . .
MR. GARRISON:	Well, very impressive, Mark. You should be able to throw the grading curve and flunk *all* these little bastards. ("Korn's Groovy Pirate Ghost Mystery")

This abuse isn't limited to children, however.

Garrison is the town's most overt adult bigot. Despite his sexual orientation, he is homophobic and his favorite abusive term is "faggot." He unsuccessfully challenged gay marriage laws. Garrison/Mr. Hat is a member of the KKK and is instrumental in ridding South Park of richers. Only in the final scene is his animosity fully revealed:

MR. GARRISON:	That's great! And now we can sell all their homes, and become . . . millionaires!
MEN:	What?
JIMBO:	But then you had us do all that for nothin'. Don't you see: If you get rich sellin' these homes, then there will still be rich people in South Park.
RANDY:	Yeah. You'd become what you hate.

MR. GARRISON: Well yeah, but at least I got rid of all those damn ni-. ("Here
                 Comes the Neighborhood")

Every Christmas he asks if they can get rid of the Mexicans, and his "Merry
Fucking Christmas" is a masterpiece of cultural and religious insensitivity:

> Hey there, Mr. Hinduist, Merry Fuckin' Christmas!
> Drink eggnog and eat some beef, and pass it to the Missus.
> In case you haven't noticed, it's Jesus' birthday.
> So get off your heathen Hindu ass and fuckin' celebrate. ("Mr. Hankey's
>   Christmas Classics")

"Merry Fucking Christmas" is, in other words, pure Garrison.

Mr. Hankey

Mr. Hankey, the cheery brown poo who wears a jaunty Christmas cap and
lives in the South Park sewer, is based on a story told to Matt Parker by his
father to teach Matt to flush the toilet. Mr. Hankey premiered in the first
Christmas episode ("Mr. Hankey, the Christmas Poo"). Mr. Hankey is the
contemporary Frosty the Snowman/Tinkerbell who requires belief and a sta-
ble sewage system to survive. He provides Christmas magic for the boys (and
the town) and even supplants Jesus, who sits alone singing "Happy Birthday"
to himself on Christmas day. Hankey's concerns are not for the boys' spiritual
well-being but for their hygiene. A chirpy shit is a fitting *South Park* icon to
bring Christmas cheer and advice on cleanliness.

The Adult Females

Most cartoon females rarely achieve their own personalities; they are usually
defined by their relationships with their children and/or their husbands—
Peg Hill, Marge Simpson. Sometimes women manage to star in their own
episodes, but these are usually aberrant and show them adopting transgres-
sive behavior (for example, Marge Simpson and Ruth Powers in "Marge on
the Lam"). South Park has a fairly diverse female population (Mrs. Crabtree,
Nurse Gollum, and Ms. Choksondik), and some have positions of authority
(Principal Victoria and Mayor McDaniels), but the majority of females on
the show are the boys' mothers. Sharon Marsh is defined by her role as
mother; she is "everymom." She is polite, quiet, supportive, and contributes
little in the way of narrative interest. Kenny's mother doesn't even have a
first name.

Kyle's mum, Sheila Broflovski, is the most vocal and politically active of the mothers. She's the nagging, overbearing Jewish mother who wha-wha-what's her way from one cause to another. No wonder Principal Victoria asks, "What's pissing you off today?" when Sheila visits the school. Sheila anthro-pomorphizes the creators' struggle against middle-class sensibilities. In Sheila's crusades against denominational Christmases and Terrance and Phillip, she is the censor cartoonized. The sheer force of her personality drives the other South Parkers to participate in her crusades, but they don't really support her; they laugh at their own toilet jokes as a counterpoint to her rigid censorship. They decry her politically correct Christmas pageant. It is no accident that as the series progresses she has receded into the back-ground; she has become virtually redundant, because the show has attracted little in the way of censorship concerns or outcries. Basically, the creators don't need her as a mouthpiece any more.

Liane Cartman, as every fan knows, is based on Trey Parker's ex-fiancée. She is the most interesting "female" character if only because she breaks every televi-sion rule proscribed for women. "Bad" mothers such as Peg Bundy usually eschew domesticity; however, Liane keeps the house spotless and endlessly bakes for her son. Women who smoke crack should live in squalor and be incapable of anything except seeking out their next high; however, Liane functions as an upright member of the community. Liane is the antithesis of the other South Park mothers. She does not mind if Cartman watches Terrance and Phillip, she farts in front of the boys and makes a joke of it ("Spontaneous Combustion"), has sex toys, and, of course, has many sexual peccadilloes. Though she's a prosti-tute, she is not defined by her sexuality and it's not expressed as power (as in the case of Mayor McDaniels); her sexuality is normalized as an economic neces-sity—she does it to support her family. The boys might make fun of her, but Liane is not reviled or rejected by the other adults. She does not prove a threat to the other families or mothers, which is strange, because Liane is the antithesis of the family unit. She does not need a male; she survives and copes well on her own.[14] If Liane were not a mother, she would be less problematic. Usually a crack-smoking prostitute produces a monstrous mother—a woman who neg-lects her children or tries to kill them. The Greek root of "monsters," *teras*, means both "horrible and wonderful."[15] Liane is truly monstrous in her maternal role as indulgent mother. As head of a nontraditional, postmodern, new-millennium family, she represents a new female potential, a socially acceptable mother who is allowed her own sexual agency and her own ambivalent gender. She might look like your average mum, but she's a sexually active sex worker who uses drugs. This is one very subversive woman.

The most monstrous mother is, of course, Linda Stotch. Outwardly a loving and caring mother and wife, Linda's mind becomes unhinged by her husband's sexual betrayal and she tries to kill her son. Her monstrosity is the result of temporary insanity; she eventually returns to her normal, grounded self. However, in later episodes the Stotches have another problem to face.

Individual Families

The dysfunctional television family is nothing new. Still, there persists the belief that *Leave It to Beaver* is the archetypal television family—in fact, the reverse is true. The nuclear family of two parents and 2.5 children at home is rarely the case on television and almost never the case when it comes to situation comedies. The jokes come at the TV families' supposed deviance from the normative nuclear family: the magic of *Bewitched*, the strangeness of *The Addams Family*, the scariness of *The Munsters*, the working-class sensibility of *Roseanne*, and the perversity of the Bundys. Playing unhappy families is part of *South Park*'s myth-debunking philosophy; behind closed doors lurk some dark secrets.

Unhappy Families?

The most terrifying family is the Stotch[16] family. Butters lives in constant fear of his parents' disapproval; he can never please them, and they ground him for many imagined transgressions ("How to Eat with Your Butt"). His parents believe in corporal punishment and, much to Cartman's delight, they beat him ("Jared Has Aides"). Butters is so browbeaten that he has learned to confess to crimes he hasn't committed. His self-condemnation shows how parental disapproval mars children: "Well, I'm just a little asshole, is what I am. When God made me, he must have not been payin' very close attention, 'cause I turned out wrong! Just plain wrong!" ("Toilet Paper"). Clearly, Butters is one disturbed child, and he commonly repeats variations of his awareness of his failings: "Why, I oughta learn to control my behavior! I should be ashamed of myself." Butters offers this plaintive description of his deep and abiding unhappiness: "I don't think I'm very happy. I always fall asleep to the sounds of my own screams. . . . And then I always get woken up in the morning by the sounds of my own screams. Do you think I'm unhappy?" ("Super Best Friends"). To say his parents are weird is an understatement; Linda tried to kill Butters ("Butters' Very Own"), and they chained him in the basement ("Marjorine"). "Butters' Own Show" perfectly mirrors the duality of the family; behind the happy tunes and the bright sitcom façade lurks a horrifying picture of American family life.

The *Marshes* are the most normal unit, an extended family of two relatively ordinary parents; a suicidal, randy grandfather; an overbearing, cruel sister; and Stan. Their problems arise as the narrative needs to explore social issues such as divorce, child abduction, euthanasia. Of the two parents, Randy is by far the worst; his predilection for violence, alcohol, and his rampant stupidity have embarrassed Stan ("Losing Edge," "Bloody Mary," "Child Abduction Is Not Funny"). However, after a recent "miracle" cure, he seems to have beaten the bottle. Randy believes in miracles because they're Roman Catholics, though they have been disillusioned and started an Atheist's Club ("Red-Hot Catholic Love"). He and Sharon support political correctness; they attended Woodstock, Randy leads the antiwar cause, and they have scolded Stan for his timecist comments ("Goobacks"). They are the typical Midwest family in that inimitable *South Park* way.

The *Broflovski* household is a Jewish family. Gerald is a lawyer but doesn't make as much money as the other South Park lawyer, Mr. Black. He has experimented sexually with Randy Marsh and suffered penile dysfunction. Like Randy, Gerald has an addiction: his is gambling. Generally, he's a fairly mild-mannered person, but he does have a tendency toward smugness ("Smug Alert"). He reads the newspaper and ignores his wife, Sheila. Sheila rules the house with an iron hand and is a strict disciplinarian, or so she likes to think. Baby Ike (a.k.a Peter Gints) is Kyle's adopted Canadian brother and the object of Kyle's favorite game, Kick the Baby. Ike hails from the mostly-silent school of cartoon babies, such as Maggie Simpson, Pebbles, and Bam Bam; largely he is a narrative device which allows Kyle to discover sibling love. The Broflovskis are of course defined by their Jewishness, and thus are separated somewhat from the other families.

Despite their seeming solidity, the *South Park* families teeter on a brink of imminent collapse. The ease and swiftness with which parents and children are dispatched gesture to the delicate fabric of family ties. Children only have to say "molestation" ("Wacky Molestation Adventure") and their parents are incarcerated; parents no sooner hear about stranger danger than they wall up the city and send their children away ("Child Abduction"); and not voting means banishment ("Douch and Turd"). The parents are so busy protesting and protecting their children that they spend little time with them, much to Stan's disgust: "'Damn it! You know, I think that if parents would spend less time worrying about what their kids watch on TV, and more time worrying about what's going on in their kid's lives, this world would be a much better place" ("Death"). Randy's drinking, Gerald's smugness, Sheila's protesting,

Liane's whoring—is it any wonder the children perform adult roles through-out the series?

The Aesthetics of Appearance

Like all cartoon characters, the *South Park* crew looks the same season after season. They don't age and they wear the same clothes; this point is made clear in "Super Best Friends." When the boys shave their heads and dress in the same clothes, they cannot tell each other apart. Only Cartman is recognizable—because of his fat ass.

Oversized people on South Park (Cartman, Chef, Sheila Broflovski, Choksondik, and Sally Struthers) embody abundance, selfishness, greed, and excess, and are paradoxically celebrated and condemned. Cartman's bloated body is a site of American excess. His eating is not the eating of hunger but of greed, of extreme consumption. Chef's generous size refers not to his eating or occupation but to his voracious sexual appetite. Sheila Broflovski's size demonstrates her power, her dominance over family and community. The corporeal flesh is graphically figured in large bodies, bodies that are symbolic of America.

Of course, the body has to be clothed. Pragmatically, clothes provide visual shorthand to differentiate among the cast, but more importantly, they impart narrative clues. Jesus and Randy wear iconic clothing: Jesus' white flowing robes and halo mark him as the Son of God, and Randy's white coat and pocket protector indicate he's in scientist mode ("Spontaneous Combustion"). Seriousness and business suits go hand in hand: Chef exchanges his chef hat and apron for suit and tie when he takes a job as an accountant ("Succubus"); the boys don dark-colored business suits and ties when they open a talent agency ("Wing") or work on a news team ("Quest for Ratings"). Gayness is illustrated through clothing as well. At the tolerance awards, Garrison wears a *South Park* version of "drag" (that is to say, it is worn over his usual clothes). His showgirl outfit is a mantle; he is performing the outrageous, camp gay—the most challenging to normative heterosexuality. More recently, Cartman has been adopting varying outfits—the disheveled look appropriate for an operations manager ("Marjorine") or stressed cop ("Lil' Crime Stoppers") and an orange pest-control suit for hippie extermination ("Die, Hippie, Die"). Lastly, the most iconic piece of clothing is the boys' headgear. Kyle wears a *Fargo*-style cap (ushanka), which is particularly functional for children in very cold weather but ultimately screams, "Kyle's mum is a controlling mum." Kenny's parka has the added advantage of having a hood that muffles his speech, and when he's shocked or wants to retreat from the world, he pulls the drawstrings tighter. When they turn into anime characters, the boys' body shapes alter but their hats remain the same (except for Kenny, whose parka is now a Japanese-style peasant hat).

Clothing is also a marker of ethnicity, politics, and culture. When Cartman seeks his father(s), he adopts various ethnic garb. His Native American outfit includes a headband with feathers, "war paint," a fringed jacket, and an eagle necklace. When Cartman performs black, he wears a tracksuit and sneakers, a Flava Flav-style large watch, a styled Afro wig, and a ring that says "pie."[17] He manages political incorrectness even in clothing. An outward sign of Chef's rejection of white culture is his dashiki ("Chef Goes Nanners"). The OC coach wears a purple and orange tracksuit and sports an earring; his outfit is street cool and particularly hip-hop cool; Randy is a contrast in his dark-colored cardigan, shirt, and nondescript pants ("You Got Fucked"). Chief Runs with Premise wears an elaborate headdress with his suit ("Red Man's Greed"). Wing, Mr. Kim's wife, wears a cheongsam ("Wing"). Jimbo and Skeeter wear the clothes of the redneck: Jimbo wears a green hunting jacket and orange cap, while Skeeter boasts the checked shirt-and-jeans version. Stuart McCormick wears a blue-collar costume: blue work pants and a white t-shirt underneath a blue work shirt that would have his name and company name embroidered on the pocket, although he's chronically unemployed; his baseball cap says "Scotch." Hippies wear headbands, tie-dyed t-shirts with peace signs, jeans, and sandals. They are the antithesis of the carefully groomed and fashion-conscious metrosexual; the unkempt hippies suggest laziness, disdain for propriety, but, most shocking of all, a lack of consumerism.

Conclusion

As *South Park* fans know, the characters are based upon the families and friends of the creators. But that alone cannot sustain the characters throughout the course of a decade. We've seen Randy Marsh develop into a pants-around-the-ankle alcoholic. As is normal in any television series of length, the cast changes over time. New characters are added for specific purposes; some allow for examination of social issues. Timmy is an example. But even Timmy was not enough. Jimmy added "handicapable" to the show's discourse about disability. Butters and Tweek became major players during the time Kenny was dead. The importance of the characters is underscored by the fandom division into Tweek or Butters factions.

In the topsy-turvy *South Park* world, the children call shenanigans on the adults and on society in general. In their roles as their town's saviors and its conscience, the boys display more maturity and wisdom than their elders.

Mostly, they have to right their parents' wrongs or guide the community on important issues such as big business takeovers ("Gnomes"), the state flag ("Chef Goes Nanners"), gay marriage ("Follow that Egg"), and war ("I'm a Little Bit Country"). They have mobilized the town when it's in danger and have saved it from mechanized monsters ("Mecha-Streisand"), zombies ("Pink Eye"), Hollywood imperialism ("Chef's Salty Balls"), Goobacks ("Goobacks"), mad planetarium directors ("Roger Ebert"), and mutant turkeys ("Starvin' Marvin"). Each week they embark on a quest to save either the town or their lifestyles. The world handed to them is imperfect, and they seem to be the only ones to see this and try to make it better.

> Poster in Mr. Mackey's office: "If you don't have a dad, you're a bastard."

Notes

1. Philippe Aries, *Centuries of Childhood: A Social History of Family Life* (New York: Vintage, 1962), 353.

2. Jake Tapper and Dan Morris, "Secrets of South Park", September 22, 2006, http://abc news.go.com/Nightline/print?id=2479197, accessed October 21, 2006.

3. Amy Jordan, "The Portrayal of Children on Prime-Time Situation Comedies," *Journal of Popular Culture* 29, no. 3, 1995: 139–47.

4. Mikhail Bakhtin, *Problems of Dostoyevsky's Poetics*, ed. and trans. Caryl Emerson (Minneapolis: University of Minnesota Press, 1984), 34.

5. Kyle's last name has been alternately given as Broslovski, Broflofski, Broflovski, and Brovlofski in the series, although the characters say "Broflovski" or "Broslovski."

6. Brian Bellmont, "TV's Top 10 Scariest Characters," MSNBC, June 29, 2002, http:// www.msnbc.msn.com/id/9699636, accessed November 1, 2005.

7. Dave Claudon, "Harlequin and Mezzetino," David's Gallimauphry, http://www.david claudon.com/arte/commedia2.html, accessed November 11, 2005.

8. Cf. Tony Montana in *Scarface* (1983).

9. He hates rainbows, dolphins, Johnnie Cochran, Dr. Lott, Kyle's mom, Butters, Tweek, Kenny, Kyle (various), and "you guys" in general. But his biggest hatred is reserved for "goddamn hippies"; when they infiltrate South Park, he realizes his finest hour.

10. Kristen Baldwin, "South Park's Problem Child," *Entertainment Weekly*, December 25, 1998, 53.

11. Allen W. Ellis, "Yes, Sir: The Legacy of Zeppo Marx," *The Journal of Popular Culture*, 37 no. 1, 2003: 15–27.

12. Diane Eicher, "'South Park' Won't Evolve This Season," *Denver Post*, April 7, 1999, F5.

13. He is described as psychologically disturbed (Eric Mink), psychotic (Jimmy Kimmel), mentally disturbed (Sylvia Rubin), "mentally unbalanced" (McFarland), demented (Deggans), deranged (Paula Span), neurotic (Patrick McDonald; Simon Yeaman the Australian). Others eschew psychological terms and consider him a jerk (Hodges), nerdy (McDonald and Yeaman),

wacked-out [*sic*] (Jeff Simon), warped (Neil Justin), and even "flaky" (Endrst and Collins). Caryn James finds him a "spookily mild-mannered teacher," a rather Superman-esque description.

14. Previously, television's single moms had developed from the 1970s' reliance on a male friend (Mrs. Partridge) to female as male friend (*Kate and Allie*). Lauren Rabinovitz, "Sitcoms and Single Moms: Representations of Feminism on American TV," *Cinema Journal* 29, no. 1, 1989, 3–19.

15. Rosi Braidotti, "Mothers, Monsters, and Machines," *Writing on the Body: Female Embodiment and Feminist Theory*, ed. Katie Conboy, Nadia Medina, and Sarah Stanbury (New York: Columbia University Press, 1997), 62.

16. Originally Swanson, Jimmy takes Butters' discarded last name in "Krazy Kripples."

17. Of course, it had to be a food item.

Chapter 12

Teaching Children to Despise Paris Hilton: The Celebrities

As part of *South Park*'s interrogation of contemporary culture, how could it ignore celebrity? Daniel Boorstin posits that a celebrity is "a person well known for their well-knownness."[1] But perhaps the best summary of fame comes during a typical *South Park* exchange. Wendy Testeburger, like many other people, does not understand Paris Hilton's appeal:

> WENDY: I don't get it. What does she do?
>
> ANNIE: She's super-rich!
>
> WENDY: . . . but what does she *do*?
>
> RED: She's totally spoiled and savvy.
>
> WENDY: What does she *do*?!
>
> MAN: She's a whore. ("Stupid Spoiled Whore")

Wendy fails to "get" Paris's celebrity status because apparently one does not have to *do* anything to become a celebrity. The puzzling answer, "she's a whore," underscores the cult of celebrity and poses the conundrum: aren't all celebrities whores, media whores?

What could be more carnivalesque than the celebrity world? It's no coincidence that the outrageous tabloids, the most non-sanctioned slice of the print media,[2] first saturated their columns with celebrity gossip. *South Park*'s theatrical rantings and ravings about celebrities expose the most seminal notions of Bakhtin's laughter and the mighty brought low. Celebrities are the sideshow freaks of the carnival—they provide laughter and as much lower body humor as a *South Park* episode can take, whether it's a turkey-inserting Martha Stewart, a farting George Clooney, or a butt-headed Ben Affleck. If you doubt the marriage of carnival with celebrity, then tune into *Celebrity Deathmatch* (1998–2002; 2006–).

When television shows used celebrities in the past, they walked on, said their lines, and walked off. However, in cartoon land, the use of celebrity is more complicated. *South Park* offers a range of "celebrity" possibilities: celebrities can appear as themselves, such as Ben Affleck does ("Fat Butt"); sometimes their looks are appropriated, such as David Hasselhoff's face on Mr. Garrison ("Tom's Rhinoplasty"); at other times, they are simply mentioned. Of course, the most popular way to use a celebrity in animation is the celebrity voice-over—the creators' least preferred option.

South Park has tried to quarantine itself from celebrity guest appearances. After only a few episodes, many stars clamored to "appear" on the hottest new television property. "We kind of realized we could probably meet whoever we wanted. And so the first person we wanted to meet was the chick from *Species*,"[3] claimed Parker. Since then, they've consistently rejected applications for appearances. Penelope Cruz[4] and Tiger Woods[5] have expressed interest, but have not appeared to date. Michael Dorn wished he had been asked to do his voice-over in "Fun with Veal."[6] Antonio Banderas is waiting for the phone call: "I love his [Trey Parker's] movies, all those Troma productions, *Cannibal! The Musical* is one of my favorites and *Orgazmo* is fantastic. If these guys call me one day I might do a movie with them. I am totally serious."[7] The difficulty of getting onto a *South Park* episode creates a desire to be on the show; it's a fascinating glimpse into reverse psychology like Cartman's "You Can't Come" technique ("Cartmanland"). Celebrities want to appear on the show, certainly not for the money as guests earn less than $300 per episode with no residuals,[8] even though they know their appearance will most likely result in ridicule.

With typical *South Park* aplomb, the creators assign the biggest names the most menial roles. These minor roles deliberately undermine a celebrity's status; some don't mind and others do. George Clooney barked Stan's gay dog and Jay Leno meowed Cartman's Kitty, but Jerry Seinfeld refused to do voice of mutant turkey #4. Parker jokes they "only do the big stars."[9] Clearly, part of their celebrity manifesto is humiliation—or at least a refusal to succumb to celebrity fascination. As Eric Mink points out, the show offers a "brutally honest commentary on the hypocrisy, rampant commercialism and cult of celebrity that infect our culture."[10]

Malcolm McDowell and Cheech and Chong pose a complex deconstruction of celebrity. In "Great Expectations," McDowell proclaims his status as "a British Person"; his accent confirms the truth of this statement. What he fails to tell the viewers is that he is a celebrated actor; by declaring himself an anonymous British Person, he negates his celebrity status. Similarly, Cheech and Chong do not perform as noted comedians in "Cherokee Hair Tampons." Cheech, a Hispanic, and Chong, an Amerasian, are deployed as Native Americans. Their celebrity status is disregarded; they represent an amorphous ethnicity. Their otherness is emphasized, not their celebrity status. The underutilization of a celebrity's fame reminds viewers that the celebrity is simply a person paid to entertain.

Personalizing Celebrity

The self-indulgent nature of the show allows the creators to target celebrities they personally find offensive. They admit that when they were struggling producers in Hollywood, they were pissed off and "just wanted to do a show which ripped on celebrities and how much people loved celebrities."[11] So now they populate Hell with an eclectic cross section: entertainers (Michael Landon, Gene Siskel, Conan O'Brien, Jerry Garcia, Tiny Tim, Walter Matthau, George Burns, Dean Martin, and Bob Hope); politicians (Hitler, JFK and Son, and Mao Tse Tung), royalty (Princess Diana), and even serial murderers (Jeffrey Dahmer and Adolf Hitler). To date they have lampooned celebrities from television, sport, religion, politics—the list is impressive (see the season-by-season summaries at the end of this chapter). Some celebrities have been more cruelly caricatured than others. Sally Struthers was so upset by her first *South Park* appearance that, it is rumored, she cried. Robert Redford is slammed for the Sundance Film Festival; clearly, Parker and Stone still smart from their rejection at the hands of the Sundance Film Festival committee. However, the most reviled *South Park* celebrity is Barbra Streisand.

In the first season, Streisand morphs into the "most threatening thing known to mankind, Mecha-Streisand" ("Mecha-Streisand"). She tries to destroy the town but is defeated by the good guys (Leonard Maltin, Sidney Poitier, and Robert Smith). But, like all feared monsters, she returns. The following season she is the spooky face of spooky vision ("Spooky Fish") and in *Bigger, Longer and Uncut*, the filthiest two words Cartman utters to defeat his enemy are "Barbra Streisand." On November 2, 2000, nearly three years after "Mecha-Streisand" first aired, Stone and Parker still described Streisand as "pure evil":

CONAN O'BRIEN: Something much more serious. Now, speaking of people that would be angry with you, Barbra Streisand. You guys have gone after Barbra Streisand time and time again. You seem to enjoy mocking Barbra Streisand.

TREY: Its not moh-, we're not mocking Barbra Streisand, we hate her.

MATT: We hate her.

TREY: And it's . . . People are like- People are always like, "Don't you get sick of making fun of, you know, of hating Barbra Streisand?" It's like "No, do you get sick of hating Satan?" "No."

CONAN: Right. When you see evil you must fight it!

TREY: She's lots of pure evil!

MATT: Yeah. Actually, we actually view our job like people who-ugh, like we are kinda freaky because we do view our job as we are fighting the good fight against evil whether its Barbra Streisand . . .

Why do Matt and Trey hate Streisand? In an interview, they explained:

[W]hen [Streisand] said she would never perform in Colorado—where she has a mansion—if a controversial ban on gay rights was passed by that state's legislature. We're both from Colorado and it was like, "Fuck you, lady! Who the hell do you think you are that you're gracing us with your presence?" She is the worst example of a celebrity who should just keep her mouth shut. She sounds like an idiot.[12]

She, in turn, is on a one-woman crusade to stop *South Park*, and calls it "an insult to a civilized society."[13] She has claimed that "shows like 'South Park' and 'Beavis & Butt-head' are the source of all negativity in society."[14] Strangely enough, she seems destined to be linked with her portrayal as Mecha-Streisand, and the show is invoked in reviews of her CDs.[15]

Trey and Matt also "really, really hate" Phil Collins. They claim that losing to Collins at the Academy Awards was an insult:

CONAN: You haven't been here since you got that Oscar nomination . . . for the song.

TREY: Yeah, it's great to write a song that like loses to a Phil Collins ballad. Like that's, like that's how good your song was, buddy!

CONAN: Well, you can't beat that man. Aaaah, you can try but you just can't.[16]

Clutching his recently won Oscar, Collins crusades against Timmy ("Timmy 2000"). He is the bad guy who campaigns against the public's support of Timmy. His appearance is comical (crossed eyes, balding pate, hairy arms, and overzealous arm waving), prompting other characters to point and laugh at him. He is a "dick" ("Timmy 2000"). When the boys start grooving to

Collins, Chef realizes something is radically wrong. He doses the boys with Ritalout and Collins's music is no longer attractive; Collins is booed off the stage. Collins's music is for the severely medicated. So obvious is the creators' dislike for Collins that fan fiction soon started making fun of him as well.[17]

By and large, music celebs draw the most criticism. Babs is an evil egomaniac with a torturous voice, Collins writes mind-numbing music, Stevie Nicks is a goat. Madonna is "an old anorexic whore who wore out her welcome years ago" ("Kenny Dies"), the creators clearly don't see her as "a site of semiotic struggle between the forces of patriarchal control and feminine resistance, of capitalism and the subordinate, of the adult and the young."[18] Notably, the *South Park* version of Madonna concentrates on her looks; indeed, female singers are more often ridiculed for their looks rather than their abilities. Jennifer Lopez is a sluttishly dressed salsa singer with a big butt; she carries the hallmark of an overindulged, wealthy, vacuous female, a small, poodle-ish dog, which she mistreats. Stan and Kyle torture a Jennifer Lopez doll when she fails to keep her promise not to make more albums or movies ("Proper Condom Use"). Probably because of their talent as musicians themselves, the creators are more sensitive to the foibles of music celebrities.

Mel Gibson has undergone a celebrity shift from hero to zero. In the earliest episodes, he was the boys' hero: his posters adorned Cartman's bedroom, Chef recreated his *Braveheart* role ("Starvin' Marvin"), and Cartman overquotes Gibson ("Scott Tenorman"). In the eighth season, he gave the creators a golden opportunity in the form of *The Passion of Christ*. Rarely is a movie so right for *South Park*; it was popular, controversial, religious, and was produced by one of the series' favorite celebrities. Now Cartman has a respected celebrity to back his anti-Semitism, and he glories in it:

> CARTMAN: Oh yeah?! My mom took me to see Mel Gibson's movie, *The Passion*, and Mel Gibson says you are a sloth and you are a liar. And if the Road Warrior says it, it must be true. . . . Mel Gibson was right, Kyle. Right now the Jew in you is screaming "No! Those [*weapons*] cost money! Get your money back!" You know this to be true. Go ahead. Prove Mel Gibson wrong, Kyle. Do it! ("Good Times with Weapons")

Though Gibson has moved from his initial sphere of influence (acting) to producing/directing, Cartman still respects Gibson's authority. Gibson is the purveyor of a religious ideology that Cartman deliberately interprets as anti-Semitic. Cartman prays to Gibson as if he is a godhead:

> I want to thank you for all the blessings you have brought me. You have shown me the way so many times in the past and . . . now you are making all my dreams come true. You give me strength when there is doubt, and I praise you

for all you have done. Only you, Mel Gibson, have had the wisdom and the courage to show the world the truth. From this day forward, I will dedicate my life making sure your film is seen by everyone. I will organize the masses so that we may do thy bidding. Hail Mel Gibson. Amen. ("Passion of the Jew")

Furthermore, the movie's box office success proves, to Cartman, that Gibson got it right, that the vast majority of people "hate Jews":

> KYLE: People don't hate the Jews!
>
> CARTMAN: Really? Three hundred million domestic box office, Kyle. The top-grossing film of all time, Kyle. Those numbers don't lie. If you're not scared of *The Passion*, then go see it. Go see it and tell me I'm wrong. Mel Gibson, Kyle. Mel Gibson. ("Passion of the Jew")

Cartman stresses Mel Gibson's name, hammering home that Kyle has been betrayed by his own hero. However, Gibson loses his fan base by the end of the movie. When he comes to South Park, Gibson is channeling various movie roles (not all his own); he lacks an identity. Gibson is now a laughing-stock. But his final act of desecration is when he farts on Cartman, a symbolic referencing of what celebrities can do to fans. Cartman has not mentioned Gibson's name since the episode.

Celebrity Allusions

As Chris Turner, Carl Matheson, and Hugo Dobson have observed, television viewers appreciate in-jokes and obscure throwaway lines, especially those that test their celebrity trivia knowledge;[19] viewers who know the latest celebrity peccadilloes garner more from quotational shows such as *South Park*. Take, for example, Kyle's remark, "Ike! Do your impersonation of David Caruso's career!" ("Anal Probe"). If a viewer does not know who David Caruso is, the visual as Ike plummets to the ground is amusing; however, if the viewer knows that David Caruso is an actor who left one of television's most popular dramas, *NYPD*, and had done little work since (the episode appeared before *CSI Miami*), then the joke has an added dimension. To fully appreciate *South Park*, it helps if viewers know that Paris Hilton loves her dog, Tinkerbell, and the rumors surrounding Gary Condit and Tom Cruise.

Celebrity allusions occur in nearly every episode of *South Park*. Many of the allusions are anchored to the meaning of celebrity:

> CARTMAN: Tom Hanks can't act his way out of a nutsack! ("Chef's Salty Balls")
>
> MRS. TWEEK: These boys are absolutely right. We've been using these poor kids to pull at your heartstrings for our cause, and it's

wrong. We're as low and despicable as Rob Reiner. ("Gnomes")

GOD: Yeah, like John Travolta before you [*Jesus*]. You are experiencing a second revival. ("Are You There God")

Other allusions are not so accessible. Sometimes a celebrity is invoked purely because he or she is a celebrity rather than for any inherent qualities. For example:

"Trees are to bushes as buildings are to houses. David Duchovny is to tampons as nougats are to chocolate." (Mr. Garrison's blackboard, "Starvin' Marvin")

pink Christina Aguilera monsters ("Timmy")

Patrick Duffy and Brent Musburger as Scuzzlebutt's leg ("Volcano")

Leonardo DiCaprio spanks Cartman/Ming Li for several hours ("Cow Days")

Mr. Garrison spends a night with Kenny G ("Worldwide Recorder Concert")

At one level, such bizarre couplings replicate the unpredictable humor of *Monty Python*, but at a more sophisticated level, the allusions indicate the undifferentiated application of "celebrity." In "Weight Gain 4000," Chef's comments about Kathie Lee Gifford are not immediately clear:

You know. Kathie Lee, you are a very special woman. I don't mean special in a Mary Tyler Moore way. Or, or special in an Extra Value Meal at Happy Burger way. Noo no no no no. I mean special. Like the song of a humming bird as it gets ready to find that female hummingbird and make sweet love to it all night long. Just two humming birds moaning and, and groaning and, and their bodies caress and touch each other in ecstasy.

What Chef means by "Mary Tyler Moore" special is unclear. Being familiar with Happy Burgers or with Gifford and Moore is not enough in this instance; how the three share specialness must be established before the allusion is understandable. Chef launches into an erotic metaphor that explains his interpretation of Gifford "special," but even this does not clarify the link between Gifford, Moore, and Happy Burger meals. This type of unanchored reference suggests that in *South Park*, the celebrity has become a free-floating signifier.

Celebrity Responses

Those celebrities who manage to make it onto the *South Park* ontological map are surprisingly grateful. Rather like Oscar Wilde, many would much rather be lampooned than ignored. When Paris Hilton visits she staggers through the town, flashes her breasts, drinks alcohol, coughs up phlegm, and is so stupid that she cannot tell the difference between a dog and a human being ("Stupid Spoiled Whore"). The episode is about as insulting as a portrayal can be, but Hilton was not perturbed at all. Rather than outraged, Hilton was "flattered." Matt and Trey were stunned by her response and iterated that she must be really "fucked up."[20] It's difficult to insult someone who refuses to be insulted.

Stephen Sondheim, Russell Crowe, Elton John, and Tina Yothers have been amused by their onscreen *South Park* appearances. Bill Kurtis laughed when told of his "appearance" on the show.[21] Ben Affleck felt that his two appearances were an "undeserved honor."[22] Of course, not everyone is flattered by a mention on *South Park*.

Alan Jackson thought the *South Park* spoof on him was in bad taste.[23] Streisand and Redford have slammed the show.[24] And, if media sources are to be believed, Tom Cruise was not happy with his caricature. Since the first celebrity savaging, media commentators have speculated as to why the celebs have "not taken a stand against" the series.[25] Perhaps the answer lies in the difficulty of winning such cases. Bing Crosby objected to his portrayal as a "vainglorious coward" in *Bingo Crosbyana* (Friz Freleng, 1936) and tried to prevent distribution of the reel, but lost the case.[26] The complexities of satire "as a form of constitutionally protected speech" continue to pose the legal question—can fictitious works be libelous?"[27]

Conclusion

The range of people who "appear" effectively demonstrates the ongoing slippage of the word "celebrity": it's a strange society in which Charles Manson, Moses, and Arthur Fonzarelli share the same televisual space.[28]

South Park raises the question: What is celebrity? It's a question considered by cultural critics such as P. David Marshall, Chris Rojek, and Graeme Turner.[29] Through the *South Park* portal, the television audience is presented with other ways of "seeing" celebrity that challenge traditional concepts of celebrity by having them appear not as themselves but as their television or movie characters. Mel Gibson is revered as Rob Roy (*Braveheart*) and the Road Warrior; Michael Dorn maintains his Mr. Worf *Star Trek* persona. The celebrity characters can act as catalysts for narratives (Mr. Jefferson/Michael Jackson) or merely as props (Garrison's David Hasselhoff face).

As part of a celebrity-worshipping society, there's nothing *South Park* appreciates more than a celebrity. But the town is too small for celebrity bull. Those celebrities who pose a threat to South Park's integrity are killed (Barbra Streisand, Robert Redford, Rosie O'Donnell, Rob Reiner). Some become victims of bizarre occurrences of the carnivalesque type of course: Eric Roberts is eaten; Paris Hilton is inserted into Mr. Slave's ass. With these metaphorical deaths, *South Park* tries to kill the media star. They expose celebrities' political beliefs as misguided, ridiculous, and posturing; in their topsy-turvy world, nobody listens to celebrities or accepts their "authority." They debunk the celebrity mythos by ridicule. Of course, much of that ridicule is of the lower body strata—John Edwards is exposed as a cold reader who preys upon vulnerable people; he is, in *South Park* terms, "a giant douche." So too is John Kerry. *South Park* rejects celebrity special-ness. Celebrities are the epitome of inauthenticity, and *South Park* defrocks the gaudily clad stars.

"What's more important? Being on TV or some stupid assassination?" ("Weight Gain 4000")

. . .

> PARKER: "The thing is we never really reached normal celebrity status. We've never reached sucky celebrity status. We're kind of like the same as Gary Coleman and people like that." "We just get bugged," adds Stone. "We don't get hot chicks coming up to us. We get 15-year-old guys asking us to do voices."[30]

Season-by-Season Guest Appearances

Season 1. Kathie Lee Gifford comes to town to present an award but finds herself the target of an assassination attempt; Cartman appears on the *Geraldo* show. Richard Stamos sings in the mid-game break (104). Suzanne Sommers appears on TV in *She's the Sheriff* (106). Tina Yothers judges the Halloween contest (107); Mills Lane, Don King, and Michael Buffer preside over the Jesus versus Satan boxing contest (108); Sally Struthers inspires the boys to feed the starving; and Vanessa Redgrave makes a surprising appearance (109). Phil Glass conducts an unpopular Xmas concert (110); Sidney Poitier, Leonard Maltin, and The Cure's Robert Smith combat Barbra; Sally Struthers does a cameo with Poitier; and Officer Barbrady admires Fiona Apple (112). Jay Leno voices Kitty while Bob Saget hosts *America's Stupidest Home Videos* (113). Jesus appears in 102, 104, 105, 106, 108, 110, 112, 113.

Season 2. Celine Dion has been Terrance's lover and Saddam Hussein tries to take over Canada for the first time (210). John Walsh and Sid Greenfield of *America's Most Wanted* come to town and Eric Roberts is eaten (202). *Cops* follows Officer Barbrady (203); the A-Team saves Mr. Mackey 204; Jesus interviews Bob Denver (206). Jay Leno, Brent Musberger, John Elway, and Arthur Fonzarelli flashback and flash sideways (207). Garrison watches Shari Lewis and Lamb Chop and admits Mr. Hat's fantasy about Brett Favre to Dr. Jonathan Katz (208). Robert Redford orchestrates the first South Park Indy Film Festival; Andy Warhol and Fred Savage attend and Tom Hanks stars in the new Mr. Hankey film (209). Robert Ebert grabs a title and a constellation (211). Fat Abbot and his cartoon friends have a crude new show (212). Leonardo DiCaprio is spanked (213). A host of musical talent comes to Chef's Aid and Johnny Cochran prosecutes (214). Barbra Streisand appears in spooky vision (215). Charlie Manson is not such a bad guy (216). Joe Camel tries to sell Harbucks coffee (217). *Crocodile Hunter* Steve Irwin makes an anonymous appearance and Marilyn Manson is seen on TV (218).

Season 3. Jennifer Aniston is not herself but Miss Stevens, the Getting Gay with Kids choir leader (301). Whoopi Goldberg's politicking is ridiculed and Nick Nolte gives out a Nobel Prize (302). Moses and Haman visit Jewbilee (309). The Japanese prime minister directs a Pearl Harbor attack (310). Sally Struthers battles Pat Robertson (311). Korn imitates Scooby-Doo and solves a mystery (312). Ronnie James Dios sings at the Bay of Pigs Memorial Dance (313). Al Gore and President Clinton find the Civil War revived; Gore thinks they don't need the South anymore (314). Hell reveals dozens of familiar faces (315); God makes a special appearance and what an appearance it is. Rod Steward is Depends-able (316). Yoko Ono and Kenny G cause the world to shit itself (317).

Season 4. Janet Reno screws up, again (403). Phil Collins, Kurt Loder, and Charlie Rose all comment on the Timmy phenomenon (404). Malcolm McDowell is "a British Person" (405). John Denver has his own special airborne ride at North Park Funland (406). Cheech and Chong pose as Native Americans (407). If the handicapped go to Hell, they'll be joining Walter Matthau, Saddam Hussein, and a host of others (410 and 411). Rosie O'Donnell and Jesse Jackson help Garrison sort out kindergarten elections (413). James Taylor sings a sexy Chef ballad; Howard Stern and Johnny Knoxville meet the latest daredevil, Kenny ("Fat Camp," 415). Fidel Castro is moved by Kyle's letter (416). The Peanuts gang inspires an animated Christmas feature (418).

Season 5. Radiohead completes Cartman's revenge in one of the most notorious episodes of all (501). Drew Carey and Mimi swear on TV (502). Steven Spielberg and Gloria Allred support gays in scouts (503). Apparently all religious deities are best friends (504). Terrance and Phillip meet Sonny and Cher (505). Cartman dresses as Justine Timberlake to make out with Britney Spears (506). Stan and Kyle still like to torture Jennifer Lopez (507). Imagine Osama Bin Laden and Stevie Nicks on the same episode (509)! Ben Assfleck helps Cartman find his funny nerve (510). A passel of financial wizards are interested in Garrison's transportation device (511). Oprah, Will Smith and family, Bill Cosby, Snoop Dogg, and Kobe Bryant upset the neighborhood (512). Madonna almost cheers Kenny up (513). John and Patsy Ramsey, Congressman Gary Condit, and O. J. Simpson appear in the "I can't believe they said that" episode (514).

Season 6. Maury Povich freaks out (601). Jared really doesn't have AIDS (602). Russell Crowe fights his way around the world (604). Cartman finally gets Michael Dorn to call him captain (605). Familiar yellow-faced cartoon cousins visit (607). The Pope is almost aware of what's going on (608). The boys meet Ted Koppel, George Lucas, Steven Spielberg, and Francis Ford Coppola (609). Alan Jackson sings and President George Dubbya's way-out accusations make people doubt his sanity (612). John Edwards is the biggest douche and Rob Schneider has his own movie industry (615). Even *South Park* is watching *The Osbournes* (616). Santa saves Christmas but Jesus dies (617).

Season 7. Cartman meets the founding fathers during a flashback (701). Christopher Reeve and Gene Hackman face off (702). A Hannibal Lecter wannabe surfaces (703). Ben Affleck falls in love with Cartman's hand (705). The crew from *Queer Eye* are not as gay as they appear (708). Metallica, Meat Loaf, Rick James, Ozzie Osbourne, Missy Elliott, Blink 182, Britney Spears, Rancid, and Alanis Morissette protest peer-to-peer file sharing (709). We learn Mormon religious leader Joseph Smith's way-out story (712). Rob Reiner really should butt out (713). Saddam Hussein is back in Canada; this time he doubles as Paul Martin, Canada's prime minister (715).

Season 8. Mark McGuire, Barry Bonds, and Jason Giambi are accused of steroid abuse (803). Mel Gibson does *Passion of the Jew* (804). Lil Kim hosts the town's dance-off (805). Bill O'Reilly chairs a debate (806). Michael Jackson moves in briefly (807). Jim Lehrer and Puff Daddy consider elections *South Park* style (808). Paris Hilton is a stupid spoiled whore (812).

Season 9. Singer Wing belts it out with Sylvester Stallone (903). Terry Schiavo appears with George Bush and Satan. Saint Peter allows Kenny into Heaven, where he rubs shoulders with archangels Michael, Gabriel, and Uriel (904). Tom Cruise, Nicole Kidman, R. Kelly, and John Travolta appear in the most-likely-to-result-in-court-action episode (912). Russian President Putin thinks George Bush is pranking him (913). Pope Benedict XVI declares a local miracle a bust (914).

Season 10. Bart, Stewie, and other cartoon characters visit (1003, 1004). Oprah, Geraldo, and Larry King meet Towelie (1005). Al Gore takes the boys hunting (1006). British nannies can't control Cartman but Cesar Millan can (1007). Conspiracy rumors force Stan and Kyle to come face to face with President George Bush, Donald Rumsfeld, and Dick Cheney (1008).

Notes

1. Daniel Boorstin, *The Image: Or What Happened to the American Dream* (London: Weidenfeld & Nicolson, 1961), 57.

2. *The National Enquirer* (of ten years ago), the *Weekly World News*. For more on the tabloids, see S. Elizabeth Bird's *For Enquiring Minds: A Cultural Study of Supermarket Tabloids* (Knoxville: University of Tennessee Press, 1992).

3. http://www.spscriptorium.com/SPinfo/SPStudiosFAQ4.htm.

4. Neil Melloy, "Rear Vision," *Brisbane Courier Mail*, December 12, 2001, 26.

5. Michael Mehle, "8-Year-Old with an Attitude," *Rocky Mountain News*, February 1, 1998, D12.

6. During an interview he admitted he'd seen the show:

> Q: Hey, Michael, did you ever see your portrayal on *South Park*?
> MD: Yes, I did. I loved it! I'm a big South Park fan anyway, and I wish they had called because I would have loved to have used my voice. Star Trek, http://www.startrek.com/startrek/view/community/chat/archive/transcript/1119.html, accessed October 22, 2006.

7. Quoted at South Park Scriptorium, http://www.spscriptorium.com/SPinfo/SPTimeline2002.htm, accessed October 22, 2006.

8. South Park Scriptorium, http://www.spscriptorium.com/SPinfo/SPTimeline2004.htm, accessed May 2, 2004.

9. Don Aucoin, "South Creators Do It for Laughs," *Boston Globe*, February 8, 1998, C8.

10. Eric Mink, "South Park on Religion," *New York Daily News*, February 4, 1998, 65.

11. *Team America* DVD, Special Features.

12. *New York Post*, May 17, 2004, quoted in "2004 Timeline," South Park Scriptorium, http://www.spscriptorium.com/SPinfo/SPTimelineIndex.htm, accessed October 24, 2006.

13. Emma Forrest, "The Way We Don't Want to Be Seen," *The Guardian*, July 13, 1998, 9.

14. Phil Rosenthal, "'South Park' vs. Subway," *Chicago Sun-Times*, March 6, 2002, 51.

15. Preston Turegano, "Streisand DVDs Recapture Icon's TV Stardom," *San Diego Union-Tribune*, November 26, 2005, E7.

16. Conan O'Brien Show, November 2, 2000.

17. South Park Scriptorium, "The Day That Changed the World," http://www.spscrip torium.com/MyStuff/TheDayThatChangeTheWorld.htm.

18. John Fiske, "Madonna," in *Reading the Popular* (Boston: Unwin Hyman, 1989), 95–113.

19. Chris Turner, *Planet Simpson*; Carl Matheson, "The Simpsons, Hyper-Irony, and the Meaning of Life," in *The Simpsons and Philosophy: The D'oh! of Homer* (Chicago: Open Court, 2001); Hugo Dobson, "Mister Sparkle Meets the Yakuza: Depictions of Japan in The Simpsons," *Journal of Popular Culture* 39, no. 1 (2006): 44–68.

20. Film Force, "Interview Trey Parker and Matt Stone," May 12, 2005, www.filmforce .ign.com/articles/612/612094, accessed October 22, 2006.

21. "A Bill Kurtis Tribute," http://pepperbay.com/billkurtis/southpark.html, dead.

22. "Paycheck Premiere," December 29, 2003, http://actionadventure.about.com/cs/ weeklystories/a/aa122203.htm, dead.

23. "Where Were You . . . When You First Heard the Song," Tennessean.com.

24. James Ross Gardner, "The Sundance Kid Stays in the Picture," *Salt Lake Magazine*, January 1, 2004, http://www.saltlakemagazine.com/index.php?src=news&prid=453&category =Features&PHPSESSID=c891bba43c4ca0d0ae7902ed0ccaa661, accessed October 24, 2006.

25. Maggie Hall, "Could this new TV cartoon show corrupt our kids?," *Sunday Mail*, Scotland, March 22, 1998, 26.

26. Karl F. Cohen, *Forbidden Animation: Censored Cartoons and Blacklisted Animators in America* (Jefferson, NC: McFarland, 2004), 39.

27. See Julie Hilden, "The Texas Supreme Court's Libel-by-Fiction Case," *Find Law*, December 9, 2003.

28. As Graeme Turner would predict, most of the celebrities come from the sports or entertainment industries. *Understanding Celebrity* (London: Sage, 2004), 3.

29. P. David Marshall, *Celebrity and Power: Fame in Contemporary Culture* (Minneapolis, MN: University of Minnesota Press, c1997); Chris Rojek, *Celebrity*, (London: Reaktion, 2001); Graeme Turner, *Understanding Celebrity* (London: Sage, 2004).

30. Dino Scatena and Allan Johnson. "Drawing on the Dark Side," *Adelaide Advertiser*, October 4, 2000, 44.

Part Three

You Bastards!

Chapter 13

Democrats Piss Me Off: Politics

Bakhtin noted the anarchical possibilities of the carnival. Carnivals crowned fools and, in doing so, they symbolically replaced the current leaders—the carnival festivities upset the normal hierarchy. Or did they? Critics such as Terry Eagleton remind us that carnivals were licensed festivals, a "permissible disruption of hegemony."[1] In other words, the wild abandon was in fact carefully contrived and controlled. Max Gluckman also points out that because the revelers crowned their own kings rather than rejecting the status quo, the status quo was reinforced, just with a different head: "the rites of reversal . . . preserve and strengthen the established order."[2] Certainly, the political tensions of carnival, though cloaked in displays of fun and feasting, demonstrated to those in authority what their underlings thought of them. Scatology and political satire have long been bedfellows. Consider Jonathan Swift's *Gulliver's Travels*, wherein a scholar of the Academy of Lagado is able to detect a man's involvement in plots against the government by examining his bowel movement: "Because Men are never so serious, thoughtful, and intent, as when they are at Stool."[3] Similarly, when *South Park* ridicules political parties, celebrity politicking, and political agendas, its writers are telling the political pundits what they (and, by association, what others) think of them. The ridicule is amusing and the episodes can be viewed for laughs, but there is more, isn't there?

Because of the show's acceptance of gays and blacks, its pro-drug and anti-hunting beliefs in the earliest episodes, viewers jumped to the conclusion that *South Park* was another leftie show, "Beneath the juvenile hijinks and violence, creators Trey Parker, Matt Stone, and Brian Garden have an unmistakable liberal agenda that's as passionate as Mister Rogers' morning soliloquies."[4] However, subsequent episodes proved that the right's fears were unfounded. The show praised big business and ridiculed abortion on demand ("Gnomes," "Cartman's Mum Is Still a Dirty Slut"). Cartman had been using "hippie" as a form of abuse since "Mecha-Streisand."

People started arguing about the show's political undertones. Was the show politically liberal or conservative? Both Democrats and Republicans claimed the show for their own—and the debate raged. The following 2003 online blogs between Jesse Walker and Greg Morrow succinctly outline the major points and episodes of contention:

> I would tend to agree with your perception that the easy shots come more often at the expense of liberals. However, I wonder how much of that is observer-effect? Both you and I are pretty solidly liberal, and we're probably more likely to recognize and remember when our point of view is being offended, and less likely to notice the opposite.

> My argument was that the show is libertarian, not conservative, and the examples you cite don't contradict that. Ritalin bashing is common among libertarians and conservatives as well as liberals. Big Gay Al declared, in one of the most libertarian episodes, that Scouts should be allowed to discriminate against gays. And the punk iconoclasm you document is hardly inconsistent with libertarianism. Parker and Stone aren't purists, and there are some exceptions to the pattern (cf. the homeschooling episode) . . .

> You yourself cited an episode—"It Hits the Fan"—that seems to hew fairly strongly anti-libertarian and pro-regulation. The episode with Mr. Garrison's "It," created to compete with the airlines, is strongly anti-market, and even the underpants gnomes episode, otherwise strongly pro-market, gets in a jab at modern business methods with "Step 2-? Step 3-Profit!" I think the show's consistent in first trying to offend. . .

> I remember thinking the episode about Mr. Garrison's invention was pretty libertarian when I saw it ["The Entity"], though that was two years ago and it's possible there was some anti-market aspect to it that I've forgotten. And "It Hits the Fan" wasn't pro-regulation—the Knights were the networks' private Standards & Practices departments, not the FCC's mandatory rules. While I'm at it, the episode where Cartman buys his own theme park seemed like a free-market fable to me and the guys I saw it with, but maybe that serves me right for watching cartoons with a bunch of libertarian filmmakers . . .

> Yeah, I'm thinking there might be more brought to the cartoon than taken from it. Witness this whole discussion about a show that at one point featured a pony fellating a hot dog. But I'm not sure that a "free-market fable"—which characterization I won't dispute—is necessarily libertarian . . .[5]

Clearly, the series is pro-personal freedom—at heart, the show is Libertarian.

Libertarian Ideology

Trey Parker is a registered Libertarian, and Matt Stone admits, "I hate conservatives, but I really fucking hate liberals."[6] Libertarians believe individuals are best able to live their lives as they see fit. Libertarianism promotes freedom of speech, no matter how offensive. *South Park*'s freedom of speech campaign has been the subject of some media controversy, usually about the show's swearing and the right to say words, no matter how offensive, well almost. In the tenth season, the creators broke the Comedy Central ban on the Nation of Islam and tried to include an image of Muhammad. The image was not shown by the network and the creators were outraged, as were many viewers.[7] The curtailment of their right to free speech pissed them off. Comedy Central had backed the Cruise satire and their shit-ful episode but had reneged on them. It was the moment the creators most feared would happen, and they almost walked out; they were ready, they told *Nightline*.[8] But the irony was, an image of Muhammad aired five seasons earlier in "Super Best Friends" and was in the opening credits of the show.

Of course, not all freedoms are created equal. The NAMBLA speaker's hypothesis that freedom means freedom to have sex with children fails to impress the boys. Randy Marsh claims his right to fight—defend himself—at a baseball match: "This is for what?! Arresting me for what?! I'm not allowed to stand up for myself?! I thought this was America! Huh?! Isn't this America!? I'm sorry, I thought this was America!" ("Losing Edge").

As the above blog shows, the market economics of *South Park* is confusing. Episodes tend to be soft around their economic edge. "Gnomes," with its predilection for homespun metaphors, gently lampoons the small business operator. Although Harbucks was given a fair chance and allowed into South Park (at the cost of the local coffee shop, "Gnomes"), it was not so forgiving with WalMart several seasons later. In "Something Wall*Mart This Way Comes," the consumers are little more than dupes who cannot control their spending[9]—it's a decidedly Marxist point of view. However, Brian Anderson argues that the episode comes down on the side of WalMart, "The lesson? Wall*Mart is successful simply because it offers consumers good deals—and beats the competition."[10] But that's only part of the story; overwhelmingly the tropes, literary metaphors, and horror clichés demonstrate a fear of WalMart. Central to the episode is Wall*Mart's power to disrupt the family and community.

In "The Politics of *South Park*," fan Michael Cust outlines the show's "manifest" political mandate.[11] He lists as examples four blatantly libertarian episodes in which outside governments and organizations infringe on personal and sometimes national liberties: environmental interference in Costa Rica ("Rain-forest Schmainforest"), enforced political correctness ("Death Camp of Toler-ance"), drug war extremism ("My Future Self and Me"), and Rob Reiner's bullying crusades ("Butt Out"). Throughout the series, episodes manifest a concern about increased government interference of personal rights because of political correctness ("Sexual Harassment Panda," "Cripple Fight," "Cartman's Silly Hate Crime"). It labels the Democrats fascists:

GERALD BROFLOVSKI: . . . Democrats make sexual harassment laws, these laws tell us what we can and can't say in the workplace, and what we can and can't do in the workplace.

KYLE: Isn't that Fascism?

GERALD: No, because we don't call it Fascism. ("Sexual Harassment Panda")

Republicans, even with their belief in limited governance, curtailed personal liberties in the Terry Schiavo case, and *South Park* responded with, "Best Friends Forever." In the Schiavo case, the husband was the legally appointed decision maker and well within his rights to decide to withdraw Schiavo's life-support system; the government had no right to interfere. And the devil whis-pers into George Bush's ear. Although *South Park* tried to present both sides, it clearly didn't have its Libertarian heart in it. When conservative Cartman wants Kenny dead, audiences know something is wrong. The moral of the episode is, at best, a cop-out:

KYLE: Cartman's side is right, for the wrong reasons. But we're wrong, for the right reasons. ("Best Friends Forever")

One of the strongest Libertarian messages comes via *South Park*'s dislike of government interference. Janet Reno removes the Romanian quintuplets, commando style ("Quintuplets"); the AFT almost relives its Waco screw up ("Two Naked Guys"):

BARBRADY: So what does the ATF do when religious fanatics are gonna commit mass suicide?

ATF LEADER: Oh, don't worry! We won't let that happen! Even if it means we have to kill each and every one of them.

But the FBI comes out worst. It has terrible negotiators ("Fun with Veal")— its cow control program causes mass suicide ("Cow Days"). Generally, gov-ernment law enforcement is shown as incompetent, ill-informed, and trigger-happy.

Local Politics

The townsfolk rely not on the strictures of government with a capital "G" but on their elected official, the mayor. The town turns to Mayor McDaniels for guidance:

> RANDY: Well, what are we gonna do, Mayor?! We have to stop these abductors from being able to get into our town!
>
> TOWNSFOLK: Rabble rabble rabble rabble rabble rabble rabble rabble . . .
>
> MAYOR
> MCDANIELS: Yes, but standing out here yelling "Rabble rabble rabble" isn't going to help anything.
>
> JIMBO: Well, we don't know what else to do, Mayor! ("Child Abduction")

Mayor McDaniels explains how local politics work:

> Look, the best I can do is create a proposition. We'll call it Prop. 10. The town can vote on it, and if it passes, we'll see what we can do. . . . So I guess you wanna do some campaigning. You can do commercials and things like that, and then we'll have a vote in the middle of town. And obviously, if more than 50 percent of the people even show up . . . and care enough to want Harbucks out, then, they're out. So, good luck to you. ("Gnomes")

Even though the Mayor is shown to be self-serving, potentially prone to corruption, and generally lacking in political savvy (she has inadvertently "sold out" the town, first to the Hollywood crowd and then to the hippies), she is their leader. She can order them to fart on a regular basis ("Spontaneous Combustion") and abolishes separation laws ("Here Comes the Neighborhood"). Mayor McDaniels is the ultimate authoritay in South Park.

The town takes the political processes seriously. Stan learns exactly how seriously when he is banished for deciding not to vote in the school mascot elections ("Douche and Turd")—though the voting process can be troublesome to a population that tends to prevaricate:

> Reporter:
> [NEWS 4 LIVE!] Tom, I'm standing out front of the South Park mayor's office, where both sides of this debate have gathered. . . . Earlier, the South Park townspeople voiced their opinion.
>
> MAN 4: Well, I think the flag is racist! Huh, but then again, it is part of our history.
>
> MAN 5: Well, I guess the flag is part of history, but I can see how it is racist.

MAN 6:   I think it is history. I think it is racist. ("Chef Goes Nanners")

Sometimes they are ignorant ("Gnomes"), sometimes they simply don't care ("Douche and Turd"), and sometimes they simply agree with everyone else:

MAYOR: All right, people. The next order of business is a very serious matter. We need to vote on whether South Park should rein-state the death penalty or not. All those in favor, say "yippee."

SOME PEOPLE: Yippee.

TARDY MAN: Wait, what was that? I missed the question. Yippee!

MAYOR: All those opposed, say "nay."

OTHER PEOPLE: Nay.

TARDY MAN: Screw you! [*punches the guy to his right*]

MAN: Ey! Screw you! [*everyone starts fighting*]

Cartman writes to Bill Clinton, "Dear Mr. President: There are times when humans can no longer endure their government's authoritah" ("Red Badge of Gayness"). That's exactly what *South Park* wants, to be left alone; the show's writers are disillusioned with the politics, political representatives, and political processes.

National Politics

Despite the wrangle over whose politics the show espouses, *South Park* gener-ally has no clear political allegiances. All leaders and all parties are found wanting. Bill Clinton was ridiculed for his sexual liaisons ("Cartman's Mom Is Still a Dirty Slut," "Chinpokomon," "Tooth Fairy's TATS") and Bush for his stupidity:

BUSH: Our intelligence tells us that when Saddam was originally killed, his soul actually went to hell. But while in hell he began a homosexual relationship with Satan, the Prince of Darkness. Satan, however, decided he didn't want to be with Hussein anymore and broke up with him about August. When Saddam became jealous and tried to kill Satan's new lover, Chris, Satan had Saddam sent to heaven to live with Mormons as a punishment. Questions? Yes?

ANOTHER
AMBASSADOR: Are you high, or just incredibly stupid?

BUSH: I assure you, I am not high. ("Ladder to Heaven")

Liberals might be douches, but Big Gay Al classes the Republicans with Christians and Nazis as oppressors of homosexuality ("Big Gay Al's Big Gay Boat Ride"), and the devil influences Republican laws and policies, especially their environmental ones ("Terrance and Phillip," "Best Friends Forever").

Generally, politicians and politics are aligned with lower body references—as Stan learns, political candidates are either douches or turds. Again, the creators turn to lower body references to demonstrate their disgust with the political system. Few speeches are more scatological than the one given at the end of *Team America*:

> GARY: Oh no, we aren't! We're dicks! We're reckless, arrogant, stupid dicks! And the Film Actors' Guild are pussies. And Kim Jong Il is an asshole. Pussies don't like dicks because pussies get fucked by dicks. But dicks also fuck assholes. Assholes who just want to shit on everything. Pussies may think they can deal with assholes their way, but the only thing that can fuck an asshole is a dick with some balls. The problem with dicks is that sometimes they fuck too much, or fuck when it isn't appropriate . . . and it takes a pussy to show 'em that. But sometimes pussies get so full of shit that they become assholes themselves. Because pussies are only an inch and a half away from assholes. I don't know much in this crazy, crazy world, but I do know that if you don't let us fuck this asshole, we are gonna have our dicks and our pussies all covered in shit.

The complex world of power relationships and shifting political ideologies is reduced to lower body references.

International Scene

In *Team America*, the misguided FAGs protect the leader of North Korea Kim Jong Il; Kim Jong Il is brought low by his depiction as an "ornery" but violent leader. Jong's plans to use weapons of mass destruction collapse him with Saddam Hussein. A previous *South Park* "guest," Saddam Hussein claims he's "just an average Joe" every time he tries to take over Canada. Hussein is a superbully who becomes sexually aroused at the thought of war and inflicting pain. The homosexual alliance between Saddam and Satan in *Bigger, Longer and Uncut* highlights the depth of Hussein's evil; he is more evil than Satan.

Hussein is one of the supervillains, as is Osama Bin Laden ("Krazy Kripples"). Despite Bin Laden's supervillain status, he is caricatured as a goofy Warner Brothers-type cartoon character who has "farty" pants; with his large ears, his Wolfie stamping and whistling, and incredible gullibility, he is not a fearful terrorist figure ("Osama Bin Laden Has Farty Pants"). He is risible rather than dangerous.

South Park also put a human face on the bombing of Afghanistan. In response to September 11, the creators offered "Bin Laden Has Farty Pants"—classical *South Park* in its juxtaposition of lower body referencing and politics. While in Afghanistan, the boys confront their Afghani counterparts who tell them their version of America's role in terrorism:

> KYLE: All right, I've had just about enough of this! They told us in school, and on TV, that most people in Pakistan and Afghanistan like America.
>
> BOY IN BLUE VEST: And you believe it? It is not just the Taliban that hates America. Over a third of the world hates America!
>
> STAN: But why? Why does a third of the world hate us?
>
> BOY IN BLUE VEST: Because, you don't realize that a third of the world hates you!

They are appalled to learn that to some, America is the "evil empire," and that their country is not universally loved and applauded for its interference. The other point they must concede is that America's values are "in the gutter" and that few countries respect a nation fascinated by celebrity excesses:

> KYLE: Do you really think your civilization is better than ours?! You people play games by killing animals, and oppress women!
>
> BOY IN BLUE VEST: It's better than a civilization that spends its time watching millionaires walk down the red carpet at the Emmys!
>
> STAN: . . . He's got us there, dude.

Celebrities and Politics

Politically active celebrities are particularly favorite targets, because they combine the creators' hatred of actors and lefty politics. Whoopi Goldberg robotically chants "Republicans are so stupid. I hate Republicans. Republicans are so stupid" ("Spontaneous Combustion"). Puff Daddy's "Vote or Die" political push was lampooned in "Douche and Turd"; he and his crew literally try to gun down reluctant voter Stan. Rosie O'Donnell is told, in no uncertain terms, that she does not have a voice in South Park politics:

> MR. GARRISON: Half the kids in the class didn't vote for your nephew, so what about them? You don't give a crap about them because they're not on your side! People like you preach tolerance

and open-mindedness all the time, but when it comes to Middle America, you think we're all evil and stupid country yokels who need your political enlightenment!! Well, just because you're on TV doesn't mean you know crap about the government! Now get your ass back on first class and respect this class's right to make up their own minds! ("Trapper Keeper")

South Park does not consider that the converse is possible: just because someone is a celebrity does not mean that they don't know about government or that they don't have the right to voice an opinion.

The most extended swipe at Hollywood royalty and politics is, of course, *Team America*. The earnest but misguided Film Actors' Guild members (FAGs) battle the blundering and inept world police, Team America. It's difficult to know which is more of a threat to the world—the self-righteous FAGs, capable and trained who support evil, or the gung-ho and stupid Team America who destroy most of the world's greatest cultural artifacts.

Symbolically, the puppets harken back to the British television series *Thunderbirds* (1965-66) whose world policing was conducted in much simpler political times—or at least that's the way it was presented to children. Now the problem of good versus evil is not so simple and the puppets (and, by extension, the viewers) have grown up. The deliberately "crappy" puppet aesthetic links the movie to its creators and suggests the amateurish attempts of Team America and, by extension, the American government, to police the world. The stilted movements of the puppets replicate the puppetry of politics. In the end, the celebs come off second best, thanks to a little politically incorrect smoking. Dozens of Hollywood actors are lampooned, even George Clooney, a longtime fan, but he continues to support the creators.[12] Not so fellow FAG member Sean Penn, whose angry response sparked another round of ridicule at Penn's expense.[13]

Conclusion

Within a year of its first episode, *South Park* was the name bandied around the political arena. For all its racial, gendered, and blasphemous commentary, politics is probably where its influence will remain most anchored. A few short months after the first episode, Libertarian candidate Steve Kubby campaigned for California governor with a *South Park*-esque advertisement.[14] The election of Arnold Schwarzenegger in California was hailed as a victory for "South Park republican/conservatism." A few years later, his failures highlighted the "limitations of the South Park conservative temperament." Chris Thompson succinclty summarized the new breed of political ideologies:

> They're socially liberal and fiscally conservative; they like their government small, their markets free, and their drinks straight up. They don't care about fags, but they get annoyed when someone says you can't say "fag." And their icons are maverick, iconoclastic political leaders who aren't afraid to call 'em like they see 'em. Think Rudy Giuliani. Or Arnold Schwarzenegger.[15]

The term "South Park republicans" has become political shorthand for "true Republicans" who

> believe in liberty, not conformity. They can enjoy watching *The Sopranos* even if they are New Jersey Italians. They can appreciate the tight abs of Britney Spears or Brad Pitt without worrying about the nation's decaying moral fiber. They strongly believe in liberty, personal responsibility, limited government, and free markets. However, they do not live by the edicts of political correctness. The South Park Republicans are an incredibly diverse group encompassing a variety of nontraditional conservatives, such as the Terminator, Arnold Schwarzenegger. Bruce Willis supported Republicans because of their commitment to lower taxes and fiscal discipline. Rap artist and movie actor LL Cool J recently endorsed NY governor George Pataki.[16]

Brian C. Anderson's book claiming South Park for his brand of conservatism hit the bookshelves the same week the show had the devil whisper in George Bush's ear. It's not safe to assume anything in South Park land. South Park is anti-extremist. Just right of center, it garners praise from both sides of the political coin.

Because of its swearing, irreverence, and challenges to authoritays, *South Park* was originally thought to have left-wing sympathies. But soon it became clear that the show was not leftist but, in fact, rather "log cabin" conservative in its values. Throughout the series, political parties *and* political processes are examined and ridiculed. Both are often found wanting. In this, the show spurns the traditional politics of the cohesive, conservative Midwestern town. National politics is of little concern to South Parkers, and whenever their small town comes to the attention of the FBI, CIA, or ATF, they suffer. In true Libertarian spirit, national interference is resented.

No matter which side will eventually claim South Park victory, one thing's for sure—when it comes to politics, *South Park* not only thinks John Edwards is a douche; Al Gore is one too. On the other hand, George W. Bush is a turd. Surprisingly, the creators are not as passionate about institutionalized politics as they are about celebrities. They don't hammer Bush or malign Clinton; they gently prod them. South Park aims, with unerring accuracy, at the very things that are annoying about liberal politics. Creator Matt Stone explains in interview with *Time* magazine:

> TIME: The book *South Park Conservatives* said your show is an antiliberal satire. Is that a fair description?
>
> MATT STONE: I think that's a fair description of some of the show's politics. But you could also easily write a book called South Park Liberals, because we've attacked a lot of funny stuff that conservative people and institutions do in America. But we're the only show that rips on Rob Reiner and anti-smoking laws and hippies, so we get that label.[17]

Mostly, South Park politics succeeds in the small touches; the conservative politics of "rednecks" Jimbo and Garrison, the more liberal ideologies of the boys, the gender/racial/social politics of the minority groups.

Increasingly, television offers complex images of government and politics. No longer are federal agencies such as the FBI considered an example of all that is good and upright (*The Untouchables*, 1959–63; *FBI*, 1965–73). In *South Park*, members of the FBI screw up more often than not. They spend time policing Internet downloading: it's easier to haul in children. The *X-Files* played to the US public's cynicism about their government and exposed their fears that their leaders lie to them.[18] So too did movies such as *Wag the Dog* (1997) and *Primary Colors* (1996). As investigative journalist Bill Kurtis shows the boys of South Park, people believe their government might not tell them the truth:

> CARTMAN: Okay, Stan . . . a UFO crash-landing card! You can deny it, or cover it up.
>
> STAN: Dude, I don't understand this game at all.
>
> CARTMAN: It's Investigative Reports with Bill Kurtis Funtime Game. You have to decide if you deny it or cover it up.
>
> STAN: Um, deny it?
>
> CARTMAN: Okay, let's see what Bill Kurtis says.
>
> ELECTRONIC HEAD: Hello, I'm Bill Kurtis. Many believe that the US Government [*pause*] covered it up. I'm Bill Kurtis. ("NAMBLA")

South Park viewers at Jump the Shark accept the show's political agenda. Given the show's lessons of tolerance (as opposed to political correctness), the viewers realize that though they might not agree with the show, its main role is entertainment—and they are prepared to laugh along. The laughter might be subversive or perhaps attack their own ideologies, but that's okay.

> FBI AGENT: Who's in charge here?
> OFFICER BARBRADY: I am. But I don't want to be.
>
> CARTMAN: It [a goat] was choking on the sweet air
>   of freedom in America, so we brought
>   it back to your crappy country.
>
> South Parkers think their choice has and will always be
> between a douche and a turd—"they're the only people
> who suck up enough to make it that far in politics."

Notes

1. Terry Eagleton, *Walter Benjamin, or, Towards a Revolutionary Criticism* (London: Verso, 1981), 148. Hugo Dobson summarizes both sides of the argument about politics and carnivals in "Mister Sparkle Meets the Yakuza: Depictions of Japan in *The Simpsons*," *Journal of Popular Culture* 39, no. 1 (2006): 44–68.

2. Max Gluckman, *Politics, Law and Ritual in Tribal Society* (Oxford: Blackwell, 1965), 109.

3. See also Claude Gandelman, "Patri-arse": Revolution as Anality in the Scatological Caricatures of the Reformation and the French Revolution." *American Imago* 53, no. 1 (1996): 7–24; Kramer Reinhold, *Scatology and Civility in the English-Canadian Novel* (Toronto: University of Toronto Press, 1997).

4. Neal Justin, "'South Park,' 'Rugrats' Are More Than Child's Play," *Minneapolis Star Tribune*, September 3, 1997, E1.

5. "Frothing at the Mouth," December 16, 2003, http://www.whiterose.org/dr.elmo/blog/archives/004954.html, accessed October 22, 2006.

6. Brian C. Anderson, "We're Not Losing the Culture Wars Anymore," *City Journal*, Autumn 2003, http://www.city-journal.org/html/13_4_were_not_losing.html.

7. For an online summary of the incident, see Michelle Malkin, "Do the Right Thing! Show Mohammed," April 13, 2006, http://michellemalkin.com/archives/004982.htm, accessed October 23, 2006.

8. Jake Tapper and Dan Morris, "Secrets of South Park," September 22, 2006, http://abcnews.go.com/Nightline/print?id=2479197, accessed October 21 2006.

9. A debate neatly summarized in Stephen Harper, "Zombies, Malls and the Consumerist Debate," *Journal of American Culture* 1, no. 2 (2002).

10. "South Park Republicans" April 17, 2005, http://www.manhattan-institute.org/html/_dmn_southpark_reps.htm, accessed October 22, 2006.

11. April 27, 2004, http://www.lewrockwell.com/orig5/cust1.html, accessed October 22, 2006.

12. "George Clooney Supports *Team America* Makers Despite Ridicule," Contactmusic.com, August 2, 2005, http://www.contactmusic.com/new/xmlfeed.nsf/mndwebpages/clooney%20supports%20team%20america%20makers%20despite%20ridicule, accessed October 22, 2006.

13. A copy of Penn's fax to Matt Stone and Trey Parker is available at Drudge Report http://www.drudgereport.com/penn.htm, accessed October 22, 2006.

14. Stills of the commercial are available at http://www.dougscribner.com/thirdwheel/stills.htm, accessed October 23, 2006.

15. Chris Thompson, "Arnold's big flameout," Salon.com, November 10, 2005, http://dir.salon.com/story/opinion/feature/2005/11/10/arnold/index.html, accessed October 23, 2006.

16. Eric Scheie, "California Dreaming (South Park Style)," October 7, 2003, http://blogcritics.org/archives/2003/10/07/191628.php.

17. James Poniewozik, "10 Questions for Matt Stone and Trey Parker," *Time,* March 5, 2006, http://www.time.com/time/magazine/article/0,9171,1169882,00.html, accessed October 22, 2006.

18. Paul A. Cantor, *Gilligan Unbound: Popular Culture in the Age of Globalization* (Lanham, MD: Rowman & Littlefield, 2001), 114–15.

Chapter 14

Tolerance, Not Stupidity: Difference

Watching *South Park* can be confronting and uncomfortable. It's meant to be. When Cartman calls Kyle a "Jew," it takes a thick-skinned person to avoid flinching. The inclusion of handicapable Jimmy and not-so-capable Timmy were tremendous risks. However, it is in these very moments that *South Park* can be at its most illuminating. As Bakhtin pointed out, the purpose of jokes is "to provide the corrective of laughter and criticism . . . to force [people] to experience beneath these [existing] categories a different and contradictory reality."[1] Furthermore, as Lois Leveen shows, ethnic humor has liberating consequences; ethnic jokes often subvert the very stereotypes they deploy because ethnic jokes and jokers confront the stereotype and, in doing so, they challenge the dominant culture.[2]

South Park Minorities

Chef was for many episodes the most visible black person in South Park. Chef, as a music-loving, libidinous Uncle Tom, does little to explore the complexities of life of a black person in a small Midwestern town. But he is the town's most sensible, respected, and loved (by the boys) adult; everyone seeks Chef's help, even the racist Garrison ("South Park Is Gay"). Chef draws attention to the marginalized and clichéd role of black people: in "Die Hippie Die," Cartman needs "a black person who can sacrifice himself in case something goes wrong," and in *Bigger, Longer and Uncut* a black regiment is used to protect the white troops. Thus, the viewers are reminded of the roles of blacks in popular cinema and the use and abuse of blacks in the military. Chef is even sent to "tolerance camp" when Principal Victoria thinks he's intolerant of Garrison's sexuality.

216

Racism is learned. The boys demonstrate this when they don't "see" color. In "Chef Goes Nanners," the boys side with Jimbo and Ned who think the South Park flag shouldn't be changed because of its historical value. The episode of course satirized the debate about the Confederate Flag and its symbolism which raged in 2000.[3] Chef is incensed and rejects the South Park "crackers." Soon, to Jimbo's horror, the KKK arrives to support his fight to retain the flag. However, the KKK proves to be more ridiculous than frightening. The hate group has cake raffles and underwear contests; Jimbo decides, "Jesus, Ned, these guys are complete nuts." But not before he wonders, if they're on his side, is his side right? At the school's debate about the issue, Chef realizes the "cracker" children didn't read the flag as racist—they didn't see the hanging figure on the flag as black:

> CHEF: I'm not mad because the flag shows somebody gettin' killed, It's because it's racist!
>
> KYLE'S TEAM: *Racist??*
>
> CHEF: Children, don't you even know what this argument is about?! That flag is racist because a black man is being hung by white people.
>
> KYLE'S TEAM: Oooooooohhh.
>
> CHEF: Oooooooohhh?!
>
> KYLE: W-we really didn't *see* it that way.
>
> CHEF: But that's a *black* man up there!
>
> KYLE: Y-yeah, but . . . the color of someone's skin doesn't matter.

They don't see Chef as black:

> STAN: We wanna talk to Chef.
>
> RECEPTIONIST: Chef?
>
> KYLE: He's a big guy, with a beard.
>
> STAN: And a chef hat.
>
> KENNY: [*And a real huge dick.*]
>
> RECEPTIONIST: Oh! The black guy!
>
> STAN: Huh? ("Succubus")

The receptionist responds to Kenny's racial stereotyping of Chef as the person "with the big dick." *South Park* provides an uneasy mix of stereotyping and racial acceptance. Chef is libidinous, has a large penis, and is musically talented. Much to Token's dismay, he too finds himself conforming to black stereotypes. Like Chef, he is musically inclined; he plays a smooth bass

("Christian Hard Rock") and sings well ("Wing"). In fact, he's talented enough to perform at the Miss Colorado pageant. On a stage of all white people, for a white audience, he provides the familiar spectacle of black entertainer. Although he is still a child, he epitomizes the black male entertainer—from his formal clothes to his smooth delivery of the Lou Rawls soul song, "You'll Never Find." Even though he is a child, he is sexualized by a white "female" when Ms. Garrison claims, "Just between us girls, nothin' gets my vadge wetter than a black man singing" ("Wing"). Token Black's heavily ironic name also counters political correctness; he is both the show's token black kid and a reminder of tokenism on television. Token's family also has the onerous responsibility of bearing the burden of blackness:

TOKEN'S FATHER: Yeah. I have a real problem with hate-crime legislation. In fact, I'd love to see you kids go down and give the governor a piece of my mind.

STAN: Well, why don't you tell the governor yourself?

TOKEN'S FATHER: Oh, he wouldn't listen to me.

KYLE: Why not?

TOKEN'S FATHER: Because I'm black. ("Cartman's Silly Hate Crime")

This episode highlights the hypocrisy of hate laws and takes swing at political correctness.

South Park deliberately turns the "there goes the neighborhood" cliché into "Here Comes the Neighborhood." Token is lonely in South Park and seeks to increase the black population, so he places an advertisement in a Forbes magazine. The advertisement attracts "richers" Will Smith, Oprah Winfrey, and Snoop Dog. The wealth of the "richers" has bought them middle-class accents and middle-class sensibilities, yet they are still subjected to racism. No sooner have they arrived than they are subjected to racist slurs, segregation laws, and KKK activity. They petition Mayor McDaniels, who agrees to abolish separation laws to "assure the nation that is watching that South Park is not a town of prejudice or bigotry." Again, the KKK-like activities, the cross burning, and the donning of white robes is rendered risible by the richers' misinterpretation. Hate groups and actions are made ridiculous and petty. There are at least two potential positions for the viewer—the episode reinforces racism by thinly disguising it or that ridiculing fear of the richers underscores the stupidity and pointlessness of racism. At the end of the episode, the boys explain to Token that their teasing is a part of friendship, not a part of race difference. In fact, the ultimate difference between the "richers" and the South Park population is not color but economics, as implied in the "underachieving" claims in the episode.

Like Token, City Wok owner Tuong Lu Kim resists stereotyping. Not only is he pranked for his accent, the residents attribute him with "authentic" knowledge of how to build walls. Kim is not impressed:

> Oh, I get it. Just because I Chinese, you think I build wall. That i' bullshit! I'm not stereotype, okay?! Just because I'm Chinese doesn't mean I go around building wall! I'm just a normal person like all o' you! I eat ah-rice and drive ah-really slow, just like the rest o' you! I'm not stereotype! ("Child Abduction Is Not Funny").

His "just like you" assertions iterate stereotype and are all that more amusing, especially when he proves to be an excellent wall-builder. Native American casino owners might wear headdresses with their suits but they are clever fiscal managers who combine astute market analysis with nature metaphors:

RUNS WITH
PREMISE: What is the state of our people?

ELDER 2:   Last night I spoke with the spirit of the Bear, and Bear said that if we do not build our highway soon, our investors may soon sell off their shares of the new casino.

ELDER 1:   Yes, and Eagle says the cumulative shared market loss on the revenue of the new casino drops 15 percent every day.

RUNS WITH
PREMISE: Then we must force the South Park people off their petty land.

ELDER 1:   But they are determined and proud. And the spirit of the wind has stated that if we use force, it could be a publicity nightmare, further hurting our net assets. (707)

Cheech Marin and Tommy Chong as Native Americans Chief Running Pinto and Carlos Ramirez exploit South Parkers' gullibility by selling them over-priced junk ("Cherokee Hair Tampons").

Cartman is a "fat racist self-centered intolerant manipulating sociopath!" ("Casa Bonita"). Cartman's abuse is so consistent that, like "shit," it tends to lose its offensive power. Kyle retaliates with "fat ass," which is a literal description of Cartman and, by association, Cartman's abuse could be taken as purely descriptive: yes, Kyle is Jewish. Trey Parker explains their rights as cultural *provocateurs*: "To me, the only thing that would be offensive is if the network called and said, 'We're getting calls from Jewish people, and we can't make fun of Jewish people anymore.' Then it becomes offensive, because we'd be saying, making fun of Jews is not OK, but making fun of fat people is."[4] If Cartman's anti-Semitic haranguing wasn't enough, the creators introduced

Connecticut Kyle ("Entity"). The whiney Jew stereotype is brought to life in all its cringing glory: Connecticut Kyle has bad hair, plaid pants, asthma, and thick glasses. He is uncool to look at and complains about everything. South Park Kyle finds his cousin unbearable:

> KYLE TWO: I can't take it anymore, Stan. My cousin's been here for two weeks and he's driving me insane.
>
> STAN: I know, dude. Every kid in school wants to kick his ass.
>
> KYLE TWO: I spent five years in this town making a good name for Jews and this . . . this . . . stereotype shows up and wrecks it all! You know what my biggest fear is? That I'll become him. That somehow his mannerisms will start rubbing off on me, and I'll become a stereotype. I mean, I'm a Jew and he's making me hate Jews.
>
> STAN: Dude, a self-hating Jew? You are becoming a stereotype.
>
> KYLE TWO: Ya see? ("Entity")

But in the end, Connecticut Kyle has the last laugh when he rejects the boys as "rednecks" and returns home with his $5 million.

It is important that racism's mouthpieces are the most despised, stupid, and least admirable *South Park* characters, Cartman and Garrison. By making them the town's racists, racism gets a bad, a really bad, name. Their offensiveness is the offensiveness of the ignorant, "The show is racist in the same way that Archie Bunker was racist. South Park is a town inhabited by stupid people, and stupid people say stupid things."[5] Garrison's garbled history lessons ("That's right . . . Engelbert Humperdinck was the first person on the moon, who was the second?") and Cartman's strange proclamations ("My mom says there's [*sic*] a lot of black people in China," 205) underscore their ignorance and stupidity. Viewers, even younger ones, understand that Cartman is not a role model:

> "We got a letter from a kid in Mississippi who said he was in a school play about Rosa Parks and played the bus driver as Cartman," Parker says. "Which shows how kids get it." Cartman dressing up as Hitler for Halloween might have alarmed some parents, but New York seventh grader Nick Farrar says, "With Cartman, you know he's just a complete idiot and you should sort of do the opposite of everything he does."[6]

To read *South Park* "straight" is to misread the show. Sure, it *might* be possible to accept Jonathan Swift's "A Modest Proposal" as a straight piece, but that is not how it was intended to be read. *South Park* takes prejudices, shouts them back to their audience, exposes the flaws of examination, and, in doing so, neutralizes their power to offend. The show turns political correctness on its head with carnivalesque humor; it holds nothing sacred and thus ridicules everything in the basest possible way.

Rednecks, White Trash, and Crackers

South Park wears its "redneck" crown proudly, if a little uncomfortably. In fact, the introductory musical number of *Bigger, Longer and Uncut* is one homage to the "redneck" town. Their redneck-ness is most obvious when contrasted with South Park visitors, such as the cool OC gang ("You Got Fucked"), the diet of the Californians ("Chef's Salty Balls"), and the vocabulary prowess of the New York kids ("Recorder Concert"). Connecticut Kyle thinks they are "all just such hick jock rednecks; it's just like you're right out of a stereotyped catalog" ("Entity"). So what exactly is a redneck?

The redneck stereotype, according to Jim Goad in *Redneck Manifesto*, is biologically different (inbred, less intelligent, unattractive, sickly), geographically different (hillbilly, southern, trailer park), and economically and culturally different (poor, lazy, superstitious, and violent).[7] Goad bundles rednecks, hillbillies, and white trash together. But the groups are different. "Redneck" literally refers to the red necks farmers get when they work in the fields; their necks became red because they do not wear collars.[8] Presidents Lincoln and Jackson "came from a southern folk the back of whose necks were ridged and red from labor in the sun."[9] Mr. Garrison, Jimbo, and Skeeter, though not rednecks in the farmer sense of the word, are the most prominent members of the redneck *genus*. They like beer (especially on hunting and fishing expeditions), support gun culture, and are always ready for a fight. They tend to be racist and homophobic, but Chef is one of Jimbo's friends, and Jimbo's relationship with Ned is suspiciously intimate. One of the hallmarks of redneckitis is their treatment of outsiders. They don't "take kindly to strangers," pandas, richers, or Goobacks. During the town's trouble with Goobacks, its redneck propensities become more pronounced. As the Gooback threat increases, the workers unite and articulate their fears with the phrase "they took our jobs," which degenerates into an indecipherable and meaningless catchcry. Basically, Jimbo's conservative politics, musical preferences, and clothing declare him a redneck. Rednecks are the American equivalent of the "common folk" as described by Bakhtin. In television land the redneck is a frightening counterpoint for the middle class.

The rural sitcoms of the 1960s played with the redneck stereotype. In *Green Acres* Oliver Wendell Douglas is continually frustrated by a community that is not lazy (the Ziffles continually outstrip his farming success) or stupid (Mr. Haney is remarkably resourceful)—they simply do not conform to his patrician idea of an orderly world of rigid rules. And no matter how much he applies his city smarts, the "simpler" folk always outdo him. He cannot function or be successful in Hooterville, though his ditsy wife can. He, the WASP, is, perhaps for the first time, the outsider. The Beverly Hillbillies[10] do the same to the Drysdales in California. So it is in South Park.

White trash has become *the* subculture for ridicule on television. The group is central to the jokey asides on the *Jerry Springer Show* and was central to the humor of *Roseanne*. Now while "white trash" was once synonymous with "po' white trash" ("cracker" in *Gone With the Wind*-speak), this is not always the case.[11] The McCormicks are South Park's white trash and they are poor. The McCormicks are the only family deserving the Chef's "crackers" label. Their poverty marginalizes them. Cartman, ever the social Darwinist, has little time for the McCormicks' poverty. White trash provides a disenfranchised group against which the other South Park families can measure their success. Stewart McCormick is chronically unemployed and unemployable, so he can perform his narrative function as counterpoint for Gerald Broflovski.

Handicapables

Two of the most controversial and most loved *South Park* characters are the "handicapable" Timmy and Jimmy. Wheelchair-bound Timmy was introduced in the fourth season, and stuttering comedian Jimmy came the following season. Timmy, based on someone *South Park* staffer Adrien Beard knew in elementary school, originally started as a one-scene joke but became so popular that he is now an integral part of the gang. Parker and Stone, who also helped fund the pro-disability documentary, *How's Your News?* (2001), emphasize that their focus wasn't Timmy, but people who don't think you can laugh at "someone in a wheelchair."[12] As Parker explains, "Our whole fight was: Here's this great kid. And I think the reason people love him is here's this kid in a wheelchair and he's just stoked to be Timmy. He's always smiling and he's always shouting his own name. It's not like we're going to do these horrible things to him and make him feel bad for what he is. And it totally worked the way we thought it would, which was great."[13]

When Timmy fronts a garage band, concert goers, like the television audience at home, are stunned and unsure how to react ("Timmy 2000"). Some leave in disgust, but the majority decide that Timmy rocks. The mixed reaction of the audience reflects society's confusion about people in wheelchairs: to look or to look away? At the end of the episode, Stan faces down Phil Collins and tells him why Timmy is cool:

> You see, we learned something today. Yeah, sure, we laughed at Timmy, but what's wrong with laughter? Just because we laugh at something doesn't mean we don't care about it. Timmy made us smile, and playing made Timmy smile, so where was the harm in that? The people that are wrong are the ones that think people like Timmy should be "protected" and kept out of

the public's eye. The cool thing about Timmy being in a band was that he was in your face, and you had to deal with him, whether you laughed or cried, or felt nothing. That's why Timmy rules!

Since his introduction, Timmy has become just another of the boys; he is included in their activities, good and bad. The boys help him put on a condom ("Proper Condom Use"), pull down his pants when they plan to harass the new teacher ("Fourth Grade"), he films Fingerbang's first video ("Fingerbang"), he adopts the metrosexual look ("South Park Is Gay"), he finds a "sponsor" in "NAMBLA," helps steal Cartman's kidney ("Cherokee Hair Tampons"), and plays the lead in *Helen Keller! The Musical*. Timmy's dilemma highlights the rigidity of Catholic doctrine in season four when the show asks "Do the Handicapped Go to Hell?" and responds with a disheartening "Probably." He might be in wheelchair and somewhat physically challenged but he's adept at Photoshop ("Cripple Fight"). He is petulant, jealous, and vengeful, and honest, caring, and righteous. He is the *South Park* token cripple. For one whole season anyway.

When Big Gay Al introduces Jimmy to Scout Troop 69 ("Cripple Fight"), Timmy is demonstrably bored and harrumps his way through Jimmy's comedy shtick. Timmy's jealousy spirals out of control, he refuses to enter into Jimmy's playful comedy and throws a cake at Jimmy at the bake sale. The climax of the episode is one of the most celebrated scenes from the entire series: a long and bloody fight between the two, mimicking the fight sequence in John Carpenter's *They Live*: every punch, swear word, and bone-crunching sound is clearly heard. The two also clash over Jimmy's steroid abuse in "Up the Down Steroid." Timmy was right to be jealous because Jimmy goes on to usurp him in the following seasons, appearing in nearly double the number of episodes Timmy does. But Timmy shouldn't despair, he is officially the "Greatest Disabled TV Character" according to *Ouch!*[14] and even has a blogsite named after him, Timmargh.net.[15]

However, the two reconcile in "Krazy Cripples" when they join forces against Christopher Reeve. When Christopher Reeve comes to South Park to promote stem-cell research, Timmy and Jimmy reject Reeve. They resent his "supercrip" status.[16] The episode was not without cultural resonances as one disabled viewer responded "so apt is their wry commentary on the 'born disabled vs. became disabled' dichotomy that often divides us. An easier target, but one skewered to equal effect, is the 'inspirational cripple' icon that gives many of us the creeps."[17] Wisely, the characters decide to "stay outta this" debate indicating even *South Park* knows when to draw the line.

Predictably, Cartman sees the Special Olympics as a way to make some money. He enters the Special Olympics convinced he can "kick ass against all the handicapped" and win the $1,000 best athlete award ("Up the Down Steroid"). His "retard" makeover involves ill-fitting and incorrectly buttoned clothes, a loping gait, a bad haircut, bicycle helmet, crossed-eyes, and speech peppered with "darh darh." He models himself on Kid Rock. Cartman looks and sounds nothing like Jimmy or Timmy. Of course, as a nonathletic person, he fails in every event—Special Olympians are true athletes.

It's the adults who don't get Timmy. His teachers wrongly label him Attention Deficit Disorder, and it's the boys who have to interpret what he says for Mr. Mackey and the others. South Park adults, in their effort to be politically correct, manage only to exacerbate the differences by drawing attention to them. They learned that people do not like being treated as "special." Nurse Gollum told them as much in the second season:

> Don't you realize that the last thing I ever wanted was to be singled out? I just wanted to do my job, and live my life like any normal person, but instead you've made everybody focus on my handicap all week long. Look, I don't wanna be treated different. I don't wanna be treated special or treated gingerly, I just wanna be ridiculed, shouted at and made fun of like all the rest of you do to each other. And take those stupid things off your heads! ("Conjoined Fetus Lady")

Generally the portrayal of disabled people in fiction has fallen into six identifiable pitfalls, according to Isabel Brittain. Disable people were portrayed as "other" than human, or "extra-ordinary," as "second fiddle" they often served as foils for the protagonist's journey, rarely were they realistically or accurately depicted, their "outsider" status translates into "alienation and social isolation," and rarely were they afforded a happy ending leading to a rich and fulfilling life.[18] *South Park* redresses that imbalance in its portrayal of Timmy and Jimmy.

Goths and Hippies

Two other subcultures to appear in *South Park* from time to time are the Goths and hippies. White-faced, black-garmented Goths are usually to be found sitting in street gutters bemoaning their terrible life. They uniformly reject conformity and refute a capitalist lifestyle: "Go ahead and wear your business suits so you can make thirty-four thousand dollars a year to buy your condominium. They're all zombies racing to their graves. . . . Have fun in your rat-race life, living paycheck to paycheck for corporate gains" ("Raisins").

Sharing the same rejection of corporate America are the hippies. Since the second episode, they've occupied an offstage role as the antithesis of the redneck. According to Cartman's typology, there are at least three types of hippies: giggling stoners, drum-circle hippies, and college know-it-all hippies;

there are also the misguided aging douches. They all have one thing in common: they espouse left-wing liberalism.

Conclusion

South Park's depiction of "difference" relies on and draws heavily on stereotypes. By deploying familiar images, the show works both within and against the stereotype. It is easy, and perhaps tempting, to be dismissive of *South Park*'s racism. When someone as oafish as Mr. Garrison sings his offensive Christmas song, he is so unworthy of respect that his opinions, all of them, are derisory. Issues that are painful to see and hear are, in effect, the performance of satire. It is easy for the television audience to feel superior listening to Cartman because the audience can see how misguided his prejudices are. Clearly, this is the intention; possibly, it fails with some viewers.

The exaggeration and proliferation of scatological references in abuse and banter refer back to Bakhtin's notions of playful parody. A monotony of stereotypes dot the *South Park* canvas and give rise to visions of a jostling, festive crowd, one that is both different and tolerant—not stupid. The shenanigans and unpredictable behavior of the community scares outsiders. No wonder Starvin' Marvin chooses to return to famine-ravaged Ethiopia.

CARTMAN: I hope they're not Austrians. That's the last thing this town needs.

CHEF: You see, it's not okay to make fun of an American because they're black, brown or whatever. But it is okay to make fun of foreigners because they're from another country. ("Conjoined Fetus Lady")

CARTMAN: Hey, Kyle. All those times I said you were a big, dumb Jew? I didn't mean it. You're not a Jew.

KYLE: Yes, I am! I *am* a Jew, Cartman!

CARTMAN: No, no, Kyle. Don't be so hard on yourself. –*Bigger, Longer and Uncut*

Notes

1. Mikhail Bakhtin, *Rabelais and His World,* trans. Helene Iswolsky (Bloomington: Indiana University Press, 1984), 59.

2. Lois Leveen, "Only When I Laugh: Textual Dynamics of Ethnic Humor," *MELUS* 21, no. 4 (1996): 29–55.

3. Kevin Alexander Gray, "Dispatches from South Carolina: Same As It Ever Was," May 2000, http://www.counterpunch.org/scflag.html, accessed October 22, 2001.

4. Michael Mehle, "8-Year-Old with an Attitude," *Rocky Mountain News*, February 1, 1998, D12.

5. Don Aucoin, "'South' Creators Do It for Laughs," *Boston Globe*, January 20, 1998, C8.

6. Rick Marin, "The Rude Tube," *Newsweek*, March 23, 1998, 56.

7. Jim Goad, *Redneck Manifesto* (New York: Simon & Schuster, 1998), 76.

8. "White collar" refers of course to office work and "blue collar" to more manual (but not field) work.

9. Jonathan Daniels, *A Southerner Discovers the South* (New York: The Macmillan Company, 1938).

10. Hillbilly culture is mountain culture and is aligned with bluegrass music, moonshine, and moon pies. Think *The Beverly Hillbillies*, Ma and Pa Kettle, *The Dukes of Hazzard*, and *Deliverance*. Hillbillies are not farming folk as such.

11. For more information see *White Trash: Race and Class in America*, eds. Matt Wray and Annalee Newitz (New York: Routledge, 1997).

12. For more information see http://www.howsyournews.com/, accessed October 24, 2006.

13. Dino Scatena and Allan Johnson, "Drawing on the Dark Side," *Adelaide Advertiser*, October 4, 2000, 44.

14. Details at http://www.bbc.co.uk/ouch/yourspace/tvvote/, October 24, 2006.

15. http://timmargh.net/, accessed October 24, 2006.

16. A supercrip is valorized for performing everyday tasks such as eating and walking and/or someone who overcomes all odds to complete an impossible task, i.e., a blind person climbing Everest.

17. Raymond J. Aguilera, "Review of Krazy Kripples," *Bent: A Journal of CripGay Voices*, September 2003, http://www.bentvoices.org/2003/09/krazy_kripples.html, accessed October 22, 2006.

18. "An Examination into the Portrayal of Deaf Characters and Deaf Issues in Picture Books for Children," *Disability Studies Quarterly* 24, no. 1 (2004), http://www.dsq-sds.org/_articles_html/2004/winter/dsq_w04_brittain.html, accessed October 22, 2006.

Chapter 15

Blessed Art Thou: Religion

F orget South Park Republicans. Are South Park atheists the next new spinoff group from the show? Unlikely.

God is not dead in *South Park*, but organized religion certainly is. The majority of religious-themed shows on television, such as *Saved by an Angel* and *Seventh Heaven*, are reverential; not so *South Park*. Maligning the sacred is a centuries old sport. Bakhtin found that the sacred was central to carnival laughter:

> . . . there was the "feast of fools" (*festa stultorum*) and the "feast of the ass"; there was a special free "Easter laughter (*risus paschalis*)," consecrated by tradition. Moreover, nearly every Church feast had its comic folk aspect, which was also traditionally recognized. Such, for instance, were the parish feasts, usually marked by fairs and varied open-air amusements, with the participation of giants, dwarfs, monsters, and trained animals. A carnival atmosphere reigned on days when mysteries and sorties were produced . . . certain carnival forms parody the Church's cult.[1]

Even the more somble "miracle and morality plays acquired . . . a carnivalesque nature."[2] Given the power of local clergyman, it is no wonder they were ridiculed, defecated upon, and laughed at during the revelries. Friar Tuck is a benign hangover from the days of the libidinous monk. One of the central figures in *Gargantua and Pantagruel* is Friar John, the lusty, imbibing, irreverent monk who can swap genital metaphor for genital metaphor and tells of using sacred scriptures to wipe his ass:

> "One day," said Friar John, "when I was at
> Seuilly, I wiped my bum with a page of
> one of these wretched Clementines that
> John Guimard, our bursar, had thrown
> out into the cloister meadow, and may all

227

the devils take me if I wasn't seized with
such horrible cracks and piles that the
poor door to my back passage was quite
unhinged."

Friar John is a travesty of the low clergy—he reworks sacred texts as obscene ones. And while Father Maxi might not be as crude as Friar John, he is as ridiculed. As Rabelais himself was a Catholic monk, he wrote about what he knew. No fewer than eighteen *South Park* episodes have religious concerns as their central narrative device, making it one of the most "religion-fixated shows on the small screen."[3]

The focus of *South Park*'s interrogation is the unquestioning acceptance of bizarre religious tenets—whether transubstantiation or the science fiction meanderings of Scientology. It's no coincidence that question marks punctuate religious episode titles. But their interrogation involves more than a religion's beliefs; central to the expositions are the role of the churches as financial corporations, brainwashing institutions, and outdated secret societies. By being equally skeptical about Judaism, Scientology, Mormonism, and Christianity, *South Park* even-handedly positions widely disparate religions on the same level playing field. The religious episodes have attracted criticism, but that's hardly surprising; approximately twenty years earlier Monty Python's *Life of Brian* (1979) also attracted widespread condemnation.

South Park is a two-religion town. The creators Trey Parker and Matt Stone confess a fascination with Roman Catholic doctrine and rely on staff member Anne Garifino to explain the complexities of Catholicism: the concepts of Limbo, confession, and transubstantiation.

Jesus in *South Park*

Throughout the ages, Jesus has been re-worked as a popular culture icon. In the mid-nineteenth century, he was the masculine Jesus who cleansed the temple and single-handedly took on the Roman Empire—the warrior Jesus. Nineteenth century writers such as Charles Kingsley thought England needed healthy Christian empire builders and promoted a philosophy of "muscular Christianity." Fast-forward one hundred years and, in the 1960s, hippie Jesus, with his narratives of love and peace, appeared in the rock operas *Godspell* and *Jesus Christ Superstar*. Although Jesus started in muscular mode as a crusader against Santa in *The Spirit of Christmas*, it's hippie-humanist Jesus who offers rich opportunities to explore Christianity and Christian values.

As Morgan Spurlock showed in *Super Size Me* (2004), younger children can identify Ronald McDonald more often than they can Jesus. No wonder Father Maxi points to Jesus, "Look, it's that guy from the public access show" ("Damien"). *South Park* Jesus tries to be relevant and reaches the community through television and telephone:

JESUS: Hello, caller, you're on the air.

ROBERT: Yeah, is, is this Jesus?

JESUS: Yes, my son.

ROBERT: This, this is Robert from Torrey Pines. I called last week asking for advice on my ex-wife.

JESUS: Of course, Robert. How are things now?

ROBERT: Well, every, everything's much better, Jesus. She hasn't mouthed off since. I just wanted to thank you for the advice. Oh, and for, for dying for my sins, that was really nice of you.

JESUS: Blessed art thou, Robert. Next caller, you're on the air. ("Big Gay Al's")

Robert of Torrey Pines might be talking to the Son of God, but he's not fazed. To Robert, Jesus is just another talk-show host. Robert's attitude reflects the town's laid-back attitude—they get more excited when J-Lo visits. It's not that people don't understand Jesus's worth; Robert even goes so far as to thank Jesus for dying for his sins, albeit as an afterthought. It's just that in a media-saturated world it takes more than the Son of God to keep viewers tuned in.

Jesus cannot provide answers to the complex questions of contemporary society. He won't answer Stan's question about euthanasia ("Death"), and Stan's question about homosexuality remains unanswered because the show has to break for *Marty's Movie Reviews* ("Big Gay Al"). Cartman is happy that *Marty's Movie Reviews* interrupted Stan's lame question; grappling with complex social questions bores Cartman. He would much rather watch something entertaining, even a show that sounds as weak as *Marty's Movie Reviews*. Entertainment is god these days, and the celebrities who entertain are the contemporary deities. So when Jesus takes on David Blaine, he fails miserably. The audience is bored because Jesus's miracles are outdated. His loaves and fishes miracles cannot compete with David Blaine's show-biz magic. Illusion has replaced reality; everything is all shadow and no substance.

Jesus is one of the good guys. He is a gentle, caring, and nice person. He has problems with an overenthusiastic producer, he worries about fighting Satan, and he has a slightly troubled relationship with his father. He suffers much at the hands of doubting South Parkers. Although he is part of the community, he stands apart from it. Visually, the *South Park* Jesus reflects traditional representations—shoulder-length hair, a beard, white robes, and, of course, the halo. His soft-spoken voice and gentle demeanor mark him as different from the other townsfolk. By presenting Jesus as a humane and caring person, the creators strip him of his awesome divinity but not of his celebrity status.

His gentility is misinterpreted in a culture where might is right. When he cannot defeat Blaine, he calls on his Super Best Friends, Muhammad, Krishna, Joseph Smith, and Lao Tse, the religious equivalent of the Justice League of America. Jesus then becomes merely another figure in the pantheon of religious leaders; therefore, Christianity is presented as another religious option rather than the one true belief. By presenting Jesus as a representative of one of many spiritual ideologies, *South Park* repositions Christianity; it is no longer the central religious doctrine.

Most importantly, Jesus is distanced from Catholicism. Jesus is never seen in the church and rarely, if ever, converses with Father Maxi. He is not South Park's spiritual advisor; Father Maxi is. This deliberately separates the political organization of the Roman Catholic Church from its Christian roots. Jesus also doesn't espouse a belief in Hell or the tortures of eternal damnation: "God doesn't want you to spend all your time being afraid of Hell, or praising His name. God wants you to spend your time helping others, and living a good, happy life. That's how you live for Him" ("Probably"). Jesus provides a much-beloved counter to Father Maxi's fiery preaching.

Catholic Church

While Jesus preaches kindness and love of your fellow man, his Catholic representative, Father Maxi, hails from the hellfire-and-damnation school of theology:

PRIEST MAXI
*[loud and
threatening voice]:*   Today, we're going to talk about Hell. Hell is not a very nice place. Burning, searing, flames. Screaming, torture. For eternity. Once you are in Hell, you cannot escape. You live forever in horrible pain, in burning agony. All sinners are there in misery, dying over and over and over. If you be cast

down into this black bog of stench, then woe is thou, for Satan has made it the most miserable place in the universe! And he will be your ruler! Your ruler of pain and agony! . . . A place of everlasting agony and pain! Hell awaits all sinners and all who do not accept Christ! Children in this town have not been attending Sunday school after Mass! And adults have not been coming to Confession! If this does not change, I promise you, you will be going to the black pit of Satan's world! That is all. Peace be with you. ("Do the Handicapped")

The "peace be with you" ending underscores the hypocrisy of a religion that seeks to control its believers with medieval images and superstitions. Maxi's sermon scares the boys into taking religion and the sacraments more seriously. But soon, the boys find the Catholic Church wanting.

In the first instance, the dogma of the Catholic Church doesn't make sense. Its teachings are confusing and illogical; especially in the modern world, where science and logic are god. When Sister Anne tries to explain transubstantiation, the boys are disbelieving:

SISTER ANNE: Now, let me explain how Communion works. The priest will give you this round cracker, and he will say, "The Body of Christ," and then you eat it.

CARTMAN: Jesus was made of crackers?

SISTER ANNE: No.

STAN: But crackers are his body.

SISTER ANNE: Yes. . . . In the Book of Mark, Jesus distributed bread and said, "eat this, for it is my body."

CARTMAN: So w-we won't go to Hell as long as we eat crackers.

SISTER ANNE: Nononono!

BUTTERS: Uhwell, uh-what are we eatin' then?

SISTER ANNE: The Body of Christ! [*confused faces all around*]

STAN: No-no-no, I get it. Jesus wanted us to eat him, but he didn't want us to be cannibals, so he turned himself into crackers, and then told people to eat him.

SISTER ANNE: No!

STAN: No??

BUTTERS: Huh-I can't whistle if I eat too many crackers.

SISTER ANNE: Look, all you have to know is that when the priest gives you the cracker, you eat it! Okay?!

KENNY, STAN,
   CARTMAN: O-kay.

SISTER ANNE: And then, you will drink a very small amount of wine, for that is the Blood of Christ.

CARTMAN: Aw, come on now, this is just getting silly! ("Do the Handicapped")

It is not difficult to see why the boys are skeptical—after all, the idea of transubstantiation is bizarre. Wafers and wine are not metaphorical representations of Jesus' body and blood but, according to dogma, are transformed *into* his body and blood during Mass. This belief is central to Catholicism and to understanding the importance of the Mass. By describing the Communion wafer as a cracker, the joke is on the Catholic Church.

But before the boys can receive Communion, they must first confess their sins because, even if they have led a blameless life, everyone is born with original sin. The problem of original sin and the innocents has long been an issue of contention in the Catholic Church. It is a cruel creed that condemns handicapped Timmy to Hell because he can't confess. The boys' dissatisfaction with the church is compounded by Father Maxi's attitude. As their spiritual advisor, he fails to evidence any compassion. He is stern and unflinching in consigning Timmy to Hell. When Kyle asks if Jews will go to Hell, Maxi is adamant: "Well, young man, you can rest assured that according to Matthew 25, when you die you will stand before God and he will say, 'Depart from me, you cursèd, into the eternal fire prepared for the devil and his angels.' Yes! As a Jew, your home will be the lake of fire" ("Do the Handicapped").

Sister Anne is the more humane voice of the Catholic Church, and she tries to soften Maxi's interpretation:

SISTER ANNE: Father, I don't know if I agree fully with what you're saying. I think that as long as Jewish people are good, they will get into heaven.

PRIEST MAXI: Sister, the Jews crucified our Savior. I mean, if you don't go to Hell for crucifying the Savior, then what the hell do you go to Hell for?! ("Do the Handicapped")

While the philosophy of Communion is strange, it does not hold the fears of Confession. Of course, Cartman has the most amusing confessional scene:

CARTMAN: No, but I'm not finished yet. I took the sandwich that the priest was eating, took the piece of ham out of it, put it between my butt cheeks, and then put the sandwich back and watched him eat it.

PRIEST MAXI: I . . . see.

CARTMAN: Yeah, and then this other time, I went pee-pee in the holy
water thing, and the priest blessed himself on the forehead
with it every day for about a week. And then this one time, I
was at the park, and the priest was out walking his dog and I
went number two on the sidewalk and then told Officer
Barbrady that it was the priest's dog. And so the priest got
fined like a hundred dollars for not cleaning it up. And then
this one time, I put superglue all over the priest's bottle of-
("Do the Handicapped")

Father Maxi grabs Cartman by the throat. Cartman is now convinced he's felt
the hands of an angry god and warns the others: "We all have to start taking
this very seriously."

In the wake of the altar boy scandals, the creators have Father Maxi pro-
pose a weekend boat cruise as part of the Young Men's Catholic Retreat.
Given Maxi's curious sexual history[4] and the latest headlines, the concerned
parents decide to introduce a counselor to probe the boys about Father
Maxi:

COUNSELOR: Okaaay, what words would you use to describe your priest?

BUTTERS: Compassionate.

COUNSELOR: Okay. And did Father Maxi, at any time, ever try to put
something in your butt? [*pause, the boys look stunned*]

CARTMAN: I-in our butt?

COUNSELOR: You don't need to be ashamed or embarrassed. Just, did he
ever try to put anything in your butt?

STAN: Like . . . money? What?

BUTTERS: You mean, like a goldfish? ("Red-Hot Catholic Love")

The counselor's searching questions do not reveal sexual abuse and only
manage to bewilder the boys. Meanwhile, their parents, dismayed by the
scandals, reject God and start an Atheists' Club. During these meetings, they
repeat platitudes against religion:

I for one can't believe I used to live my life by what a very old and very fictional book used to say . . . what do a bunch of stories about people in robes
slaughtering goats have to do with today's world . . .

We're worried we might have a hard time raising our son atheist . . . it could
end up being very difficult raising an atheist child in such a Christian society.
I feel that everywhere my poor son goes he's being persecuted for his beliefs.

I don't want him saying "under God" every day at school. That could really
damage him.

We can't let the religious right corrupt our kids. ("Red-Hot Catholic Love")

During their self-congratulatory statements, crap literally comes out of their mouths, providing a visual representation of the verbal metaphor.

In a typical *South Park* turnaround, Father Maxi becomes the hero of this episode. He visits the Vatican to exhort the religious leaders about their outdated beliefs. They refuse to listen to him, and Father Maxi undergoes a computer adventure; again, the carnivalesque is invoked, and he retrieves ancient documents that he destroys in frustration. The Vatican crumbles while Maxi exhorts the Cardinals:

> All that's dead are your stupid laws and rules! You've forgotten what being a Catholic is all about. . . . You see, these are just stories [Bible]. Stories that are meant to help people in the right direction. Love your neighbor. Be a good person. . . . And when you start turning the stories into literal translations of hierarchies and power, well . . . Well, you end up with this [the ruins of the Vatican]. People are losing faith because they don't see how what you've turned the religion into applies to them! They've lost touch with any idea of any kind of religion, and when they have no mythology to try and live their lives by, well, they just start spewing a bunch of crap out of their mouths! . . . I'm proud to be a Catholic. But I'm a Catholic in the real world. In today's world! It's time for you all to do that, too. It is time . . . for change.

A lowly priest challenges the Church's authority, and, in doing so, he destroys the Church as institution.

Needless to say, all of this is done with lashings of lower body humor. The Galgamek's *vagina dentata*, the priests' pedophilia, and, of course, the aetheists' crapping. Later, in "Bloody Mary," the lower body is further indulged when a statue of the Virgin Mary bleeds from its ass and onto the Pope's face. The Catholic Church offers little help in coping with contemporary life; for compassion or spirituality, for comfort and advice, people in South Park go to Chef, Jesus, or God (in that order).

Alternative Christianity

Disgusted with the Catholic Church and Father Maxi's hypocrisy, Cartman starts his own religion. Soon he is on a soapbox preaching his brand of hell, fire, and damnation. Cartman enacts another type of religious leader, the Pentecostal, revivalist preacher—most widely recognized today as the television evangelist. He has Elmer Gantry's charisma, Pat Robertson's business acumen, and Jimmy Swaggart's evangelical zeal. He gives a performance of persuasive rhetoric, dramatic monologues, and theatrical gestures. He holds his Bible aloft and intones:

CARTMAN: Many of you knew Kenny McCormick. He was a playful, school-going eight-year-old. And then yesterday, he was [*prostrates himself*] smacked down by the Lord-uh! God bitch-slapped him right to the fiery depths of Hell. So when will *you* go?! Tomorrow?! Ten years?! Does it mattah?! No! Because unless you give this life to the Lord, that life belongs to Satan-a! But we cannot worship God in that church where that priest of sin resides, so we will build a new church-a. With crystal walls, a ceiling 80 feet high, and a slide that connects this part hmya to this part hmya. Who will help us? ("Probably")

He affects an evangelist patois and adds a syllable at the ends-a of certain-a words-a. He also has the whole hypocrisy thing going, too. When his mother tries to tempt the boys away from religion with food and toys, Cartman refutes her temptations . . . between bites of powdered doughnut pancake surprise.

Cartman conducts his services in his version of Robert Schuller's Crystal Cathedral. He includes a healing ceremony, which parodies (or replicates?) the evangelic ritual. He smacks people on the head and "cures" Kyle of his "Jewness," a girl of her "ugliness," and Timmy of his "affliction"—that is, until he falls down. All of the cures are clearly a sham, but his child-only congregation believes because they want to believe. He then receives a message "directly from God-uh! God is telling me that . . . each and every one of you is to walk up to the stage, and give me one dollar!" ("Probably"). Donations are now linked to salvation; just like the money changers in the temple buying plenary indulgences. Cartman mines Christianity three seasons later, with his Faith +1 band. Christianity, as Cartman knows, always offers the potential for profit.

Judaism

While the dogma, politics, and personnel of Roman Catholicism are foregrounded, the Jewish religion is inferred. We do not know the name of the rabbi and rarely see the synagogue. Most of the signifiers of "Jewishness" come from Cartman's stereotyping. Visually, Jewishness is defined by Gerald's skullcap and Sheila's Jewish-mother performance and cousin Kyle's whiney Jew.

The most information about Jewish doctrine (as opposed to Jewish culture) is in "Jewbilee," where the different sects, "Orthodox Jews, Hasidic Jews, Northern Italy Cave Jews," gather. Elders from each sect argue; they gang up on the new radical anti-Semitic sect that follows the teaching of Haman.

Throughout the episode, Kenny plays the viewer's cipher; through his non-Jewish eyes we witness the silliness of Judaism—the campfire adoration, the soap offerings, and the carrot cake. But Moses is much more impressive than God. He is a gigantic orange and yellow five-sided geometrical figure with eyes, nose, and mouth, very different from the animal-like god of Catholicism ("Are You There God?").

After seeing *The Passion of The Christ*, Kyle questions the role of the Jews in Christ's death and approaches Father Maxi. An unusually understanding Father Maxi explains the historical roots of the passion play and its role as an anti-Semitic performance piece ("Passion of The Jew"). Armed with Father Maxi's advice about atonement, Kyle addresses a Jewish congregation and suggests that it is time for the Jewish community to apologize for the death of Jesus. The congregation is appalled. At the standoff outside the Bijou Theater, Jews and Christians face each other; the burning question, should the Jewish community apologize, is averted by the arrival of Mel Gibson. His daffy behavior is reason enough for them to question his sanity and, by association, his film. Stan delivers the ultimate religious lesson: "[Y]ou should follow what Jesus taught instead of how he got killed. Focusing on how he got killed is what people did in the Dark Ages and it ends up with really bad results" ("Passion of The Jew").

A Different Kind of God

In a world of cruel deaths, unexplained misery, and horrific violence, *South Park* asks: Can there truly be a God if such evil exists? South Parkers battle with the age-old philosophical dilemma of the problem of evil, and each has a slightly different version of God. Father Maxi describes his warped-sense-of-humor god:

> It is sometimes hard, in times like these, to understand God's way. Why would he allow nine innocent people to be run down in the prime of their lives by a senior citizen who, perhaps, shouldn't be driving? It is then that we must understand God's sense of humor is very different from our own. He does not laugh at the simple "man walks into a bar" joke. No, God needs complex irony and subtle farcical twists that seem macabre to you and me. All that we can hope for is that God got his good laugh and a tragedy such as this will never happen again. ("Grey Dawn")

Chef explains his pissed-off god:

> CHEF: Stan, sometimes God takes those closest to us, because it makes him feel better about himself. He is a very vengeful God, Stan. He's all pissed off about something we did thou-

sands of years ago. He just can't get over it, so he doesn't care who he takes. Children, puppies, it don't matter to him, so long as it makes us sad. Do you understand?

STAN: But then, why does God give us anything to start with?

CHEF: Well, look at it this way: if you want to make a baby cry, first you give it a lollipop. Then you take it away. If you never give it a lollipop to begin with, then it would have nothin' to cry about. That's like God, who gives us life and love and help just so that he can tear it all away and make us cry, so he can drink the sweet milk of our tears. You see, it's our tears, Stan, that gives God his great power. ("Kenny Dies")

Jimmy's parents think that God is a cruel teacher, that he is a revengeful God:

RYAN: Uh, Jimmy, we've told you before. God made you the way he did for a reason!

JIMMY: Right. Because you and Mom used to make fun of crippled kids in high school.

RYAN: That's right. You were sent here through the vengeful and angry hand of God to teach your mother and I a lesson. And that's a big responsibility, son. ("Krazy Kripples")

When Jehovah gives Kyle an infected hemorrhoid and Cartman $1 million, to Kyle, no justice means no God.

Despite the town's disdain for God, they still want him to appear on the eve of the millennium. In this carnivalesque-inverted world, God is not the anthropomorphic Christian God; he is a snaggle-toothed, hippopotamus-like creature. Neither is he all knowing; instead, he is gullible and accepts Saddam Hussein's denial that he has a chemical weapons plant. Hussein thinks God is "a stupid asshole" ("Ladder to Heaven"). Hussein is the epitome of pure evil, not Satan.

Satan is impressive. He is a red, huge, barrel-chested satyr with yellow horns and eyes and pointy white bottom teeth; his hoofed feet are a nice touch. Satan lives in the River Styx Condominiums in a blue oasis of townhouses. He collects Hummels and lives with his lover, Chris. Chris is understanding and patient; in fact, Chris is so nice that he could be a Mormon. One can only assume he's in Hell because he's gay. Satan finds Chris's Sensitive New Age Guy persona grating; he misses his bad-boy ex-lover Saddam Hussein. Actually, he's cowed by Hussein. Like Jesus, Satan's relationships and personal problems make him human—no longer the demonic Prince of Darkness, he's no more frightening than Jesus.

All About Mormons and Scientologists

When Satan visits Heaven, he is met by a crowd of cheery people. They welcome Satan, offer him cookies and punch, and invite him to join their charades and sing-a-long. Needless to say, he rejects the invitation. All the people in Heaven are dressed in white, short-sleeved shirts, black pants, and clip-on ties; their uniform dress sends visual cues that they are a unified group. One of them wears a bicycle helmet. They are now identifiable as Mormons—the man with the bicycle helmet is a missionary. Mormons consider Satan a "nice fellow." Yes, the Mormons are the only people allowed into *South Park* Heaven. The newbies in Hell soon learn that their religions have failed them:

MAN 4:   Hey, wait a minute, I shouldn't be here. I was a totally strict and devout Protestant! I thought we went to heaven!

HELL DIRECTOR: Yes, well, I'm afraid you were wrong.

SOLDIER: I was a practicing Jehovah's Witness.

HELL DIRECTOR: You picked the wrong religion as well.

MAN 5:   Well, who was right? Who gets into Heaven?

HELL DIRECTOR: I'm afraid it was the Moooormons. Yes, the Moooormons were the correct answer.

CROWD: Awww. ("Probably")

Throughout the series, the Mormons are depicted as happy, kind, and thoughtful; they are thoroughly nice people who live their value system.

The only thing strange about the Mormons is their dogma. In "All About Mormons," the Harrisons re-tell the Joseph Smith story. Though intrigued at first, Stan rejects Smith's increasingly weird story. Stan is the mouthpiece of nonbelievers; he invokes a crisis of faith and faith is, of course, central. No matter how ridiculous the Joseph Smith story is, however, the Harrisons' family spirit supersedes their "whacky" religion. Gary responds to Stan's cynicism:

> Look, maybe us Mormons do believe in crazy stories that make absolutely no sense, and maybe Joseph Smith did make it all up, but I have a great life and a great family, and I have the *Book of Mormon* to thank for that. The truth is, I don't care if Joseph Smith made it all up, because what the church teaches now is loving your family, being nice and helping people. And even though people in *this* town might think that's stupid, I still choose to believe in it. All I ever did was try to be your friend, Stan, but you're so high and mighty you couldn't look past my religion and just be my friend back. You've got a lot of growing up to do, buddy. Suck my balls.

Succinctly, Gary extols the virtues of his religion. Ultimately, it is not the Mormons' history that gets them into Heaven, it is their hands-on application of their beliefs that wins God's approval.

Joseph Smith's story is positively sane compared to L. Ron Hubbard's. After recruiting Stan and performing quasi-scientific tests, the Scientologists are convinced that Stan is the reincarnation of their leader, L. Ron Hubbard. The elders want Stan to continue their scriptures where Hubbard stopped, and so they explain the roots of their religion to him:

> It all began 75 million years ago. Back then, there was a galactic federation of planets which was ruled over by the evil Lord Xenu. Xenu thought his galaxy was overpopulated, and so he rounded up countless aliens from all different planets, and then had those aliens frozen. The frozen alien bodies were loaded onto Xenu's galactic cruisers. . . . The cruisers then took the frozen alien bodies to our planet, to Earth, and dumped them into the volcanoes of Hawaii. The aliens were no longer frozen; they were dead. The *souls* of those aliens, however, lived on, and all *floated up* towards the sky. But the evil Lord Xenu had prepared for this. Xenu didn't *want* their souls to return! And so he built giant soul-catchers in the sky! The souls were taken to a huge soul brainwashing facility, which Xenu had *also* built on Earth. There the souls were forced to watch days of brainwashing material, which tricked them into believing a false reality. Xenu then released the alien souls, which roamed the earth aimlessly in a fog of confusion. At the dawn of man, the souls finally found bodies which they can grab onto. They attached themselves to all mankind, which still to this day causes all our fears, our confusions, and our problems. L. Ron Hubbard did an amazing thing telling the world this incredible truth. Now all we're asking you to do . . . [hands Stan a pen and some paper] is pick up where he left off. ("Trapped in the Closet")

Throughout the narrative, "Scientologists actually believe this" appears at the bottom of on the screen.

But this is no benign Mormon group; Scientologists have a history of protecting their institution by suing anyone who questions its tenets. The crowd rejects Stan's assertion that "Scientology is just a big fat global scam" and threatens to sue him. Stan, obviously the mouthpiece of the creators, dares them to sue him.

After the show, Scientologists were outraged, and Isaac Hayes (who did not appear in the episode) showed his displeasure by leaving *South Park*. How could *South Park* leave it at that? So they retaliated with an episode about the brainwashing activities of a "fruity club," and Kyle gives a fitting eulogy:

> We're all here today because Chef has been such an important part of our lives. A lot of us don't agree with the choices Chef has made in the past few days. Some of us . . . feel hurt . . . and confused that he seemed to turn his

back on us. But we can't let the events of the last week take away the memo-
ries of how much Chef made us smile. *I'm* gonna remember Chef as the jolly
old guy who always broke into song. *I'm* gonna remember Chef . . . as the guy
who gave us advice to live by. So, you see, we shouldn't be mad at Chef for
leaving us. We should be mad at that little fruity club for scrambling his
brains. ("Return of Chef")

Christian Charity

Christian charity is portrayed through the figure of the starving Ethiopian,
Starvin' Marvin. Appropriately, the two Marvin episodes are Thanksgiving
ones; the USA's celebration of plenty provides the perfect vehicle to examine
how the Christian South Parkers treat the less fortunate. In the first episode,
the boys donate to Feed the Children Foundation—not out of Christian
charity, but because they want the sports watch ("Starvin' Marvin"). Charity
is giving money, not caring, explains Principal Victoria. It's even better if the
money you give is not your own, but your parents'.

Two seasons later, Ethiopians are still suffering famine and privation, and
the "help" America sends is misguided. The culturally insensitive Sister Hollis
bribes the Ethiopians with food: "reading Bible plus accepting Jesus equals
food" ("Starvin' Marvin in Space"). The missionaries just do not get the
nature of real charity: heathens are given Christian names and taught "God's
language," English. Marvin leaves Sister Hollis's classroom in disgust; he's
been to America and he's seen the American life of plenty. She admonishes
him: "Where are you going? Back to your life of sin? Don't you understand
that unless you find Christ, you and all your people are doomed to eternal
hellfire?" She doesn't understand that Marvin's Earth is Hell. His country is
flat, dry, hot, and denuded of trees; there is no food.

Ironically, the Ethiopians' solution is otherworldly, but not in the way
Christianity would have us believe. The inhabitants of Planet Marklar haven't
heard of God or Jesus, but they demonstrate Christian spirit when they agree
to take in the Ethiopians. Their dismissal of the Christian missionaries is a
poignant mixture of disinterest and politeness:

> HOLLIS: Alien friend, we are here to spread the word of Jesus. He
> died for your sins.
>
> MARKLAR: Who? Marklar? . . .
>
> MARKLAR: You marklars must leave. [*points to missionaries, Sister Hol-
> lis*]
>
> HOLLIS: But you will all burn forever in eternal hellfire.

MARKLAR: Yes, that's nice. Thank you for stopping by.

There seems no answer to the Ethiopian problem on this planet. It is only in another galaxy that people are caring enough to truly help.

Conclusion

For a show that has children blaspheming, graphic sexual overtones, and lots of inappropriate behavior, *South Park* spends a lot of time in its churches. Through religion, the creators examine what contemporary society offers in the way of spirituality. The problem is not divine leadership—God, Jesus, Moses, and other religious deities fare pretty well—but earthly hypocrisy. *South Park*'s secular humanism offers every religion equal opportunity. Belief in a higher deity or deities is fine, even encouraged, but be wary of politicized religion, warns the show. Religion is just another powerful institution that needs to have its cages rattled. The show's irreverence promotes a healthy skepticism about religious dogma. The morality of a culture is reflected in the ability of its adherents to learn simple moral lessons and to lead "good" lives.

South Park seeks out the hypocritical and examines various belief systems for logic. The show also considers how people perform their religions because for many, religion is ultimately a performance. If we window-shop religions via *South Park*, Mormonism triumphs because it seems to be the only religion that is a lifestyle.

The series' scathing attacks on the Catholic Church are another reworking of the carnivalesque. During medieval festivals, sinners in priestly vestments preached nonsensical or blasphemous sermons. Carnival is a reminder that the pope's shit stinks, too. And nonbelievers literally and figuratively crap out of their mouths. Stan tells viewers:

> You don't need David Blaine to tell you how to live. See, cults are dangerous because they promise you hope, happiness and maybe even an afterlife. But in return, they demand you pay money. Any religion that requires you to pay money in order to move up and learn its tenets is wrong. See, all religions have something valuable to teach, but, just like the Super Best Friends learned, it requires a little bit of them all. ("Super Best Friends")

Throughout the seasons, *South Park* episodes ridicule, mock, explore, and explode religious dogmas.

CARTMAN: Many of you knew Kenny McCormick—yesterday God bitch-slapped him right to the fiery depths of Hell. ("Probably")

CARTMAN: Right here we have a little girl who is very, very ugly! Do you believe he is gonna cure your face of the uglies?!

UGLY GIRL: Yes!!

CARTMAN: He is gonna take that ugly face and make you reasonable to look at! [smacks her on the face] Bah! ("Probably")

KYLE: Hey, Jesus, if you win the fight, can you turn Kenny back to normal?

JESUS: What the hell do you mean, "if I win the fight?"

CARTMAN: Don't mind him Jesus, [whispered] he's Jewish.

JESUS: Oh. ("Damien")

Notes

1. Mikhail Bakhtin, *Rabelais and His World,* trans. Helene Iswolsky (Bloomington: Indiana University Press, 1984), 5–6.

2. Ibid.,15.

3. Mark I. Pinsky, "Jesus Lives in South Park," www.beliefnet.com/story/174/story_17498.html, accessed October 23 2006.

4. In "Cripple Fight," Maxi refers to his homosexual past.

Chapter 16

South Park Is Totally Gay: Sex and Gender

In his celebration of the joys of living—feasting, farting, and fucking—Rabelais did not shy away from considering the role of the body in the human condition. The folkloric celebration of the lower body embraces reproductive organs and anuses. And Rabelais often gave the bodies of his grotesque characters both sets of genitals:

> Gargantua's hat has an emblem which portrays a man's body with two heads facing one another, four arms, four feet, a pair of arses and a brace of sexual organs, male and female. Such, according to Plato's *Symposium*, was human nature in its mystical origins.[1]

This duality represents the grotesque body at its most transformative. Furthermore, Bakhtin's grotesque affirms both body and gender transgressions:

> the grotesque body is not separated from the rest of the world. It is not a closed, completed unit; it is unfinished, outgrows itself, transgresses its own limits. The stress is laid on those parts of the body that are open to the outside world, that is, the parts through the world enters the body or emerges from it, or through which the body itself goes out to meet the world. This means that the emphasis is on the apertures or convexities, or on various ramifications and offshoots: the open mouth, the genital organs, the breasts, the phallus, the potbelly, the nose. The body discloses its essence as a principle of growth which exceeds its own limits only in copulation, pregnancy, childbirth, the throes of death, eating, drinking, or defecation. This is the ever unfinished, ever creating body.[2]

Certainly in *South Park,* some bodies are a little more unfinished than others.

Because of censorship issues, television has been limited in its exploration of sexuality. Married television couples slept in single beds until the radical

Bradys. In the 1990s, sex became big on television; first it was heterosexual sex (*Seinfeld*, *Sex and the City*), then homosexual lifestyles (*The L Word*, *Queer as Folk*, *Will and Grace*), suburban sex (*Desperate Housewives*), and even religious sex (*Big Love*). Predictably, *South Park*'s takes on sex and gender issues push the boundaries of good taste. Few shows have dared to go where *South Park* goes.

Sex and the Single Person

The two most sexually active singles are Chef and Liane Cartman. Chef has bedded most of the South Park females. Unlike the other males, he prefers bed to bars, and is often seen in the company of more than one female ("Summer Sucks," "Die Hippie, Die"). He remains a confirmed bachelor, though he was convinced by his fiancé that "Meaningless sex is fun for twenty or thirty years, but after that, it starts to get old" ("Succubus"). Chef's sexuality might be racial stereotyping, but it's a celebratory sexuality—he is the most caring of the town's males. He is so constituted by his sexuality that his solution to raise money is to "whore myself to every woman in town" ("Chef Aid"), which he does successfully.

Liane Cartman is the town's whore and the town's most intriguing person in terms of gender. She has multiple sex partners, uses sex to get favors, likes dildos and blow-up Antonio Banderas dolls. When it is revealed that she is a hermaphrodite, all of the males in the room are sickened at the thought that they had sex with someone who had both sets of genitalia; however, her hermaphroditism doesn't seem to have hampered her, as she continues to have sex with Chef and other men since the revelation.[3] She is treated as a female because she *performs* the female-gendered role: she bakes, wears female clothing, has a high-pitched voice, and is a mother.

Other single females in South Park, including Mayor McDaniels, Ms. Choksondik, Mrs. Crabtree, and Principal Victoria, have all had heterosexual encounters. Mayor McDaniels has a varied sex life. She conducts an ongoing affair with the married Officer Barbrady and pays Chef for an extra session. In fact, the women of South Park are not averse to paying for sex, even if only to demonstrate their community spirit ("Chef Aid").

Sex and the Married Couple

Viewers have come a long way since the days of *The Dick Van Dyke Show* and twin beds for married couples. Even family sitcoms such as *Everybody Loves*

Raymond contain jokes about married sex. The sexual revelations reflect the changing sexual mores in contemporary society.

Throughout the series, viewers learn that Randy and Sharon spice up their sex lives with a little porn; Sharon's willing acquiescence demonstrates that porn is not for males only. Gerald Broflovski's erectile dysfunction ("Spontaneous Combustion") mirrors society's uptake of Viagra. The episode in which Mr. Stotch experiments with gay sex collapses several sexual issues: it explores married gay sex and Internet sex and suggests that sexuality is not rigid.

Nothing is simple or straightforward in the town of South Park—sex is handled with typical *South Park* humor and verve. When Randy and Sharon "bed" down for the night, they discover a video mix-up. They call the other parents and explain the problem, but instead of horror, several men indicate familiarity with *Back Door Sluts 9* and porn videos in general—a fact not appreciated by their wives:

GERALD B., CHRIS S.: *Back Door Sluts 9!!!*

> LINDA: Is that bad?

> CHRIS: *Back Door Sluts 9* makes *Crotch Capers 3* look like *Naughty Nurses 2*!

> GERALD: I-it is the single most vile, twisted, dark piece of porn ever made.

> SHEILA: [*slaps him*] How the hell do you know?! ("Return of the Fellowship")

Clearly not every wife has Sharon's proclivity for porn in the bedroom. The video causes Butters the first flutterings of sexual awakening; he doesn't understand what's happening, but he becomes addicted to his "precious." Token has a totally different reaction. At the end of the show, the parents (fearing the children have watched the video) explain sex to their children:

> RANDY: A-alright, now, now listen, kids. There's some things we need to put into context for you. You see, a man puts his penis into a woman's vagina for both love and pleasure. But sometimes the woman lays on top of the man facing the other way so that they can put each other's genitals in their mouths. [*the boys are stunned*] Uh this is called "sixty-nin-ing" and it's normal.

> SHARON: See, boys, a woman is sensitive in her vagina and it . . . feels good to have a man's penis inside of it.

> SHEILA: That's right, but sometimes a woman chooses to use other things. Telephones, staplers, magazines. It's because the

> nerve endings in the vagina are so sensitive, it's like a fun tickle.
>
> GERALD: Now, on to double penetration, boys. You see, sometimes when a woman has sex with more than one man, each man makes love to a different orifice.
>
> RANDY: That's right. It's something adults can do with really good friends in a comfortable setting.
>
> SHEILA: It's also important that you understand why some people choose to urinate on each other.
>
> RANDY: Going number one or number two on your lover is something people might do, but you must make sure your partner is okay with it before you start doing it.
>
> GERALD: Okay, boys. Do you have any questions?
>
> STAN: . . . Wwow. [*stunned silence*] ("Return of the Fellowship")

The explanation is politically correct but is clearly way too much information for children; it is totally inappropriate. What the parents describe is the spectacular sex of porn, not the "normal" sex usually explored in sex education, which the children received the previous season ("Proper Condom Use")— also with disastrous results.

At the center of many of the *South Park* displays of male sexuality is the possibility that all men have homosexual thoughts, if not actual experiences. Many of the males are presented with ambivalent sexual possibilities. Jimbo seems to live with his Vietnam buddy Ned; in several scenes, his homosexuality is inferred: he isn't beeped when he says fag, his metrosexual outfit says he "takes it in the butt," and he admits, "We're all a *little* gay" ("Two Guys Naked"). Gerald Broflovski and Randy Marsh share a homoerotic in Mackey's hot tub:

> GERALD: I wish. That's the one thing I've always thought of experimenting with. A threesome.
>
> RANDY: With two girls or two guys?
>
> GERALD: Huh, well, two girls, of course! I mean . . . with another guy, you know, that'd be . . .
>
> RANDY: You, you never have a homosexual fantasy? Not that I have.
>
> GERALD: You haven't?
>
> RANDY: *No*, I mean . . . Well, they say everybody has at some point, don't they?
>
> GERALD: Well, I never really wanted to experiment with anything too crazy. You know . . . maybe just . . . I don't know . . . masturbate in front of another guy.

RANDY: Yeah, well, that, that's not really . . . gay, is it?

GERALD: NO, no, uh I don't think so.

RANDY: . . . Well, it is a night for experimenting.

GERALD: Sure is.

RANDY: Okay, I'll start. ("Two Guys Naked")

Mackey and Ned admit they've watched men masturbate. And later, Ned masturbates in front of Jimbo (though the two men are watching a woman undress). Father Maxi has had homosexual encounters and heterosexual ones. Married Mr. Grazier, a.k.a. Mr. Slippy Fist, takes photos of naked boys ("Cripple Fight"). But the man with the most confused sexuality in South Park is the schoolteacher, Herbert Garrison.

Gayness

Garrison provides a complicated exploration of gay issues. Through the seasons, viewers have witnessed his evolution from firmly closeted gay:

STAN: What's a homosexual?

MR. GARRISON: Ho-well, Stanley, I guess you came to the right person. Sit down.

MR. GARRISON: Stanley, gay people . . . well, gay people are evil. Evil right down to their cold black hearts, which pump not blood like yours and mine. . . . But rather a thick, vomitous oil that oozes through their rotten veins and clots in their pea sized brains which becomes the cause of their Naziesque patterns of violent behavior. Do you understand?

STAN: I guess.

MR. GARRISON: Good, I'm glad we could have this little talk, Stanley. Now you go outside and practice football like a good little heterosexual. ("Big Gay Al's")

While Garrison was emotionally unable to recognize his sexuality, no one else was:

CHEF: Well, you know what they say: you can't teach a gay dog straight tricks.

MR. GARRISON: Oh, stop filling his head with that queer-loving propaganda.

CHEF: Say what?!? You of all people should be sympathetic.

MR. GARRISON: What do you mean?

CHEF:	Well, you're gay aren't you?
MR. GARRISON:	What?!? What the hell are you talking about?!? I am not gay.
CHEF:	Well, you sure do act like it.
MR. GARRISON:	I just act that way to get chicks, dumb ass. ("Big Gay Al's")

For the next several seasons, Garrison continues to pretend he's straight, aggressively straight. He claims all he wants to do is "hang out and screw hot chicks" ("Tom's Rhinoplasty"). He even claims to have slept with Cartman's mum ("Cartman's Mom Is a Dirty Slut"). Finally, he seeks professional help when Mr. Hat goes missing:

MR. GARRISON:	At first I was sure one of the children took him, but then I remembered that Mr. Hat and I actually had a fight that morning.
DR. KATZ:	Um, ahem. Are you gay?
MR. GARRISON:	What?
DR. KATZ:	It's, it's just a question.
MR. GARRISON:	Are you propositioning me?
DR. KATZ:	No.
MR. GARRISON:	Well, I can tell you that I'm 100 percent not gay.
DR. KATZ:	Well, I believe you. I absolutely believe you.
MR. GARRISON:	Mr. Hat, on the other hand.
DR. KATZ:	Mr. Hat was gay?
MR. GARRISON:	Sometimes he fantasizes about same relations.
DR. KATZ:	I see.
MR. GARRISON:	Sometimes Mr. Hat liked to pretend he was in a sauna with Brett Favre, in a bottle of a Thousand Island dressing.
DR. KATZ:	That I did not need to know.
MR. GARRISON:	Well, I'm just saying.
DR. KATZ:	Mr. Garrison, I think that Mr. Hat was actually your gay side trying to come out. You see, it's you that's gay, but you're in denial, so you act out your gay persona with a homosexual puppet. What do you think about that?
MR. GARRISON:	I think you're the loony one in this room. ("Summer Sucks")

Mr. Hat not only allows Garrison to fantasize, Hat is in fact Garrison's only sexual outlet and is the visual reminder of Garrison's autoeroticism. This is clear when Garrison writes his erotic novel. Mr. Hat gives Garrison relief. Garrison then decides his sexual problems are due to his father *not* molesting him, and he begs his father to remedy the situation ("Worldwide Recorder Concert").

Half a dozen episodes later, Garrison is again in sexual trouble. This time, he's made an appointment to meet with Cartman. It's clear now that Garrison's sexuality is multidimensional: he's had sex with ducks, women (?), a paraplegic uncle, and is now soliciting a young boy. Garrison is one confused site of sexual aberration.

He is given a break from teaching until his little "child molestation" thing dies down. While on break, he writes a romance novel, but is appalled when it receives a Pulitzer Prize for the "best homoerotic novel since *Huckleberry Finn*." The prize causes him to have a breakdown—he retreats to nature and goes to the mountains, where of course he will find himself. But even then he argues with his alter ego:

UNKEMPT GARRISON:	But I'm not gay! Everyone just thinks I am!
"GAY" GARRISON:	Oh, stop it! What about the time you looked at Counselor Mackey's penis in the men's locker room?!
UNKEMPT GARRISON:	I was just comparing size!
"GAY" GARRISON:	For seven minutes?!
UNKEMPT GARRISON:	Aaaaaarrrh.
"GAY" GARRISON:	And what about the time you masturbated to the men's 100-meter swimming relay at the Olympics?!
UNKEMPT GARRISON:	I was beating off to the chicks!
"GAY" GARRISON:	THERE WERE NO CHICKS!
UNKEMPT GARRISON:	OH, DAMN YOU SPIRIT! HAUNT ME NO LONGER!
"GAY" GARRISON:	ADMIT IT!
UNKEMPT GARRISON:	NO!!!
"GAY" GARRISON:	YOU HAVE TO STOP LYING TO YOURSELF AND GET A G-
UNKEMPT GARRISON:	ALRIGHT, ALRIGHT, I ADMIT IT! I'M GAY!!! I'm . . . gay. I'm gay! I am gay! You hear that everyone? I'm gay! I'm gay! I'm gay and it . . . and it feels good. ("4th Grade")

From this moment, Garrison embraces his sexuality with fervor. He relishes being "gay" and is thrilled when the metrosexual craze fills his bar with new men. However, he becomes angered when his sexual advances are rejected. Garrison does not understand the difference between sexuality and gender.

He believes that if a male is well dressed, meticulously groomed, and drinks shiraz, that the man must be gay. Now he is confronted with men who perform gay but aren't gay. Could it be that "sexuality" is merely performance? He challenges the *Queer Eye* guys: "Look, us gays have created a lifestyle, a-a culture that is uniquely ours. If we keep trying to make straight people into us, well, we're gonna have no identity left." Gender, as Judith Butler has pointed out, can be performed.[4] And so on to Mr. Garrison's next performance, that of a woman.[5]

In season eight, Garrison fulfills his previously unspoken dream, that of being a woman. He has a vaginoplasty because he wants to be "well again"; to Garrison, to be "well" is to be female—he has internalized his homophobia. Garrison apparently confused sexuality with gender. He claims he is a transsexual not a homosexual and confesses as much to his partner, Mr. Slave.

Mr. Slave dresses in black leather chaps, vest, cap, and chained boots. He has a square jaw and muscular body; he's hirsute and has a handlebar moustache, sideburns, and hairy chest. Can you guess who he is? Yes, Mr. Slave is the embodiment of a Village People stereotype, "the leather/biker guy." Despite his hypermasculine appearance, Mr. Slave is given to exaggerated wrist flapping, pursing his red lips, and has a lisp. True to his eponymous persona, Slave is masochistic and enjoys being spanked. But mostly, he enjoys having things shoved up his ass. Slave performs a different kind of gay to Garrison's gay. And he most definitely does not want to make love to Mrs. Garrison.

Aside from Garrison and Mr. Slave, the other *South Park* gays are Big Gay Al, Sparky, Sadam Hussein, Satan, and Chris.[6] Sparky, Stan's gay dog, is the first gay dog on television and introduces viewers to the show's homosexual agenda. Homosexuality on *South Park* couldn't be presented as a human being—that would be too predictable. Better to use a dog and preferably a dog voiced (or barked) by George Clooney.

Sexual tolerance does not mean unmediated acceptance, though, as Garrison explains: "Look, just because you have to tolerate something doesn't mean you have to approve of it! . . . 'Tolerate' means you're just putting up with it! You tolerate a crying child sitting next to you on the airplane or, or you tolerate a bad cold. It can still piss you off!" ("Death Camp of Tolerance"). Nor should tolerance engender oppression, as Big Gay Al explains when he wins a court case against the Boy Scouts:

> . . . this isn't what I wanted. I'm proud to be gay. And I'm proud to be in a country where I'm free to express myself. But freedom is a two-way street. If I'm free to express myself, then the Scouts have to be free to express themselves, too. I know these men. They are good men. They are kind men. They

do what they think is best for kids. No matter how wrong we think they might be, it isn't right for us to force them to think our way. It's up to us to persuade, and help them see the light, not extort them to. Please, don't cut the Scouts' funding. The Scouts help and have always helped a lot of kids. That's why I love them. I will continue to persuade them to change their mind, but this is the wrong way to do it. So, I am hereby dropping my case, and allowing the Scouts their right to not allow gays into their private club. ("Cripple Fight")[7]

The boys enjoy having Big Gay Al as their troop leader. Despite male parental misgivings, they accept him in the same unconditional way they accept Chef.

Children and Sex

Children and sex are an uncomfortable mix. Though they are only third/ fourth graders, the boys have had quite a range of sexual experiences. In ten seasons they have learned about heterosexual intercourse, sex toys, porn videos, homosexuality, bestiality, and even alien sex.

Kenny is the most sexually sophisticated of the boys. Many of his mutterings are sexually loaded. He is fixated on large-breasted women and is thrilled to visit a strip club ("Lil' Crime Stoppers"). However, his "deviant" sexuality is performed as part of his white-trash heritage, especially his familiarity with incest:

> KYLE: Stan, you can use family love as a weapon against Shelley. The next time she's gonna kick your ass, just tell her, "Shelley, you're my sister, and I love you."
>
> KENNY: And I want to take off your bra.
>
> STAN: Sick, dude, she's my sister. ("Big Gay Al's")

As the boys inch towards sexual maturity, the parents fear the children's increasing sexuality. They demand sex education—at school, of course. In this comedy of sexual errors, the parents and the educators get it horribly wrong, and the boys and girls end up at war. But the boys and girls are culturally destined to be on opposite sides.

After a brief interest in Bebe's boobs, the boys reject female sexuality ("Bebe's Boobs"). Females are threatening creatures and South Park even has its own disturbing *vagina dentate*,[8] the Gelgamek female who has "a vagina . . . three-feet wide and filled with razor-sharp teeth. Do you really expect us to have sex with them?!" ("Red-Hot Catholic Love"). Girls in *South Park* have limited sexual agency—when they express their sexuality, the boys look incredibly uncomfortable ("Stupid Spoiled Whore").

Kenny might be the most developed sexuality, but Cartman offers the most aberrant sexual knowledge. Cartman's sexual referencing lacks Kenny's knowledge but provides plenty of laughs: "Yeah, if some girl tried to kick my ass, I'd be like, 'Hey, why don't you stop dressin' me up like a mailman, and making me dance for you while you go and smoke crack in your bedroom and have sex with some guy I don't even know, on my dad's bed!' ("Elephant Fucks"). He has heard of a dildo and carries around an anatomically erect Antonio Banderas doll ("Korn's Groovy Pirate Ghost Mystery"). He names his band Fingerbang, a term that Kenny explains but which is rejected out of hand by the boys. Viewers might not be sure exactly what happened during "his" night with Leonard DiCaprio ("Cow Days"), but his first confirmed sexual encounter is with Ben Affleck ("Fat Butt"). Cartman, unwittingly, introduces the boys to pedophilia. Cartman is certainly headed for a strange adolescence.

In "Cripple Fight," a very different (and more dangerous) pedophile comes to South Park. After Big Gay Al is dismissed from the South Park troop because he's gay, the fathers are much happier with Al's replacement, Mr. Grazier:

HEAD SCOUTMASTER: Parents, this is the new Scout leader, Mr. Grazier. He will be taking over for the homosexual.

RANDY: Nice to meet you.

MR. GRAZIER: Marsh, right? We kind of actually know each other. Your wife and mine are friends.

STUART: Your wife, huh?

HEAD SCOUTMASTER: Carol is the head of a girls' Mountain Scouts troop.

MARSH: Well, I guess we're off to the bar until nine, then.

MR. GRAZIER: Gonna go pound some brews, huh? ("Cripple Fight")

Mr. Grazier performs heterosexuality: he is married, and he looks and acts like a marine drill sergeant with his buzz cut, stern countenance, clipped sentences, and deep, authoritative voice. The fathers feel that here's a man's man; they exchange knowing looks, smile, and nudge each other in their mutual recognition of Grazier's obvious masculinity. Grazier is a direct contrast to the simpering Al, but Al is a homosexual, not a pedophile. In the end, Grazier—not Al—proves to be a controlling pedophile who photographs naked children.

But the biggest betrayal comes from Chef. When he returns and tries to have sex with the boys, at first they are disbelieving. Chef has never acted like that before, so something's changed him. Sexuality is fixed—Chef can't simply "become" a homosexual pedophile. Of course, the whole episode is a ruse to explain Isaac Hayes' departure from the series, and, in typical South Park style, it has a sexual dimension.

Gender in *South Park*

Sexuality is not gender. Both Garrison and Liane Cartman have ambivalent sex organs and have decided to perform as females. Garrison is a prime example of the confusion between the two. Gender is therefore something performed, and Garrison's operation demonstrates his confusion.

Garrison reveals her change in a typical feminized space, the supermarket. She stands in the doorway and strikes an apparently typical female pose to show off her new appearance. She has feminized clothing: her brown pants have been shortened into capri pants and considerably tightened; the shirt is tighter to emphasize her new breasts; she wears white shoes (not brown) and carries the ultimate marker of a female, a handbag. She has accessorized with earrings and, of course, she wears makeup. Her glasses and hair haven't changed, but s/he now "looks" like a female. To celebrate her new gender, Garrison heads straight for the feminine products aisle where she approaches and hugs two females; she cannot wait to have her first period. Feminine physiology obviously escapes her.

Throughout the episode, she is treated as a freak. Her behavior is off-putting to other women: she is both too masculine (aggressive) and too feminine (caring). Garrison just can't seem to get it right. She brings home the groceries, talks about "sales," wants to see sad movies, talks "female talk" about men, and claims "girl power": "Men are all the same. My boyfriend walked out on me! Turns out he was a fag. But I've been livin' it up ever since, havin' sex with all kinds of different guys!" The gender differences are highlighted during her bathroom visit; Garrison's loud farting and noisy shitting disgusts the females—for some reason, shitting and farting remain the province of males. Overall, her performance of a female is not believable; she remains an aggressive, farting male. Her insistent hyper-femininity is not the glamorous performance of drag but the mimicry of the acolyte.

After she realizes she cannot have a baby, Garrison is mad. She has paid "five thousand dollars to be a woman"; in her worldview, one can buy "gender." An angered Garrison confronts Dr. Biber. Biber explains that a sex-change operation does not "make" a woman. Garrison is appalled. She calls herself a "freak"; she is "a guy with a mutilated penis." But by the end of the episode, Garrison accepts that being a woman is more than having periods and abortions (the reduction of "woman" to child-bearing propensities is disturbing). She concludes: "You know what? I'm okay. Even though I'm not truly a woman, I think I still like the new me. I'd rather be a woman who can't have periods than a *fag*. Hey, guys! This girl is staying a woman! Who wants to pound my vadge! Girl power!" ("Mr. Garrison's Fancy New Vagina").

The always politically challenged Garrison decides that even though he's "not truly a woman," he'd rather be a "woman who can't have periods than a *fag*." Garrison now rejects the former gayness that she had so wholeheartedly embraced. "Woman" is now his new gender central. He tries female-gendered rituals—he appears on a *Girls Gone Wild* video and tries to bond in bathrooms, bars, and supermarket shelves. Garrison's "revenge" on the male race is to have indiscriminate sex with as many men as possible. His version of girl power is to have his "vadge" pounded. Will Garrison ever accept that he wants to have sex with men, no matter what genitalia his body displays?

Gender is part of the show's masquerade performance. Liane Cartman and Garrison are complex sites for gender display and gender issues—Garrison because of his confused sexual identity and Liane because the hermaphrodite presents a unique version of the grotesque—hers is a body that usurps normative and notional forms of identity.

Gender socialization starts at South Park elementary. Boys and girls are divided and sent to gender-specific classes: the boys attend Shop and the girls, Home Economics. The boys learn to cut wood and do things with tools. The girls learn how to be "women." The lessons focus on finding a rich husband. Kenny doesn't want to be in shop for one reason, the dangerous tools; however, he seems to enjoy the female activities of Home Ec. Eventually, Kenny is dismissed from Home Ec because of poor performance:

> PEARL: Well, your cooking is unsatisfactory, your sewing skills are below average, and, frankly, I don't think the odds of you marrying a nice rich man in the future are very, well, good. ("Tweek vs. Craig")

The joke of course is that Kenny doesn't want to marry *any* man. He is puzzled and a little disheartened at Pearl's dismissal. Wendy, on the other hand, wants to take Shop because she's trying to reject traditional female roles. Given *South Park*'s conservative gender values and strong socialization program, it's highly unlikely, Wendy, you've already been pushed into the background.

Conclusion

No sexual practice is too taboo for the *South Park* humor mill. Episodes explore a wide variety of sexual issues in varying degrees: homosexuality, heterosexuality, pedophilia, bestiality, even necrophilia. Similarly, people are presented on a sexual continuum. Characters experiment with sexual options (Steve Stotch), have ambivalent gender (Liane Cartman), even change their physical gender (Mrs. Garrison). While most of the sexual activity is relegated to the adults, the children aren't immune. Some are starting to experience sexual feelings ("Return of the Fellowship," "Lil' Crime Stoppers," "Erection Day"), and they are potential prey for sexual predators ("Cripple Fight," "NAMBLA"). While the show as a whole espouses conservative political beliefs, sexual politics in *South Park* is anything but conservative. Indeed, *South Park* celebrates sexual diversity, is all its characters, white or black, handicapable or not, young or old, are portrayed as having sexual agency. As Rabelais wrote, "If the head is lost, all that perishes is the individual; if the balls are lost, all of human nature perishes."[9]

Notes

1. From book 1, chap. 8, quoted in Mikhail Bakhtin, *Rabelais and His World*, trans. Helene Iswolsky (Bloomington: Indiana University Press, 1984), 323.

2. Ibid., 26.

3. Liane's ambiguous genitalia also very subtly refers to cartoon characters of questionable gender, such as Bugs Bunny, Tom and Jerry, and Daffy Duck.

4. Judith Butler, *Gender Trouble: Feminism and the Subversion of Identity* (New York: Routledge, 1990).

5. It is interesting that Garrison, old conservative that he is, adopts Mrs. rather than Ms. Garrison.

6. The gay minority are lesbians. The only lesbian character has been Miss Ellen ("Tom's Rhinoplasty).

7. This is of course based on the *Boy Scouts of America et al. v. Dale* case.

8. Literally, "toothed vagina." Sigmund Freud's term for the mythos of women whose toothed vaginas can castrate men.

9. Panurge to Pantagruel in François Rabelais' *Gargantua and Pantagruel*, book 3, chap. 8.

Conclusion: You Know, I've Learned Something Today

So, after viewing hundreds of hours of *South Park*, reading thousands of media print articles, and browsing hundreds of Web sites, blogs, fanzines, and the like, what have I learned about *South Park*?

It is a phenomenally successful television show. Few can argue with that. Since it first premiered, it has become one of the most recognizable shows on television. In 2006, it celebrated its first decade. Other animated television shows have been going as long, but *South Park* has managed to carve a special niche, a niche helped by its ability to keep constantly in the media—few episodes go by without the series generating some press. Success is more than print inches, however; high ratings translate into big income—whether from merchandising sales, advertising dollars, or program syndication. *South Park*'s early ratings soon had networks in the rest of the world clamoring, and it has enjoyed similar success in the United Kingdom and Australia. *South Park*'s success is ballyhooed by Comedy Central, and each contract renegotiation comes with much fanfare and patting of backs. Will it last much longer? The creators must certainly hope not, after ten years of hard work. With long days, impossible hours, and relentless deadlines, the two creators must secretly cry to be released from the television servitude to which they've become indentured. It would be surprising to see the show last past fifteen years. But stranger things have happened. What *South Park* leaves in its wake is a generation of adult animations, a new(ish) television genre.

South Park's heritage is a legacy of adult television animations; it, *The Simpsons*, and *King of the Hill* demonstrated that cartoons can draw big television ratings. *South Park*'s distinctive style—popular cultural references, social commentary, adult situations and language—created a space for a different kind of animation. Of course, it wasn't the first show to have pretty crappy animation, *Beavis and Butt-head* beat them to it, but *South Park* elevated crappy to an art form. The colorful cardboard cutouts encapsulate the show's aesthetics and ideology of crap. Not surprisingly, a handful of similar animations soon followed (*Bro'town*, *Bromwell High*, *Chilly Beach*). And in a final ironic twist, it's a crap that sells, sells, sells.

When *South Park* reset the animation bar, the creators probably didn't realize that they would also be recalibrating censorship zones. For a show given to offending and the offensive, it has remained remarkably censor free. Even syndication warranted only fairly minor cuts, minor enough for the creators not to be able to see them. To date, no celebrity or organization has made a concerted or successful attempt to curtail the content; even Tom Cruise's tantrum over his portrayal did not prevent "Trapped in the Closet" from airing around the world.

Part of *South Park*'s appeal is its irreverent humor. It challenges hypocrisy without blinkers or hesitation. It takes on the mighty and the small. And though some issues might be personal bugbears of the creators, the show is known for its ripped-from-the-headlines content.[1] Fans now expect to see news items animated within weeks and sometimes in hours—including the Terry Schiavo debate, Hurricane Katrina issues, or a George Clooney speech. "How will *South Park* deal with x" has become a common catch phrase. *South Park* does not hate God or politicians; it's just not keen on religious dogma, outrageous pretensions, or liberal douches. It does, however, hate celebrities; they're just too darned smug.

Toilet humor: it's the mantle *South Park* will forever wear. And while I maintain it's not a fair one, the show does have many potty moments. Crassness is the show's *raison d'être*. But toilet humor is much more complicated; jokes that focus on the lower body are many hued. When a character literally craps out of his/her mouth, it's a common metaphor made visual. *South Park* reminds us of the crude origins of "talking crap." Despite its predilection for the lower body stratum, it doesn't have many purely sexual episodes. It's pretty mild when compared to shows such as *Sex and the City*.

Perhaps the most astonishing aspect of this case study to me has been the revelation of how little humor has changed. Nothing seen or heard on *South Park* is new; people have joked about bodily functions probably since the beginnings of humankind. *South Park*'s situations, obscenities, and observations echo Aristophanes, Juvenal, Erasmus, Rabelais, Swift, and other great satirists, people who have farted on society's hypocrisies. What remains a mystery is how students can catch every subtle nuance and every ironic moment of *South Park* and still misread Swift's "A Modest Proposal." Now is the time to teach "A Modest Proposal" alongside "Cartman's Mom Is Still a Dirty Slut"; eating babies and eating Eric Roberts aren't really that far removed.

What *South Park* offers is an aggressive pastiche. It's part comedy, part satirical observation, served with lashings of music, parody, irony, and self-mocking awareness. The multiple layering of meaning gives fans and viewers (especially those nostalgic for the 1980s) the opportunity to smirk knowingly and then rush to their computers to recap the latest episode, replete with popular culture references—*à la* comic book guy.

South Park arrived at a particularly pivotal time in Internet history. By 1997, the Internet was being loudly proclaimed as a truly democratic space. It was no longer the provenance of the technologically elite; new software applications, cheaper computers, and broader access enlarged the World Wide Web. Corporations such as Comedy Central were keen to scoop the Internet pool but unsure how to capitalize on the new media users. Consequently, the network (inadvertently perhaps) alienated fans, and many fans rejected the official Web sites. Much of the Internet of the mid-1990s has gone; it's not the same wild and crazy rabble of an Internet that it once was. Today's Web sites are informative, functional, and way too sterile. Gone are the flaming wars, the experimental software, and the delightfully amateurish fan sites.

South Park has finally grown up. It's come a long way since its premier as an unpredictable cartoon with lots of child swearing, cow suicides, perky poo, and mutant turkeys. The first two seasons put the program on the media map, but it faltered in its third and fourth seasons. It came of age in seasons five and six, when the show developed more focused narratives. But in doing so, it lost some of its Pythonesque unpredictability. Seasons six, seven, eight, nine, and ten offered much in the way of social commentary. Indeed, the show has become a little preachy, something it recognizes in "Cartoon Wars II."

South Park is a "classic"—it is the poster child for the controversial and the crude; even its crappy style has become a benchmark for its many imitators. It is now its own genre: part sitcom, vaudeville routine, comedy skit, and satirical political show. It was ranked third in *The London Independent's* "Greatest Cartoons of All Time."[2] *South Park* stepped into a discursive space and filled a political and cultural void.

Whenever I mentioned that I was writing a book on *South Park*, people routinely condemned it as a childish show full of swearing and bum jokes. Then they admitted they either hadn't seen it or watched only one or two episodes. Initial perceptions can be misleading. I, too, was one of those. I surfed on after watching a snippet in which Satan and Chris washed up ("Do the Handicapped"), it didn't grab me. However, a year later I was oh-my-god-ding when Mr. Stotch virtually accused a slack-eyed O. J. Simpson of murder. I was intrigued, but not enough to become a regular viewer. After becoming indoctrinated into the *South Park* world, I have a fuller appreciation for what the show does and how it does it. No matter how exasperating I might personally find its politics or how frustrating I might find its fuzzy logic, I still admire the series and the creators. The series can best be described as a call-and-response show. It demands howls of indignation, agreement, and disgust—sometimes simultaneously. Its mission is to attack everything, keeping nothing sacred, even itself. *South Park* demonstrates how little the world changes and how much hypocrisy, bigotry, and folly remain embedded in the human psyche.

Notes

1. Perhaps too much so. Matt Stone admits, "What happened was that we started procrastinating really bad. We started doing the show the week before it aired." In Terry Morrow, "Respect Their Authority!" *Knoxville News Sentinel*, October 20, 2005, http://www .knoxnews.com/kns/tv_and_radio/article/0,1406,KNS_357_4170956,00.html.

2. Jonathan Brown, "From Homer to *Scooby Doo*," *The London Independent*, February 28, 2005, http://www.findarticles.com/p/articles/mi_qn4158/is_200502/ai_n11831122.

Select Bibliography

Adamson, Joe. *Tex Avery: King of Cartoons*. New York: Da Capo, 1975.

Bakhtin, Mikhail. *Problems of Dostoevsky's Poetics*. 1963. Edited and translated by Caryl Emerson. Introduction by Wayne C. Booth. Minneapolis: University of Minnesota Press, 1984.

————. *Rabelais and His World*. 1965. Translated by Helene Iswolsky. Bloomington: Indiana University Press, 1984.

Barney, Richard A. "Filthy Thoughts, or, Cultural Criticism and the Ordure of Things." *Genre* 27, no. 4 (1994): 275–93.

Beardsworth, Alan, and Teresa Keil. *Sociology on the Menu: An Invitation to the Study of Food and Society*. London: Routledge, 1997.

Bell, David, and Bill Valentine. *Consuming Geographies*. London: Routledge, 1997.

Bell, Michael Mayersfeld. "Deep Fecology: Mikhail Bakhtin and the Call of Nature." *Capitalism, Nature, Socialism* 5, no. 4 (1994): 65–84.

Bucher, Bernadette. *Icon and Conquest*. Chicago: University of Chicago Press, 1981.

Billig, Michael. *Laughter and Ridicule: Towards a Social Critique of Humour*. London: Sage, 2005.

Boorstin, Daniel. *The Image: Or What Happened to the American Dream*. London: Weidenfeld & Nicolson, 1961.

Butler, Jeremy. *Television: Critical Methods and Applications*. Mahwah, NJ: Lawrence Erlbaum Associates, 2002.

Cantor, Paul A. *Gilligan Unbound: Popular Culture in the Age of Globalization*. Lanham, MD: Rowman & Littlefield, 2001.

Chapman Antony J., and Hugh C. Foot, eds. *Humour and Laughter: Theory, Research, and Applications*. London: Wiley, 1976.

Cholodenko, Alan, ed. *The Illusion of Life: Essays on Animation*. Sydney: Power Publications/Australian Film Commission, 1991.

Clarkson, Jay. "Contesting Masculinity's Makeover: Queer Eye, Consumer Masculinity, and 'Straight-Acting' Gays." *Journal of Communication Inquiry* 29, no. 3 (2005): 235–55.

Crafton, Donald. *Before Mickey: The Animated Film 1898–1928*. Chicago: University of Chicago Press, 1993.

Creeber, Glen, Toby Miller, and John Tulloch, eds. *The Television Genre Book*. London: British Film Institute, 2001.

Cowan, Douglas E. "*South Park*, Ridicule and the Cultural Construction of Religious Rivalry." *Journal of Religion and Popular Culture* 10 (2005).

Dobson, Hugo. "Mister Sparkle Meets the Yakuza: Depictions of Japan in *The Simpsons*." *Journal of Popular Culture* 39, no. 1 (2006): 44–68.

Feinberg, Leonard. *Introduction to Satire*. Ames: Iowa State University Press, 1967.

Fiske, John. "Madonna." In *Reading the Popular*, 95–113. Boston: Unwin Hyman, 1989.

———. *Television Culture*. London: Methuen/Routledge, 1987.

Frame, Donald M., ed. *The Complete Works of François Rabelais*. Berkeley and Los Angeles: University of California Press, 1992.

Freud, Sigmund. *Jokes and Their Relation to the Unconscious*. Hammondsworth, New York: Penguin, 1976.

Furniss, M. *Art in Motion: Animation Aesthetics*. London: John Libbey, 1998.

Gardiner, Judith Kegan. "*South Park*, Blue Men, Anality, and Market Masculinity." *Men and Masculinities* 2, no. 3 (2000): 251–71.

———. "Why South Park Is Gay." *Quarterly Review of Film and Video* 22, no. 1 (2005): 51–62.

Jackson, Wendy. "Dig This." *Animation World Magazine*, September 1, 1998. http://mag.awn.com/index.php?ltype=search&sval=south+park&article_no=411.

Johnson-Woods, Toni. *Big Bother: Why Did That Reality TV Show Become a Phenomenon?* St. Lucia, Australia: University of Queensland Press, 2002.

Klein, Norman M. *Seven Minutes: The Life and Death of the American Animated Cartoon*. London: Verso, 1993.

Korenman, Alicia. *Princesses, Mothers, Heroes, and Superheroes: Images of Jewish Women in Comic Books and Graphic Novels*. Master's thesis, University of North Carolina at Chapel Hill, 2006. http://hdl.handle.net/1901/308.

LaPorte, Dominique. *History of Shit*. Cambridge, MA: MIT Press, 2000.

Leacock, Stephen. *Humor and Humanity*. New York: Holt, 1938.

Leslie, Esther. *Hollywood Flatlands: Animation, Critical Theory and the Avant-Garde*. London: Verso, 2002.

Levy, Emanuel. *Small-Town America in Film: The Fall and Decline of Community*. New York: Continuum, 1990.

Lorenz, Konrad. *On Aggression*. Translated by Marjorie Wilson. New York: Harcourt, Brace & World, 1966.

Marc, David. *Comic Visions: Television Comedy and American Culture*. New York: Routledge, 1992.

Matheson, Carl. "The Simpsons, Hyper-Irony, and the Meaning of Life." In *The Simpsons and Philosophy: The D'oh! of Homer*. Chicago: Open Court, 2001.

McAllister, Matthew P., Edward H. Sewell Jr., and Ian Gordon, eds. *Comics and Ideology*. New York: Peter Lang, 2001.

Montanari, Massino. *The Culture of Food*. Oxford: Blackwell, 1994.

Persels, Jeff, and Russell Ganim. *Fecal Matters in Early Modern Literature and Art*. Aldershot, England: Ashgate, 2004.

Pilling, Jayne. *A Reader in Animation Studies*. Sydney: John Libbey, 1997.

Rabelais, François. See Frame.

Rapp, Albert. *The Origins of Wit and Humor*. New York: Dutton, 1951.

Solomon, Charles. *The History of Animation: Enchanted Drawings*. New York: Wings Books, 1994.

Stallybrass, Peter, and Allon White. *The Politics and Poetics of Transgression*. London: Methuen, 1986.

Tropiano, Stephen. *TV Towns*. New York: TV Books, 2000.

Turner, Chris. *Planet Simpson*. London: Ebury Press, 2004.

Turner, Graeme. *Understanding Celebrity*. London: Sage, 2004.

Twitchell, James B. *Carnival Culture: The Trashing of Taste in America*. New York: Columbia University Press, 1992.

Wells, Paul. *Animation and America*. New Brunswick, NJ: Rutgers University Press, 2002.

————. *Understanding Animation*. London: Routledge, 1998.

Wolfe, Charles K., and James E. Akenson, eds. *Country Music Goes to War*. Lexington: University Press of Kentucky, 2005.

Index